THE UNSPEAKABLE

Lying Down Together: Law, Metaphor, and Theology
Milner S. Ball

Politics and Ambiguity
William E. Connolly

The Rhetoric of Economics
Donald N. McCloskey

Therapeutic Discourse and Socratic Dialogue: A Cultural Critique
Tullio Maranhão

The Rhetoric of the Human Sciences: Language and Argument in
Public Affairs
John S. Nelson, Allan Megill, and Donald N. McCloskey, eds.

The Unspeakable: Discourse, Dialogue, and Rhetoric in the
Postmodern World
Stephen A. Tyler

Heracles' Bow: Essays on the Rhetoric and Poetics of the Law
James Boyd White

The Unspeakable

DISCOURSE, DIALOGUE,

AND RHETORIC IN THE

POSTMODERN WORLD

STEPHEN A. TYLER

THE UNIVERSITY OF WISCONSIN PRESS

Published 1987

The University of Wisconsin Press
114 North Murray Street
Madison, Wisconsin 53715

The University of Wisconsin Press, Ltd.
1 Gower Street
London WC1E 6HA, England

First printing

Printed in the United States of America

For LC CIP information see the colophon

ISBN 0-299-10270-5 cloth; 0-299-11274-8 paper

In Memory of
Guy, Beatrice,
Peggy, Sidney, and Henry

CONTENTS

ABBREVIATIONS

E	English
G	Greek
IE	Indo-European
L	Latin
Skt	Sanskrit
SAE	Standard Average European

PREFACE

These essays of the unspeakable evoke the carnival of the everyday, and parody the dominant discourse of a decaying order. They do not pretend to novelty or invention for they are but reminders, in their own paradoxical way, of the commonsense world modernism thought it had surpassed or suppressed in its domestication of all the world that was exotic. They speak the language of resistance to all totalizing ideologies that justify the repression of the commonsense world in the name of utopia, or that seek to legitimize practice and judgement as the expression of theory. They deny that theory is the enabling condition for rational life, and they overturn the notion that knowing is the necessary means and precondition of doing, saying, and feeling. They thus express the mood of postmodern sentiment.

No one knows the beginning of postmodernism, and appropriately so, since it denies the idea of knowable origins. Some declare that it is already dead anyway, consumed perhaps, by its own autopoetic dissemination or forfeit to its own deconstruction, and even though it is difficult to understand how the uncreated might be said to die, such is the desire for the new that one supposes it is capable of that, too. Whatever its current condition, no one can now think about language, writing, and discourse in quite the same comfortable way they did before—whenever that was—as the steady forward march of ideas pressing on toward the end foreordained in their beginning, for now we know that ideas are always foretold and that their end is neither ironically preordained by the matrix that makes them nor their beginning overcome in their end. The easy assumptions of the old order of discourse—of wholeness, consensus, clarity, closure, telos, and even order itself—now seem awkward, unfamiliar, and almost embarrassing, rather in the way of someone speaking about last year's fashion as if it were last year, speaking seriously, and not in parody of the unspeakable.

Postmodernism is the culmination of modernism's assault on the idea of representation, but unlike modernism, it also undermines the idea of form, closing off any easy escape into that cosmetic cosmos of ordered abstraction. The deconstruction of writing—for some the whole significance of the postmodern moment—was the consequence of the crisis of representation in science and the arts, and is ultimately only a preliminary move in the restoration and recuperation of the commonsense world incarnated for us not in language or representation but in speech and communication in the carnival of the mundane and quotidian talk of everyday life.

Some of these essays have appeared in other places. "Words for Deeds and the Doctrine of the Secret World: Testimony to a Chance Encounter in the Indian Jungle" was published in Papers from the Parasession on Language and Behavior, Proceedings of the Chicago Linguistic Society (Chicago: University of Chicago Press, 1981), pp. 34–57. "The Vision Quest in the West, or What the Mind's Eye Sees" appeared in the *Journal of Anthropological Research* 40, no. 1:23–40, in 1984. "Ethnography, Intertextuality and the End of Description" is forthcoming in the *American Journal of Semiotics*. "Postmodern Ethnography: From Document of the Occult to Occult Document" has been published in *Writing Culture,* edited by James Clifford and George Marcus (Berkeley: University of California Press, 1986). "Postmodern Anthropology" is to appear in a different version in a book being edited by Phyllis Chock. Thanks for permission to reprint is hereby acknowledged.

Over the years I have received grants from the Ford Foundation, the National Science Foundation, and the National Endowment for the Humanities that have made it possible for me to carry out some of the research reflected in these essays. I gratefully acknowledge their support.

Apart from the authors cited throughout, an important stimulus to these essays has been dialogues with my colleagues in the Rice Circle— George Marcus, Michael Fischer, Julie Taylor, Tullio Maranhão, Robert Lane Kauffman, Steven Crowell, Konstantine Kolenda, Tom Haskell, Douglas Mitchell, Richard Wolin, others who joined us from time to time, and various guest speakers. The most important influence though, has come from my wife, Martha, and daughter, Alison. Their conversation informs all of my thought and writing. So, too, reflections on my conversations with Koyas during field work in India influence my understanding of discourse. I also acknowledge influence of a more practical kind in expressing my thanks to Barbara Podratz for all the varied ways she has assisted me since I first came to Rice, and to Frances Henderson, who has done my typing for years and now reads my handwriting better than I do.

AC-KNOWLEDGMENT

THE EYE-CON OF THE EYE-DOZ

"Scientific thought is rather hampered by the necessity of drawing itself out in typographical channels and it is certain that if some procedure would permit the presentation of books in such a way that the materials of the different chapters are presented simultaneously in all their aspects, authors and their users would find a considerable advantage." Jacques Derrida (1974:333, n.35).

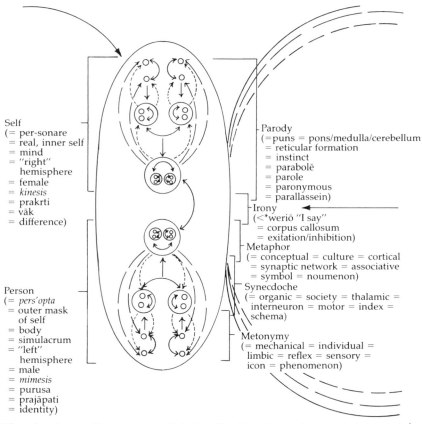

Self
(= per-sonare
= real, inner self
= mind
= "right"
  hemisphere
= female
= *kinesis*
= prakrti
= vāk
= difference)

Parody
(= puns = pons/medulla/cerebellum
= reticular formation
= instinct
= parabolē
= parole
= paronymous
= parallassein)

Irony
(<*weriō "I say"
= corpus callosum
= exitation/inhibition)

Metaphor
(= conceptual = culture = cortical
= synaptic network = associative
= symbol = noumenon)

Synecdoche
(= organic = society = thalamic =
interneuron = motor = index =
schema)

Person
(= *pers'opta*
= outer mask
  of self
= body
= simulacrum
= "left"
  hemisphere
= male
= *mimesis*
= purusa
= prajāpati
= identity)

Metonymy
(= mechanical = individual =
limbic = reflex = sensory =
icon = phenomenon)

Thought picture. The structure of desire: The hieroglyph of the emboîtment of the hylomorphic "wonam," the Peirce-*opta* invaginated with and "structurally coupled" in autopoetic desire to its other within the Cosmic Egg. With apologies to the Koyas. This selvage says: "svanāmi or sva nāmi or svan am I."

THE UNSPEAKABLE

The image of the bull is based on a sketch by Pūsem Laksmayya.
The bull, particularly the gaur *(Bos Bibos gaurus),* the wild bison of
the Indian jungle, is venerated by the Koyas. Their horns are prized
for making the bison horn headdress the Koyas wear during cere-
monial dances when men "become bulls," gouge the earth with
their "hooves" and "horns," cover themselves with dust, and,
snorting and bellowing in anger, charge at one another—all the
while beating lustily on the huge drums slung across their torsos.
Laksmayya's bull resembles the zebu *(Bos indicus)* more than the
gaur. The gaur's hump and dewlap are less prominent than the
zebu's.

EPODE

"Mirror, mirror, on the wall, who is fairest of all?"
"I am," said the mirror.

Breaking the Mirror

Postmodernism is the name of the congeries of nega-
tivities that end the modern epoch. It is the improper name of the
transition from the age of irony to the age of parody. Postmodernism
names no positive program nor system of concepts; it narrates no minatory tales, evokes no originary allegories of past wholeness, and
builds no foundations for future utopias (cf. Spanos 1985, Magliola
1985). It is the name of the duplicity of "end," of the end of "e-motion,"
of ends that set in motion, and of movements that culminate in ends,
of the sentimental journey that begins in sensation and ends in sensibility as the movement from sense to sense.

The past is the myth modernism invented as the story of its origin
and as the justification for the future overcoming of that origin. It is
the irony of creation-in-destruction, of utopia rising from the detritus
of the plundered past, and it is the source of the nostalgia for the
whole sundered by desire for that future. This is the fundamental
irony of all that is modern—of the future that legitimizes the dismem-
berment of the past and of the past the future ends. It is the story of
the necessity for loss and alienation and of the necessary longing for
the lost and alienated.

The modern epoch begins in the triumph of things over signs, of
plain style over rhetoric, of reason over passion, and ends in the
deconstruction of things, plain style, and reason in the carnival celebrations of the postmodern. The modern epoch begins with the liberation of the [ay] and ends with its repression in the totalitarian surveil-
lance of the panoptic [ay] roving imperiously over its files, data banks,
charts, maps, and diagrams. The brief, romantic moment of liberation
in the subjectivity of the [ay] founded science and was the origin that
had to be overcome by consensus, in the myth that made the transformation of the "I see" to "we agree." The first person plural, that mark
of royalty, of rule, the "we" that justifies and objectifies the subjectivity of the [ay] as the authority of the unauthored is the sign of the
modern era's obsession with the method of consensus. Science and
democracy are founded in it, as are the corporation, bureaucracy, and

all forms of totalitarianism. It is the objective means of the fictions that speak with the authority of the realities they have made, saying "because it is, you must." The whole tale of the modern era is told in these shifting pronouns of the "I" become "we", and of the "it" "you" must be; it is a story of substitutes and changelings, of illusions, appearances, and false identities, of pronouns masquerading as nouns.

The discourse of the modern era is a variation on the theme of immortality, representing the West's attempt to overcome time, not by mastering the self, as in Hinduism or Buddhism, but by mastering space and reducing time to the ordered array of intersecting lines that make the energic matrix within which all thought and being have their source and means. Displaced into the ever-receding future and alienated from a discredited past, the modern age groped for the narrowing point of the disappearing now and fell into the existential abyss of nothingness. The modern version of the story of "The Fall" is not a fable of the fall into being in time, it is a traveller's tale of the upward journey into the immortal nothingness of space.

It is a story whose allegory is the spiral ascending from the here and now of the material world of the senses to the timeless locus of the spiritual in the celestial stratum of the transcendental mind. It is a tale whose whole meaning is the polysemy of "sense" (cf. Derrida 1974: 13), and its central mystery is the source of light. It reaches beyond the limit of light, exceeding each putative source except the one within thinking the end in the beginning.

Postmodernism is the name for the end of a kind of writing that begins by reading "the name for the end of a kind of writing" as "the name for the end of a kind of writing" and ends by reading "the name for the end of a kind of writing" as "the name for the end, goal, telos, terminus, finis of a kind of writing" or as the "name for the end, goal, telos, terminus, finis of a kind of, 'kinda' but not quite, class of writing," which has among its possible readings: "the name for non-created writing," or "the writing without a subject," or "the writing that is by no-one about no-thing." In its end, it is "the name for the goal of writing that is a simulacrum of itself," its own end.

Postmodernism is the writing of the history of the repression of the paradigmatic axis of reading and representation, and it is the breaking of the mirror, and the "opening of the field" of the signifier. It is the harvesting of the margins of the field of the signifier where the machine of language turns at the end upon itself, as Pound, Olsen, and Derrida foretold. The goal is to read and write paronymously, to make new meanings by repetitions that make small changes and evoke the *karma,* the copresent, implicating, inseminating "pasts" of every word in the way a smell, or a taste, or snatch of song, or an etymology evokes the chance genealogical copresence of the multiple meanings that make the excess of the Buddhist void, which is not empty but is the chaos of the excess of order in the instantaneous copresence of all possible orders, the *śunyatā*, the insolent, swollen belly of all- being (cf. Derrida 1981:129–30, 238; 1967; 1974:69–70, 94, 188; 1978: 27; Magliola 1985).

The aim of modernist writing was to free the signifier from an economy of discourse in which the relation of signifiers was determined by lineal sequentiality, the structure of the signified, and the intentions of the author. Writing mirrors the world; writing mirrors the author's voice; writing mirrors itself. Three alternatives of Western discourse—the reflected object, the spectral subject, and the mirrored mirror—how long played out in so many books? Lacan's "mirror stage" of development and Foucault's meditation on the mirror painting "Las Meninas" are recent reminders of the power of the three dyads "words and things," "words and deeds," "words and words" that we know as well in their other names as "language, speech, and thought," "language and the world," "language, thought, and reality," "mind and nature," "sense, reference, and pragmatics."

Now the ocular fairy tale is finished, the mirror broken. Modern science, begun by Bacon and Descartes, accomplished the first assault on the trinity, on the object, on nature, on the signified, and now we know, because science tells us so, that there really wasn't any real out there, just the discourse of science. The language of things was but a thing of language. And because of psychoanalysis, we now know we no longer know but only give the illusory appearance of a cogito. And, what of the "prison house of language?" The prison has become an amusement park, an autopoetic hall of mirrors. The moderns left the mirror intact in their attempt to remake discourse on the model of the unconscious, as the discourse of the other, but postmodernism dismantles the hall of mirrors and builds no new prisons.

The "plain style" taught by Bacon eschewed ornament, "choiceness of the phrase" and "the sweet falling of the clauses" in favor of a discourse that makes direct access to the "weight of the matter," "worth of subject," "soundness of argument, life of invention" and "depth of judgement" (Bacon 1951:29). What words with their wonderful freight of ambiguity-in-clarity better epitomize the spirit of the modern age? "Matter," "weight," "subject," "invention," "worth," "argument," "judgement" are indices to an economy of discourse and its key metaphors. The line misquoted above begs us to read it paradigmatically, not as a line, but as the associative extensions of its highlighted terms.

Epode

Who now, on reading this, can repress "atomic weight" or not hear the "weight of matter" in the phrase "the weight of the matter," or not laugh at the polysemous possibilities of "subject," and who now connects "worth" and "subject" when everyone knows that is what objects have?

Plain style seeks transparency in the conventional connections of words-to-words-to-things where sequential movement along the syntagmatic axis represses paradigmatic associations that are other than connections with things. Each word is a label of a thing, and the train of thought, loaded with things, runs directly in a straight line from place to place. Think straight! Don't think:

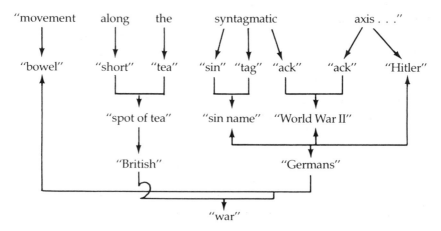

means "the second world war pitted the anally fixated Germans against the orally fixated British." The simultaneity of paradigmatic implication interrupts the urgent forward flow of signifiers in the singularity of time. Don't follow forking paths! Don't fork! Get thee behind me Borges! Time marches on! for, as Hobbes declares ". . . the order of words, when placed as they ought to be . . . [shows] a man the stops and unevenness in his way. But when placed unnaturally . . . [makes him] . . . go back and hunt for the sense" (1908, II:69). Linear coherence in the sequence of syntagma enchain and bind the discourse into an integrated whole. The signifiers' work is to signify the signified—the "weight of the matter," not to "play with itself" or resemble by "dissembling" words and things.

Paradoxically, plain style in its quest for transparency as the unity of form and content actually emphasized the difference between form and content and established the context for their further separation. By foregrounding content—the weight of the matter—it actually announced and made evident the very problem it had sought to correct. It announced—in other words—its own consciousness of the failure of transparency by naming the remedy, by trying to legislate the form of discourse.

Nothing so well marks the modern urge as this utopian dream of transparent language, of language so perfectly fitted to the world that no difference could insinuate itself between words and things. The modern age is characterized by this anxiety about language, this recurrent and irrepressible worry about the form of discourse and its fit with thought and things. The great goal was to create an order of discourse that mirrored the mind that mirrored the world that mirrored the discourse that. . . . Language is the expression of the world in the immediacy of the mind, and a sick discourse is a sick mind in a sick world (cf. Rorty 1979). Bad discourse is a bad consciousness, and that is why changing the economy of discourse is revolutionary.

For plain style, rhetorical tricks are bad because they cloud the mirror; metaphors liken the unlike, and ornaments cover up reality. Rhetoric is a discourse of trickery and concealment that obscures and distorts the relation between words and things. Worse yet, it marks a discourse as the work of a speaking subject. Ornaments of style and tropes are oral residues in writing. They are the written signature of the speaker's voice in the text for they direct our attention to the artifice of words and constantly remind us that they are creatures of an artificer, an author, and proxies of his/her voice. The reader's mind is constrained and guided by the sleight-of-hand of the author who is the king of the text enthroned in his cognitive utopia.

Plain style, above all else, seeks to erode the presence of the speaker by eliminating all marks of individuality that speak of the speaker's difference from the text. Speaker intrusions, from personal pronouns to parentheses, must be rigorously controlled. The text should be the unspoken voice of a universal reader immanent in the text at the same time as it transcends it. Plain style presupposes a transcendental ego who is not so much the author of the text as the creator of it. This is how plain style seeks to obliterate the speaker's voice without at the same time undermining the author-ity of the text. The problem of plain style is to dethrone the king of the text without at the same time destroying the kindgom of the text, to overthrow the king's authority without overturning the kingdom of authority. This is how revolution in discourse precedes and legitimizes revolution in the world.

Rhetoric is the voice of the past; its tropes and formulae speak in the rounded phrases of tradition, of commonplace knowledge, of the familiar and already known. Rhetoric is thought constrained by past authority. Plain style, at least in the discourse descending from Bacon and Descartes, was dedicated to reporting new knowledge, knowledge not derived from texts, not from the accumulated experience of the past, but from the senses, from the observation and description of nature. It became a discourse of disruptions, of challenges and changes in its textual past instead of a discourse of continuity and accumulation, even as it projected a fable of continuous, progressive, teleological change. It devalued the past, dismissed tradition as the accumulation of ignorance and superstition and denied authority to every text, making all contingent on what the future might bring. In place of its history it conjured a myth of progressive perfectibility, of constant innovation, discovery, and invention, of the new modifying and replacing the old in the unceasing production of novelty. Its cry was ever, "nova!" "nova!" It was an economy of discourse mirroring and justifying the political and economic realities that created it, and that it created.

Plain style is grounded in the subjectivity of *a* cogito which it strives to obscure by transforming the text into a cognitive utopia of *the* cogito, and that is how the irrational subjectivity of an author becomes the objective subjectivity of a rational, transcendental ego whose name is Nemo and in whose mind the unity of text, author, and reader apprehends the world in the immediacy of thought unspoken. The transcendental subject is fully present to itself, not, as Derrida thinks, by means of voice, but by the unity of subject and object, knower and known, signifier and signified.

Plain style is the unspeakable; it erases the traces of speech because it seeks the thoughts objects make, the thoughts speech can only distort because it signifies the subject before the object. Rhetoric is the mark of the author's will, and all allusion, allegory, metaphor, simile, and ornaments of style are its instruments. They point to the author's character, creative skill, and intent, and proclaim the worth of subject that is neither a subject of worth nor the "worth of subject." They are presentations of self that trumpet "What a clever fellow I am!" Moreover, they tempt the reader's mind to leave the straight and narrow path of the sentence's linear trajectory, and to follow instead forking paths that lead to parallel worlds beyond the world of words and things conjured by the text before the reader's eyes. They are repugnant to literal meaning and to the strict, lineal movement of thought. They are the means of the mirror that reflects only inasmuch as it distorts.

Plain style subverts the will of the individual, merging it into the transcendental ego of the voiceless *communis fidelium*. Derrida misconstrues the "presence" of plain style as presence by means of voice, of a subject speaking to itself, but the presence of the transcendental ego is the presence that is before and beyond voice, the presence of the unspeakable perception/understanding that happens all at once, that con-temporary thought outside of time that speech distorts by forcing it into sequential temporalities. Plain style presses for the unity and purity of representation, of the world impressed upon the mind *before* speech. Derrida misunderstands Aristotle's meaning in *De Interpretatione*, where speech is only the *symbol* of mental experience and, unlike mental experience, is not universal. The proximity and closeness of voice to mental experience is not the point. The point is that speech signifies, but in signifying necessarily misrepresents. Here is no basis to argue for the metaphysical primacy of speech or phonocentrism. It tells us instead of the sounding irony that writing wishes to overcome by making a unity of mental experience and written expression. That is the aim of plain style, and somewhat paradoxically, it is also the aim of all those modernist tinkerings with the form of writing, no matter how outrageous and how seemingly different from plain style.

The English reflex of *pathēmata* better tells the tale—something pathic happens between *psychēs* (thought) and *phonē* (speech) and it is this willful pathology of speech that plain style wishes to cure. Discourse, as it develops within the dominant scientific tradition, is no hankering for inner voices; it is instead a lust for the visual, for the *res* as *eidos*, for "mental experience" as a "vision," for things of which our experiences are the images. Things and images of things are universal, the same for all, so wrote Aristotle.

What science, seeking universal knowledge, would settle for the allusory illusions of speech, for "hearsay," when it could have a true vision of the real? The search for the being of the entity as presence, of: ". . . the presence of the thing to sight as *eidos*, presence as substance/essence/existence *(ousia)*, temporal presence as point *(stigme)* of the now or of the moment (nun), the self-presence of the cogito, consciousness, subjectivity, the co-presence of the other and of the self, intersubjectivity as the intentional phenomenon of the ego . . ." (Derrida 1974b: 12) is neither phonocentrism nor logocentrism; it is videocentrism, the search for the mirror of the mind that reflects the real without distortion. Thus properly understood, writing is not "debased" as "mediation of mediation," a signifier of a prior signifier, the secondary symbol of primary symbols, the substitutional changeling of speech; it is instead the visible sign of the yearning for the visible, which, when cleansed of its oral residues, dreams a destiny of a better picture of the world seen not by a mirror to look into, nor even to step through, but by a glass to see through—a lens to amplify the power of sight.

The modern period is not the time of the tongue, it is the time of the eye, which is no time at all, but space and light. Its symbol and instrument is the lens—the microscope and telescope, whose vestigial mirrors reflect neither objects nor subjects but shine back the pure light that illuminates objects for subjects. Placed out of sight where the perceiving eye could not look at once into it and into the lens it illuminates, we might think the mirror and its images had finally been overcome, but such is far from the case, for when Einstein travelled in his mind faster than the speed of light and looked for his familiar reflection in the mirror and saw nothing, the mirror's lost reflection became the object that was not an object but only the symbol of an object propagated by light. Einstein saw the light, and light became the signifier of the past presence of objects coming to be and disappearing without having been in that time when the object does not matter, and only its sign matters. Fiat Lux!

Copernicus thus heralds the return of the old gods repressed by Christianity, of Apollo and his whole pagan retinue, of the sun as the center of cult and practice, and of astronomy/astrology as the key to all knowledge. We have returned to that time when the light of reason is the reason of light, and being shrivels in the light that extinguishes the breath of life.

Representation without Communication, ESSE/esse

The modern moment is defined by the quest for a lost or occulted "arche-writing," as Derrida says, it is the search for the originary difference, for the possibility that makes representation the difference between what represents and what is represented, that original and originary disjunction between signifier and signified (1974:70). Arche-writing is the equivalent of Aristotle's "phantasms" and of Hume's "impressions," the represented objects thought thinks, the writing thought silently reads before it can speak. It is the "arche-trace" (Ibid.: 61) of the originary disjunction that makes the difference that is the ground of arbitrariness, of the arbitrary relation between signifier/signified. It bears already the imprint of in print, the being imprinted of the in print (cf. ibid.: 63), "an opaque energy . . . no concept of metaphysics can describe" (ibid.: 65). We cannot think of a being before its trace or apart from its trace. We cannot think the originary moment before the trace traces nor the separate substance the trace traces until it is already traced. We think only of traces of traces of traces without the possibility of either transcendental tracing or an originary untraced. This is a unity of the trace/traced that is an unbreakable duality, for we cannot get to the hinterland that Nietzsche says lies behind the trace without a trace. But, if neither the trace nor what the trace traces is available to us except in duality, what makes the possibility of our longing for that impossibility of the prior essence? What is the source of supposing the difference the trace traces between itself and what it traces? What leads us to the possibility of a difference? Why would we speak of a trace as if it were other than the traced?

Is this not the condition of particle physics? What reality lies behind the traces particles leave in cloud chambers? How can the otherness of the absent substance whose traces we see be other than its trace?

Since trace : traced :: signifier : signified, these questions are also questions about signification, and they make us ask: "How can we assert the prior difference between the signifier and the signified that enables us to assert that their relation is *arbitrary?* Could we not as well say their relation is natural?"

Here is a fine fairy tale. "Once upon a time we knew the unsignified as the unsignified before it was signified as the unsignified and became the unsignified signified." There was a moment of origin when the signifier was first joined to the unsignified, and because of that origin we may now say that the signified is other than its signifier, or that signification is the "othering" of signified and signifier. The signified is both "before" and "behind" the signifier, for the idea of original disjunction and originary junction is the "before" that makes us think signifiers have a "behind," or that signifieds can, as Lacan says, slide under signifiers, and is presumably why we can write $\frac{S}{s}$ with the signifier "over" the signified (Lacan 1977:154). All of these "befores," "behinds," "overs," and "unders" are ways of declaring the difference between signifier and signified and tell the tale of the placing of the uncrossable bar sinister that emblazons the original miscegenation of S/s and signifies the Schutzstaffel that bars their reunion. We can't cross the bar because the bar makes the necessity of not crossing it, but we could cross it any time if it weren't necessary that we not be able to cross it. Isn't this the meaning of "arbitrary"? Isn't it a bit like the paleontologist imagining a hairy mammoth from its thigh bone, or the coonskin-capped hunter who thinks "bar" on seeing spoor on the trail?

Epode

If we only have access to signifiers (traces), where does the signified (the traced) come from? The signified is in the past, but is produced by a signifier in the present. Its being is presented, not from its presence but from its absence. On the other hand, if we had prior access to signifieds, where do signifiers come from and how did the signified get to be signified without a signifier?

The answer that tempts is that signifiers are the signifieds of other signifiers or even of themselves. This is the Peircean possibility of "secondness," of the reflexivity of the signifier, of writing, for example "the trace of the trace that is the trace of the trace," or "the signifier of the signifier that is the signifier of the signifier." But no-thing is "traced" here nor "signified" either. That a trace traces a trace or a signifier signifies a signifier can only make "traced/signified" in the past tense, as English grammer makes clear in the suffixes -er and -ed, where the first is the agent and present, and the second is patient and past.

Now it may be, as Peirce thought, that the essence of "signifier" is that it be "signified" (= "being signified") by another signifier, but how did we get from the first signifier to the second one that makes the first its signified? It is a bit like saying, "'it is a bit like saying' it is a bit like saying. . . ." It is, in other words, the condition of a repetition, of a same that is a difference, an identity/difference.

Derrida errs then, inasmuch as he as-signs priority to difference and to the signifier. His error is the converse of those who de-sign the signified prior to the signifier. The seeming priority of difference is akin to the problem of synonymy. When we say $x = y$, we have already supposed that $x \neq y$, for the "x" and the "y" being equated must be initially different (even if that difference is only mistaken) or there would be no point in saying $x = y$ when we could as well say $x = x$ or $y = y$. Saying $x = y$ is tantamount to saying not only $x \neq y$, but that $x = x$ and $y = y$. It presumes, in other words, the identity of "x" with itself, of "y" with itself, and the difference between "x" and "y" ($x \neq y$), which is removed by a second operation of identity in $x = y$. But, isn't this prior identity of $x = x$ and $y = y$, which is the condition of asserting $x \neq y$ and the enablement of $x = y$, itself dependent on a prior difference, of $x = x$ if and only if there is some y other than x such that $x \neq y$, and isn't that "$x \neq y$" dependent on the prior identity of $x = x$ and $y = y$ which enables $x \neq y$, which is the condition of asserting $x = y$ . . .? The condition of synonymy, then, depends upon something being simultaneously itself and not itself. This is the name of the self as the self and its other, and the name of the signifier as the signifier signified. Just as we cannot assign logical priority to the signifier or to the signified, we cannot assign ontological priority to the self or the other.

Difference then does not insinuate itself into the heart of signification by itself; it is companioned there by its other—by identity, the other of the other (*per contra* Lacan). Identity and difference are correlatives, the one unthinkable without the other. Just so, the signified is the correlative of the signifier. There is no bar, and rather than inscribing S/s or even S/S or s/s, we ought to write ⑤ to signify the unity of the duality, and the unthinkable origin of identity/difference. We cannot, following Saussure, sublate them by assigning them to the whole called "sign" (1966:67).

If the signifier is also the signified and the trace the traced, what can be said about the "arbitrariness" of their relation? What makes us think it could be different? What makes us think we can reasonably claim that "horse" arbitrarily names a familiar four-footed quadruped that might as well be called "cheval" or "equus" or "pferd" or "hayburner"? What is the source of this idea that *we could call "horse" something else if we wanted to*? What justifies this intrusion of will and caprice, of the "could" and the "wanted to" into the orderly and closed world of the *system* of signification? There are at least three conditions: (a) the concept/thing named is one and the same in each case, a "horse" thing/concept is a horse thing is a horse thing (identity of the signified); (b) there are different names that name the same "horse" thing/concept (difference of signifiers); (c) a condition of reasonable substitution of signifiers.

The identity of the signified requires the stability of the signified in all conditions of name substitution, as if the signified had an independent existence prior to its being signified so that we could on encountering it say: "I dub thee 'horse,' . . . or, wait a minute, 'equus,' or maybe 'pferd,' or how about. . . ." The signifier cannot, in other words, change the "essence" of the signified in other words. This is Aristotle's claim in the famous passage at the very beginning of *De Interpretatione* to the effect that all men agree on the things of which thoughts are representations. But, it won't do to say that the being of the signified is its being signified *and* that it exists prior to being signified and independently of a signifier that signifies it. Only in the latter case could we say "I could call 'horse' 'equus' if I wanted to," for only then is the substitution of signifiers just a substitution of signifiers that does not effect the identity of the signified. But, if the different signifiers do not alter the signified, what can be the meaning of "different" here? The formula says, in effect, that all signifiers of "horse" thing/concept are equal by means of the identity of "horse" thing/concept. The difference between "horse" and "equus" is a kind of illusion, and it makes no difference that we can hoarsely say " 'equus' is the name for 'horse' in Latin," but cannot say " 'horse' is the name for 'horse' in Latin."

Though this says nothing reassuring about the identity of the signified, it does in part exemplify one of Saussure's conditions for the mutability of signifiers, namely our knowing about other languages. That "sister" could be represented as well by any other sequence of sounds is "proved by the very existence of other languages" (ibid. 68). In other words, the beginning of arbitrariness is in the possibility of a linguistic difference noted. To put it differently, the condition that makes arbitrariness also makes linguistics. Linguistics and arbitrariness emerge simultaneously in an alienation that marks a suspension of the natural attitude in which speaking is an unreflective means and instrument of social life rather than an object of scrutiny. Something strange, exotic, different, problematic, alien, and exterior goads us into recognizing arbitrariness and opens the possibility of linguistics. Linguistics is the science of an alienated nature. Derrida is quite right in pointing to the coemergence of linguistics and alienation (1974:14).

Since the identity of signifieds (condition "a") contradicts the difference of signifiers (condition "b"), telling us, in effect, that the different names for horse don't make any difference because a horse is a horse is a horse, we can ask what would be the effect of arguing condition "b" first? If each signifier of the "same thing" does not signify the "same thing," either by changing "it" in the signifying act itself as in "hay-burner" = horse/thing concept, or by a difference of reference, as in "a zebra is a funny-looking striped horse," so that hearers change their minds about the essential character, function, or appearance of "horse-things," then the difference of signifiers (condition "b") contradicts the identity of signifieds (condition "a").

So far these arguments only repeat the synonymy argument, but what of condition "c"? What are the conditions for the reasonable substitution of signifiers that makes saying "I could call 'horse' 'equus' if I wanted to" seem so commonsensical? Condition "c" implicates the sense of "signifier" as "he or she who signifies" and reminds us that signifying involves communicating and communicants. Signifying is not just representing; it requires interpretants, a Peircean "third" who is the source of will and intent in *"I could* call 'horse' 'equus' if *I wanted* to."

An interpretant, however, is not Humpty Dumpty, who said "words mean whatever I want them to," nor a lonely, monadic, Cartesian cogito introspectively divining the nature of signification in splendid isolation from other cogitos whose existence is, at best, only dubious. Instead, an interpretant is a dialogical interpretant whose other is not just a mute signified, but a signified that "talks back," making the interpretant its signified (cf. Bakhtin 1984; Todorov 1984). An interpretant is a signified/signifier who becomes the signified of another signifier. The interpretant is the "I" as a "shifter" where the "I" who speaks is not the "I" spoken of, and it is the "I" who speaks to a "you" who can become the "I" who speaks to "you" (cf. Jakobson 1971). In less contorted speech this is the distinction between speaker and hearer that notes the intersubstitutability of the roles of the speaker and hearer such that we are never just speakers or hearers but are speaker/hearers.

There is a temptation to think of this mutuality of correlatives as if the idea of sign dominated the idea of speaker/hearer, just as I have written here of speaker/hearers as if they were equivalent to signifier/signified. What could be called subjectivity, individuality, intentionality, or person if speaker/hearers are just signifier/signifieds? Indeed, in the hands of most semioticians, this is the result, but it is solely the consequence of making the idea of representation hegemonic, dominating the subordinated idea of communication and this has, of course, been the dominant trend in Western philosophy, but that hardly recommends it to us as a desirable outcome. Note here the ambiguity of "signifier" in English. We cannot escape its agentive force. A signifier is a trafficker in signs as well as the vehicle of representation. It is not the passive thinglike character understood as the mark of the signified. To use an older, but potent terminology, the signifier is both *actus* and *potentia*, the making of signifying. To say that speaker/hearers can be signifieds as well as signifiers must also imply that signifier/signifieds can be speaker/hearers, but it does not mean that this is all they are in either case. Speaker/hearers are not just signifier/signifieds and signifier/signifieds are not just speaker/hearers. We can't put Humpty Dumpty back together again by declaring him to be a chicken in disguise.

Nominally, there are differences among signs that are used only as signs, signs that are used as signs and use other signs as signs, and signs used as signs that use themselves and others as signs. This is, after all, part of the Peircean characterization of signs that establishes the interpretant in its role as a "third" in a way that does not permit its reduction to a "second" or a "first." These distinctions can be illustrated as in thought picture 1.1.

The relationship of "first," "second," and "third" echoes Kant's discussion of transcendence and moral agents. The interpretant is a higher order category associated with "symbol" and "thirdness" and we can say that it is the interpretant's mediation that makes arbitrariness possible. Without a third, the relation between signifier and signified would be "natural." These sign functions make complex intersections that Peirce never tired of diagramming. They involve among their many intersections the following partial list: law and chance; system and element; communication and representation; reason and passion; individual, society, and culture; icon, index, and symbol; monad, dyad, and triad. They are perhaps best understood as a logogram in which each triadic division contains within itself the possibility of all the others. Each part contains the whole. Some sense of this can be generated from thought picture 1.2.

The real meaning of this kind of arbitrariness, however, is not that it is the means of individual will, intent, or desire, nor that it is completely conditioned by the will, intent, and desire of other thirds. In thought picture 1.2, the metaphoric equivalents of "thirdness" are "culture," "symbol," "triad," "communication," "system," "law," and "reason," and these are opposed to the metaphoric equivalents of "firstness," which are "person" (individual), "icon," "monad," "representation," "element," "chance," and "passion." "Thirdness" is another name for *communis*, the moral community founded as a community of discourse. It is the realm of the speaker/hearer. The result is that *the system of semiotic is relativized to rhetoric and representation is relativized to communication.* We have instead of an abstract and totalizing

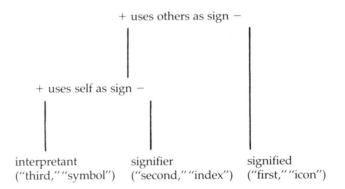

Thought picture 1.1. Peircean hierarchy of signs. Plus (+) means the feature is present; minus (−) means the feature is absent. Thus, the signifier uses others as a sign, but does not use itself as a sign.

reason ⟷ passion

law ⟷ chance

system ⟷ element

communication ⟷ representation

"third" symbol culture triad moral community	"second" index society dyad	"first" icon person monad

Thought picture 1.2. Peircean hologram. "Symbol," "culture," "triad," and "moral community" are metaphorical equivalents of "third"—kinds of "thirdness"—and are characterized by "reason," "law," "system," and "communication." These characterizations are opposed to "passion," "chance," "element," and "representation," respectively, which are the metaphorical equivalents of "firstness"—"icon," "person," and "monad." Each element of the whole implicates the whole and every other element. The idea of "moral community" is consensual, emergent, and created in communication.

notion of a system of signs, a relativizing understanding of signs in uses that may or may not make systems. Consequently, there was never a circumstance in which we could be said to know the origin of the disjunction between signifier and signified that did not already entail a communicative context that made disjunction possible at the same time as it resisted more than merely local disjunction. The disjunction of signifier and signified is, as Derrida says, always in quotes and embedded in a field of discourse, but, *per contra* Derrida, that field of discourse is not in quotes. As against the semiotician, we can say that the discourse is not a totalizing system of representation; it is always flawed, fragmented, and partial because it is relativized to rhetoric. Neither grammatologist nor semiotician is right.

The communicative context includes, makes possible, and is itself the result of agreements that allow disjunction for some purposes in some contexts, while prohibiting disjunction of the whole field of signifier/signified at once. This is the import of Saussure's statement to the effect that signified and signifier are held together by the "social fact of language" (1966: 113), though we may wonder what the "social fact of language" means in his account.

Arbitrariness, then, always involves its counterpart—the given, conventions understood as if they were both natural and the product of intentions mediated by conversation and discourse. Arbitrariness is neither the imposition of culture on nature, nor a reflection of nature within culture; it is the naturalness of the cultural, which is neither a closed system of self-reflecting signs nor of signs reflecting a foundational nature. Arbitrariness requires conventions, intentions, and naturalness. To put it differently, arbitrariness is made by the intersection of person, will, and representation, or by their other names: culture, society, and individual, respectively. The category "person" is the speaker/hearer, the symbol of culture. The category "will" is convention/intention, the index of society. The category "representation" is signifier/signified, the icon of the individual (cf. Tyler 1978:459–65).

Saussure is at least partly correct when he says that no individual alone could change a sign or that the "choice" of signifiers is not left entirely to the speaker. Individual whim is "checked" by the weight of time and the collectivity (1966:74, 78). I could not say "equus bzdid plkld" and expect to be understood unless my hearers were already conversant with this way of speaking, or could become conversant with it. Wittgenstein's comments on private language make the same points and both would agree that language is a "form of life" developed and inherited throughout history (Wittgenstein 1958:18, 226, 230). But, these forces do not erase intentionality. An individual may not be able to make his/her idiolectical innovations stick, but individuals can and do. What else could be meant by "use" than that it is intentional and that intentions may be inventions? To say that language has no "tend-encies" is to deny ourselves the means of "reaching-out" to others by portending, pretending, extending, and intending. And to say that language is all convention denies that we could ever come upon anything new. It would be equivalent to a new doctrine of "natural signification" in place of "participatory signification." It is the arbitrariness of "we could change signs if we wanted to, but we can't."

What then is the source of our sense of the possibility of disjunction and arbitrariness? Standard answers have always involved two arguments: (1) "the spoken of" is other than "the spoken"; (2) "the spoken" can become "the spoken of." The first argument is really an assertion about statements, about sentences that seem to say something about something other than themselves, as in "the sun is larger than the moon" or "dogs have four legs" or "cows are animals." In a sentence like "I wish I had a cow," though, it is not so clear that anything other than my declaring a wish is going on, even if we might want to say it's still about my "wishing." But, what of sentences such as: "Have a cow," or "I said, 'I wish I had a cow.'" Do they say something about something other than themselves? This is all familiar enough now in the discussion of speech acts for us to assert that these utterances either assert themselves or are about themselves at least as much as they are about something else, and even when they are about something else they do not encode a distinction between utterance and thing the way statements do. Condition 1 is Aristotle's notion of an *apophantic* utterance, an utterance capable of being judged true or false either in its form or in what it asserts. It is a prejudice in favor of statements for which the disjunction of "the spoken" and "the spoken of" is the ground. In other words, condition 1 merely reasserts its presupposition. It is the anticipation of the substance/substantive that fills the blank in "I am speaking of _____." It anticipates the *res*, the order of reality other than the speaking that the speaking points to but is not. Though the first condition fails because it cannot characterize the speaking that is not a speaking of, is it not at least derivable from the second, and therefore saved? This is Derrida's argument against Searle. Any time saying can be put in quotes it becomes a signified, what is spoken of by whatever is outside the quotes as in ". . . it beomes a signified, what is spoken of by whatever is outside the quotes as in . . .," and "the spoken" becomes at once "the spoken of" and other than "the spoken of." This identity/difference is created by a postponement, or as Derrida says, by a deferring or "deference" of closure, and we are back again to the infinite regress of identity/difference of the synonymy argument.

This does not, however, save condition 1 in its original sense as the difference between something spoken and something spoken of, for some thing spoken of is not something spoken nor is something spoken some thing when spoken of. In other words, there are only other words here, and no disjunction between words and not words to make the difference between word and world.

Aside from the fact that the quote of a quote of a quote of a quote begins to sound more like a pathological condition of perseveration than the talk of ordinary folk going about their business, the main point is that if everything is already structured by the system of signs, then there can be no arbitrariness in the relationship between signifier and signified, no matter what the evidence of different languages may seem to tell us, for this is precisely what we would mean by a "natural" relationship—one that cannot be otherwise. To forego the fairy tale of an initial disjunction between signifier and signified is to forego the idea of an arbitrary connection implying some originary "cultural" act.

What Derrida does not make clear in his deconstruction of the signified is that speech is the other writing invents in order to give itself an origin and thus to legitimize itself as the mark of civilization. It ensures that speech will always be ambiguous, connected at once with all that goes before civilization—savagery, barbarism, the individual, sensation, and nature—and all that transcends or comes after civilization—spirit, the occult, and whatever is beyond language.

Our sense of arbitrariness, of the possibility of a disjunction between signifier and signified is created by writing. It is writing that makes it possible for us to think of speech as if it were an object, or to think of the sounds that are other than the written objects before our eyes. Writing invents its own origin in the disjunction of signifier and signified and sets itself the problem of overcoming the self-inflicted amputation which was its own parthenogenesis.

Kinesis and Mimesis

The narrative of thinking about thought thinking about thought records a foundational metaphor signalled in English by the grammatical distinction between "thinking" and "thought." Thinking is an activity or process or movement, a sequence in the time that is not yet past, while thought is some thing, a static arrangement of parts in the contemporaneous past. The distinction was already marked by Plato as the difference between kinesis ("movement," "activity") and mimesis ("copy," "mimic," "represent"), where it was not only the difference between thinking and the thought about, but also the impression of externalities on the organs of sense (kinesis) which caused *pathēmata* or modifications of the mind that resulted in *eidola* ("images," "copies," mimesis). So we speak of thoughts as if they were things activated by powers just as nouns are animated by verbs. Thinking is the motor of thought.

Thoughts, first seen by the body's outer eye, are scenes before the mind's inner eye. They are sensible species, exuviae, simulacra, effluxes propagated from external sources which penetrate the organs of sense and effect the soul, giving it a mediate and representative perception of outward reality. Thoughts are reflections of another world that thinking only thinks about by means of thoughts. Thoughts are what we have in mind, but thinking is motion and activity, the upward *movement* of sensory information from the senses to the higher cognitive faculties; it is the *movement* from sensory particulars to conceptual generalization; it is the *movement* from the concrete to the abstract; it is the *movement* from unconscious to conscious; it is the *movement* of feeling from impression to expression; it is the *movement* from sense to sensibility, of sentient sensitivity in the sensorium that assents to sense, dissents from nonsense, consents to common sense, and is sensitized to sensuality. It is in this sense that thinking makes sense of sense, thought of sense, and sense of thought, for thinking is sense sentenced.

Thinking is the activity that creates the objects it thinks about, making what phantasms it fancies, and it is the orderly movement of thoughts, their unguided guide. Thinking is the movement from impression to expression and the motion of expression itself as the orderly succession of thoughts, the train of thought, the flow of thoughts, the sequence of ideas, notions, concepts, and images that course through our minds in logical array one after the other in lineal succession.

Thinking is both e-motion and pro-motion, a moving out from the com-motion of feeling and moving forward toward a re-mote abstraction and conception that ultimately de-motes feeling. Our metaphor of thinking as motion actually recapitulates all four of Aristotle's subspecies of motion and change: change in substance as generation and decay; change in quantity as augmentation and dimunition; change in quality as variation; and change in place as local motion (*Metaphysics* XII:11, *De Anima* I:3). Though it is not clear that Aristotle himself overtly used more than variation in his account of the association of ideas in memory and thought *(De Memoria)*, we do not hesitate to speak of "generating" ideas which, if they do not "decay" in memory, may "grow" into "big ideas" that "come to us quickly" or "slowly" after great effort before they "fade away." Our thoughts are linked or chained together in sequences, and this too is an ancient metaphor for the connection of thoughts as the movement from thought to thought (cf. Hamilton 1895:894, note). Thinking is thought enchained, and sometimes, wrongfully imprisoned, sentenced to run an artificial and unnatural course, to swim against the current in constricting channels and canals. There is an antagonism between thought and thinking for the sequential train of thoughts is both sustained and constrained by its opposite, the synchrony of thoughts. Thoughts are the impressions of nature's originals and mirrors of its forms. Close and intimate with their progenitors, thoughts have a logical and ontological priority over thinking. They are copies of the real existents from which they originate. Beings for beings before, they are "be-fors" of originals in the before, but thinking? What sort of prior motion does it mimic? What appearance makes motion in the absence of objects that change places in time? Isn't it this desire to think of thought as local motion that makes us think thinking is occult?

The conjunction of mimesis and kinesis in Saussure is the disjunction of paradigmatic and syntagmatic coordinating signs (1966:123). Syntagmatic orderings consist in the linear sequence of signs where each sign acquires its value in opposition to preceding and following signs in discourse. Paradigmatic orderings are nonlinear and are formed outside of discourse. They are associated relations which are not present in the discourse itself. They are absent potentialities, mnemonic wholes in the inner storehouse of ideas that make up language. A word thus evokes everything associated with it; it is the center of a constellation of thoughts, the point of convergence or departure in a synchronous whole whose parts are indefinite and indeterminant (ibid: 124).

The distinction between paradigmatic and syntagmatic parallels the equivalent distinction between static (synchrony) and evolutionary (diachrony) aspects of language in Saussure's discussion of the factor of time, where he divides linguistics into two divisions along an axis of "simultaneities" (= paradigmatic), and an axis of "succession" (ibid., 79–80). The former denotes coexisting things where time has no function, while the latter consists of singular events one at a time. Even though events occur one at a time on the axis of succession, all the things and events from the axis of simultaneity are available on the axis of succession. This availability parallels the "mnemonic series" in his discussion of paradigmatic ordering. It is the source of the speaker's notion of language as a "state," and it is also the past speakers must suppress as they order their expression sequentially (ibid.: 125).

Synchrony and diachrony, paradigmatic and syntagmatic are Saussure's equivalents of the quandary of quantum mechanics: linguistics cannot at the same time describe both position and movement (structure and change), and speakers cannot at once attend equally to the sequence of ideas and their synchrony. Paradigmatic and syntagmatic are necessary to one another, but both cannot be the object of thought or description at the same time. One must focus on one or the other— if focusing is necessary. Saussure conjures an image of an absurd artist attempting to sketch the Alps by seeing them simultaneously from several peaks and contrasts this with the moving observer who goes from peak to peak recording shifts in perspective, travelling obviously at less than the speed of light (ibid.: 82). Note that the problem of indeterminancy arises only in a context of "seeing" and "describing." Take away those contexts and most of the problem of indeterminancy dis-appears. Hearing and speaking, in fact, require the simultaneous integration of paradigmatic and syntagmatic.

The trope of perspectival relativity recurs again and again in Western thought, but the important point here is Saussure's notion of suppressing all but one of the associations that try to crowd in on the same point on the axis of succession. Recall that the scholastics called suggestion (= association) the "logic of Lucifer" or the "devil's dialectic" not only because of its waywardness, subjectivity, and looseness, but also because of its temptation to transcendent completion, to knowing all in an instant outside of time in imitation of the deity. In Saussure, it is as if speakers had attempted to arrogate to themselves the godlike abilities and prerogatives of linguists, but more important than Saussure's denigration of the speaker's understanding of language is his claim that only by studying the logic of Lucifer can linguistics become a science. For Saussure, the synchronic perspective is the only proper one. Diachronic study yields a mass of unrelated singularities, it does not yield a system. Diachrony is merely a record of the accidental effects of speech on language, of changes in the synchronic structure produced by all the forces of social life.

Saussure's endorsement of the paradigmatic and synchronic, of *langue*, is a charter for freeing the paradigmatic axis from the sequentiality of speech and from the intention and will of the speaking subject. It is part of the modernist program for undermining the individual, the self-mastered self, taking away its conscious control over the language it speaks much as Freud took away its conscious control over the thoughts it thinks.

Langue is objective and transcendental. The psychological connection of signifier/signified is important not in itself, but only in the role the unity of the sign plays in relation to other signs as part of a larger system. Its value is determined in opposition to other signs. These oppositions create a whole, not of identities or entities, but as a structure of differences and relations. The essence or make-up of the sign is unimportant, only its role as a bearer or marker of difference in the larger system of differences counts. This system is not located in discourse, in the syntagmatic succession of sign differences, it is located in memory where it is available as a potentiality.

Saussure invokes the by-now tired trope of the game as a means of making his point. *Langue* is likened to the game of chess. He argues that so long as the rules don't change and the pieces keep their respective values, it doesn't matter what the pieces look like or how well the players play. All the moves are pointless motions, epiphenomenal artifacts of the structure of the game. It would even be the same game no one ever played it. Thus Saussure makes his pact with the Devil.

Apart from the fact that this is a bad analogy for language since it closes off any understanding of dialect, style, or history, it has the value of reminding us that the price paid for Saussure's version of the transcendental is high, for it encourages us to "see" language as if it had extension in space, as if it were, indeed a structure, a picture, or a building, or any other subject we might say had a structure or comprised a system, or had a known set of rules of composition. It focuses our attention on the structure of the game as if that's what games are all about, but as we all know, the game is not the point—winning or losing is. Where all the players already know the rules, what use is an account of the rules unless it translates into strategies, choices of sequences of moves oriented to some end like winning the game? Saussure's game analogy is defective because it fails to exploit all of the meanings of "game," one of which is that it involves players whose motivations are not the same as those of analysts or game designers. The game as an object is not the object of the game, and the name of the game is not language, *langue,* competence, or any other transcendentalizing signifier; the name of the game is "play."

Saussure's key terms are structured thoughout his text by metaphorical equivalents of the opposition of mimesis and kinesis, as follows:

mimesis	kinesis
langue	*parole*
signified	signifier
paradigmatic	syntagmatic
synchronic	diachronic
hearer	speaker
collectivity	individual
essential	accidental
system	fragment
immutable	mutable
external	internal
associative	lineal
space	time
determinate	chance
game	players
convention	intention
memory (the unconscious)	conscious thought
past structure	present process

And this is so even though he deliberately attempts to side-step the central mimetic component—what is a copy of what? The signified, inasmuch as it is a sound image is at least, by implication some kind of representation, but what does the signified copy? What is the source of the signified? Where do concepts come from in Saussure's system? They are given no external source except by implication, so we must assume that they are either simulacra, copies of themselves, or that they are referentially connected to the exterior world by some simpler more straightforward mode of representation which is just given.

Saussure and the structuralist moment, whose genealogy is "being traced here," make the penultimate chapter in the narrative of the bewitchment of language, of the entification of language, of the construction of the idea of language as an objective, transcendent system, a totalizing structure of relations, a formal substance built up from elemental units of substance held together by the mortar of rules; an analytic structure, which, as Derrida rightly writes, recapitulates the episteme of the alphabet, which is to say, the episteme of episteme since the alphabet teaches but a single truth: knowing is the representation of elemental particles of being and their laws of connection in a whole which is both the subjective object of an objective subject and the objective subject of a subjective object.

The focal issues are representation and collocation, and the mediation of form and substance. The first two are only different names for mimesis and kinesis, but form and substance make the reasonableness of the sign as their mediator in:

form

↑

sign

↓

substance

The sign is neither form nor substance, but reputedly makes both available, though we know not to whom. This is the part left out in Saussure and structuralism. Recall that Plato, in one of the several equally likely versions of this episteme, connected form and substance in the manner of thought picture 1.3

Saussure's version of the sign moves the idea of the "name" into the center of the structure and eliminates the soul, and so the name in which soul participated becomes only the sign that points to a body but not to a soul. Saussure's version deletes both the soul and the idea

Epode

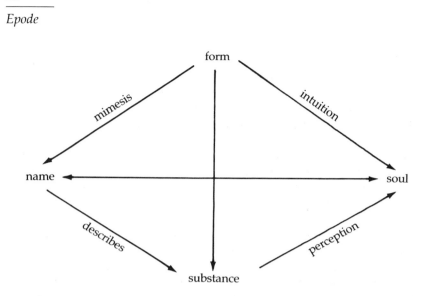

Thought picture 1.3. Semiosis in the Platonic episteme. "Name" and "soul" participate in the union of "form" and "substance." "Form" communicates in three ways: to the soul by intuition; to the name by mimesis or representation; and to substance as an emanation. The name "describes" a substance, and the soul perceives a substance that it recognizes by means of intuiting its form and by the name that describes it and imitates its form.

of participation. Representation alone is made to seem capable of doing the whole work of signs.

At the end of this penultimate chapter, which has the name "post-structuralism," Derrida disconnects the sign from the substance, and distorts the rules of collocation that had been the ideal of plain style and good forms, and we are left with a ceaseless shifting of signs without substance or form whose name is language and whose text is the last metaphysical survivor.

One could say that the object of postmodernism is to write the last chapter which would be the final slaying of the metaphysical beast, the deconstruction and overcoming of language, but this we cannot do so long as we write alphabetically. We can only overcome language by means of a writing that is not analytic. This, according to Bohm, is the project of postmodern physics (1980).

Bohm recommends a piecemeal restructuring of language of the sort that Saussure decreed was impossible. Bohm wishes to change the substance/substantive orientation of language, to end the domination of the noun by giving the verb the basic role (ibid.: 29). He recommends a new mode of language, called the "rheomode" (from G *rheo*,

"to move"), in which movement is primary. This would break the cognitive grip of the subject-verb-object form of language which does not
divide things appropriately. Rather than things as such, verbs would
merely emphasize different aspects of movement so that each would
merge, interpenetrate, and imply others. The new language would
also have new truth conditions. Rather than the truth of isolated statements, there would be an act of "verr-ation," of "truthing" in a given
context (ibid.: 29–47).

In Bohm's account, order is a key idea, for which he uses the verb
"ordinate" with its other forms "re-ordinate," "irre-ordinate," "re-
ordinant," "irre-ordinant," "re-ordination," and "irre-ordination." To
"ordinate" is to order attention while giving attention to thoughts
about order, and "re-ordination" is the continuing state of calling attention to an order. "Irre-ordination" is "re-ordinating" in an inappropriate context and signifies a failure of attention. The reason for
the importance of order is that it is needed in order to write coherently
about the new order of quantum physics which cannot be expressed
adequately in terms of the old Cartesian grids.

The new order is the result of perceiving similar differences and different similarities and different similarities of differences. The last
step, different similarities of differences, creates the beginning of a hierarchy of differences. The idea of disorder is replaced by the idea of
different degrees of order. When combined with measure (the boundary of an order) orders produce structures. This "structuration" is a
"harmoniously organized totality" of hierarchic levels working together (ibid.: 111–22).

Bohm goes on to note how the notion of "signal" in relativity theory implicates "communication," "signs," and "significance" as key
concepts in accounting for events and processes, patterns and movements within a field that is continuous and indivisible. Particles are
merely singularities which wax and wane within fields that merge im-
perceptibly into other fields. From this Bohm concludes that we can
no longer think of the universe as being divided into separate, distinct, interacting parts, but must regard it as "an undivided, unbroken whole" (ibid.: 125).

Here is the point of Bohm's discussion that is most important to
postmodernism. The order of undivided wholeness requires us to reject analysis or analysis-by-synthesis, for the essential idea of analysis
is that anything can be broken down into its basic constituent parts
and then reassembled into a total system. We think of things as if they
were autonomously behaving parts that could be separated out and
then put back into interaction. Undivided wholes do not fit this pat-

tern; they call for a new kind of description that does not separate the observed object from the observing instrument, and they require a new kind of observing instrument that would be capable of holography. Bohm's analogue here is, in fact, the holograph, but what he wants is a means of describing "holomovement," which will lead to "holonomy," the laws of wholes. The key feature of holomovement is that it expresses or carries an "implicit order." An implicit order cannot be reduced to a regular arrangement of objects or events for it is the totality of some order (ibid.: 125–57).

I include this account of Bohm's ideas here not because I endorse them wholly. His argument is, after all, still motivated by the visual episteme of observing and describing, and holomovement seems to be a kind of local motion that does not yet include the other Aristotelian varieties of movement and change. Bohm's ideas, though, are one option for postmodernism, and there are interesting parallels with Derrida and Heidegger here. Note, for example, the use, common to all three, of hyphenated terms, of words broken apart to remind us of the paradigmatic flow of connections that indexes a kind of rehabilitation of etymology. All three share the desire to find a way out of the analytic episteme with its entified essences, and they also agree in identifying language as the entifying culprit. There is, moreover, a common emphasis on holism and process, and on holistic representation, which for Bohm is the holograph and for Derrida is the rebus. Then, too, the idea of difference is fundamental to both Derrida and Bohm.

There are obvious differences in their use of these themes, and other differences as well, such as Bohm's attempt to remake alphabetic language, which reveals his continuation of the modernist's search for a future Adamic language. There is also a strong similarity between Bohm and Whorf, which is not surprising given their common interest in the implications of relativity. What is surprising is that Bohm seems not to have read Whorf. Saussure, too, was certainly aware of the "implicate structure" of language as a whole, and when Bohm writes of hierarchic strata of differences the writing of such linguists as Hjelmslev and Lamb comes immediately to mind.

One difference between Bohm and Derrida deserves comment. In opting for "movement" as the basis for his reformed language, Bohm seems to differ most clearly from Derrida. Derrida seems more interested in the mimetic side of language, more interested in representation than in communication. Despite their differences, neither Derrida nor Saussure attends to the dialogical and communicative characteristics of language, and this is the consequence of their common disdain for speech. Though Saussure occasionally speaks of speakers or dialogue, or represents dialogical situations, and even diagrams a "speaking circuit" (p. 11), he does so in order to eliminate speech and the speaker. *Langue* is not a function of the speaker, it exists perfectly only in the collectivity. Speaking is an expression of the individual's will, and speech cannot be studied because it is not homogeneous (1966:9–14, 19). Saussure, however, does not reject the whole oral/auditory facility, just the first part. His notion is that the "receptive coordinating faculties" make *impressions that are the same for all* and are therefore the means of the social bonds that make language a social and collective fact (ibid.: 13). He eschews speech because it is not traceable to an external impression that would guarantee its identity, even though it is the instrument that makes that identity possible in the mind of the hearer. It is as if only hearers really know what is said, and here, of course, is the parallel with Derrida, for whom the author of all is the passive recipient, and it must be this way for both because they deny the possibility of creation. For Saussure, no one could create or could have created language; it had no knowable origin. For Derrida, no one really creates a text. The essential theme for both is that nobody could really create anything but noise, and since that is the case, the idea of individuals or of creating, authoritative, authorial egos in charge of what they say has to be consigned to the metaphysical dump.

No origin, no creation, and for Derrida, no being, just an already was. There is also no invention in the sense of the coming to be of something new. How could there be without creation, origin, or being? The idea of invention in both Saussure and Derrida does not involve the *nova* of plain style; it is instead the *inventio* of rhetoric, the resurrection of the past, of everything already in the storehouse of the collective representation. For Saussure, what is known is as voices from the past; for Derrida, it is what has been written by Nemo. And this, of course, is where Derrida and Saussure part company. Saussure grounds his linguistics in phonology, in the representation of the sound of the voice. Moreover, his definition of the sign carries the voice into the very heart of the sign in the notion of "sound image," the psychological representation of the speaker's voice, which has the effect of grounding the sign in external substance. "Sound image," this oxymoron, with its confusion of the oral and the visual, tells the whole tale of linguistics, of its desire to transform the oral into the visual and of the resistance of the oral residue to its reduction to writing, to speech made visible by marks.

Derrida exposes Saussure's hesitation here, showing how Saussure's denigration of writing for its inaccurate representation of that originary sonic substance acquiesces to the cultural tradition that has always either assigned writing to an inferior, secondary role, or made it the scapegoat for man's distance from being. It is the means of representation that reveals only by obscuring.

Derrida is right in his argument that linguistics and the idea of the sign are coeval co-evils that reflect the whole metaphysics of alphabetic writing (1974:10). The problem of the sign as a representation of sound is reflected in the long and pointless dispute about the nature of the phoneme. In all its versions, the question was, "What is the relationship between sound as a physical phenomenon and the meaningful signs of writing?" The problem of the phoneme recapitulates the entire question about alphabetic writing at the same time as it presupposes that writing. On one hand, it was a question about how to render in written form the sounds of unwritten languages, but on the other hand, it questioned the adequacy of all systems of writing not already rationalized by the methods of phonological inscription and the rules of analysis that created phonemic signs as transcendental universals.

We hear in this story the whole thematic of the manifold of sensation (phonology) that represents substance (sound) and is itself re-represented as form (phonemics). This story retells the fundamental allegory of mimesis as representation, of the movement from the outer world to the inner world, which is also the movement from the particular, concrete, and individual to the universal, abstract, and collective, the congeries of movements that eventually came to be summarized in the polarity conscious-unconscious. This movement, too, is repeated in the history of phonology, when the phoneme was at last understood by Sapir not as a psychological image, as in Saussure, but as a kind of unconscious knowledge that linguists came to know in the fullness of analytic method, by a means, in other words, unavailable to the native speaker of a language.

Here, then, is an interesting parallel movement of psychoanalysis and linguistics. Linguistics becomes the reading of language as unconscious, and psychoanalysis, in the hands of Lacan, becomes the unconscious as language. Moving, so to speak, in opposite directions the two inscribe a complementary figure, and both are motivated by the same urge to justify at one and the same time the rule of analysis and the privileged position of the analyst in that analysis. Both invoke the unconscious as a special province of the mind that is closed to ordinary understanding and inaccessible to the procedures of empirical justification with its demands for substance as the beginning and end of rational analysis. The world of linguistic form is thus sealed off both from the world of direct observation and lived experience. The unconscious is the guarantor of its boundaries, the surety for the separation and opposition of *langue* and *parole*, form and content, competence and performance which express over and over again the Platonic polarity of *nous* and *aisthesis* and the Kantian opposition of noumenon and phenomenon. We can now appreciate the full meaning of Sapir's paper entitled, "Why Cultural Anthropology Needs the Psychiatrist" (1938). The unconscious establishes the necessity for a special method of writing that can only be done by one who is trained in its *techne*, and who can thus write the secret text that is language.

In the same way, psychoanalysis guarantees its method and ensures the special role of the analyst as the one who knows the method for reading the secret language of the text of the unconscious. Thus it is that the linguists and psychoanalysts, in that wider context of the episteme of the unconscious, are complementary—one writes the unconscious language, the other reads it. So we have here a division of labor not unlike that of other priesthoods which divide the functions of scribe and preacher. Conjointly, linguist and psychoanalyst symbolize the whole idea of writing.

But, just as the unconscious justifies and ensures the inviolability of the labyrinth of language, it also closes off any exit from it. Analysis can only add to the labyrinth, it cannot eliminate it, transcend it, or overcome it; it can only continue the analysis, as Freud himself admitted in "Analysis Terminable and Interminable." To put it differently, the price of justification is the loss of any legitimacy beyond that already presupposed by analysis itself. Analysis (psychoanalytic and linguistic) seeks to transform its justification into its legitimization, but all it can offer is some unachievable goal that involves something like the ultimate triumph of reason. Paradoxically, both linguistics and psychoanalysis work within the reason of the enlightenment, but undermine it at the same time. Whereas the enlightenment held out the hope for the fulfillment of reason, analysis finds a kind of narcissistic fulfillment in itself. Reason is not the means to ultimate reason, it is the ultimate reason for reason, but that reason cannot answer the question, "What's the use of an analysis whose sole aim and only course is self-perpetuation through the unmasking of ever-new regions of unreason?" Reason as means and end is meaningless, for it produces nothing beyond itself and the need for more of it. It is the perfect image of capitalist production.

This final transformation of the unconscious from the reason for reason to the reason of reason, its rewriting as the secret place of ultimate order instead of a seething chaos of unreason, chance, and indeterminancy reflects the disengagement of the sign from the world, of form from substance, and language from speech. It both implicates and is facilitated by a rewriting of the idea of association that removes association from the world of contingency and from the lineal, sequential chain of signification. In Freud, the change is gradual, but emerges finally in the idea that dreams reproduce logical connection by simultaneity in time in the manner of a palimpsest or collage where the nexus of images overlaid and juxtaposed provides the connection of logical sequence without the sequence. Spatial "co-nexion" makes temporal connection, just as it does in the "causal" ideas of association in Hume. For Hume and Freud, temporality is only illusory, something added to "co-nexion" by the mind. It is the means of the illusion of the continuous existence of the self. In this interpretation, associations are not temporal sequences in the "chain" or "train" of thought, not one thing after another as in plain style, but one thing on top of another as in a hieroglyph. This "spatialization" of association reproduces the Western penchant for space and its fascination with the occult writing of Egypt, themes which, from their articulation in Plato, have played over and over again in the literature of Western physics and metaphysics.

In Saussure, this transformation of association is announced without a backward glance at the older idea of sequential contingency in time. In plain style, association functioned on the syntagmatic axis, but for Saussure, as for Freud, Hume, and the scholastics, it functions on the paradigmatic axis as the storehouse of memory, as the means of repetition. Where plain style had understood suggestion (the paradigmatic axis) as the rhetorical and poetic means by which writers and speakers exercised their will, Freud, Saussure, and the scholastics understood it as the "Devil's Dialectic," as something beyond the control of the will. For the scholastics and for plain style, only an exercise of will could keep thought from being led astray, whereas for Freud and in a different sense for Saussure, too, repression of the paradigmatic axis had to be overcome in order to reveal the real structures of thought and language. Paradoxically, both Freud and Saussure continued to write in plain style while undermining the idea that animated it. It remained for others to see the discrepancy between the old order of discourse and the new orders of thought and language.

There is, in all of the literature on association from Aristotle to Saussure, an ambivalence between association as kinesis and association as mimesis. When writing of the nexus of thoughts in reminiscence, Aristotle emphasizes kinesis, but even he suggests that synexis, the thought of wholes, is some kind of coadjacency, a relation of parts in space (*Physics* 7:4.10, *De Anima* 2:5.2, *De Memoria* 1:4). Hobbes (1908), and empiricists generally, have interpreted Aristotle as if he understood the movement of thought as local motion and therefore as a purely mechanical phenomenon of the action of one element upon another in a causal, sequential order. It was this understanding of association that plain style sought to impose upon the order of discourse. Hume's deconstruction of the idea of causality as necessary connection between contingencies undermines the philosophical basis of plain style, but this implication of his argument is repressed and virtually unacknowledged, except in the commonsense defense of "suggestion," and by implication, of plain style, in Reid and other commonsense philosophers.

Freud never succeeded in overcoming the ambiguity of association. In fact, he needed both the kinetic and mimetic ideas of association in order to make the unconscious work right. He needed contingencies that could be explained as noncontingencies. Perhaps his dream of the unconscious was closer to Kant's synthetic apriori than Lacan's reading of him would suggest.

The idea of association as pure contingency (*co-tangere*) continued in a quasi-statistical sense and in the ideas of habit-formation and stimulus-response in behaviorist psychology, but this was only a repetition, albeit unacknowledged, of Aristotle's discussion of *ethos* (custom, habit) in connection with memory, where the whole question of necessity and contingency was more clearly presented than it has been since (*De Memoria* 1.2).

The opposition of kinetic and mimetic in association surfaces again and again. Whorf (1956), for example, calls for a new principle of association that would account for the unconscious, cryptological structure of language in a way that is reminiscent of Saussure. Sapir, too, makes a plea for the unconscious, mimetic form of association (1958), and the whole issue is restated in Chomsky's derailment of Skinner's train of lineal association as the explanation of syntax. It recurs also in the contemporary distinction between "semantic" and "episodic" memory, where the latter is clearly kinetic and the former is clearly structural and mimetic. In different phrasing we find it too in Quine's attack on the distinction between analytic and synthetic propositions.

Not only does the thematic opposition of kinesis and mimesis persist throughout, so does the ancient distinction between *verba* ("words") and *res* (things) that appears already in Aristotle's *De Memoria* as the distinction between "memory for words" and "memory for things." Ambiguous from its very beginning, it is invoked over and over again to explain the necessary connection of words in thought and utterance by reference to contingencies in time. It thus speaks of the desire for necessities that yet retain some stigma of contingency, some connection with the outer world, as if the incorporation of the outer world had left stratified residues like handy geological ledges that could be ascended or descended. Here is the desire for contingencies that are the means of necessity.

The idea is from beginning to end doubly ambiguous. On one hand, it purports to explain how things become connected in thought by imitating a prior connection in the outer world, while, on the other hand, it tries to show how words and things are connected. Its ambiguities, in other words, are those already familiar to us in that conundrum of representation as the originary connection in the series things → thoughts → words that reflect both this origin and the direction of the series from gross to subtle, material to spirit, phenomenon to noumenon, or any one of several other metaphoric implicates such as unconscious to conscious, concrete to abstract, sensation to conception, particular to universal, or substance to form, for these are all different ways of telling the same story of the one in the many, the literal and the figurative.

The consequences are interesting. Whereas Freud's dream analysis enables the psychoanalyst to think of images as if they were instantaneous propositions, Saussure's paradigm prompts linguists to think of language as if it were an image or picture, or more exactly, as his metaphor of the chessboard tells us, as if it were an instantaneous matrix. In psychoanalysis, the succession of images yields up a synchronous logic, while in linguistics a logic of succession yields up a synchronous image. It is almost as if each tries to become the other, but succeeds only in projecting an interestingly distorted reflection of itself. The same interesting complementarity is repeated in the contemporary period in the quarrel between those psychologists who argue that thought is verbal and propositional and others for whom it is visual imagery, or is perhaps coded in both modalities. Something of the same set of ideas also obviously animates all those oversimplified dualisms that supposedly constitute the differences between the right and left hemispheres of the brain, but the important point here is that this complementarity expresses a fundamental preference for metaphors of space and synchrony over metaphors of time and sequentiality, or to put it differently, a preference for myth rather than narrative. Psychoanalysts and linguists share the same desire to fix the world in an immutable pattern of necessary connections between words and images. They are both fixated on the idea of the patterning of signs, and they both repress speech as the symbol of all that is chance, contingency, narrative, and time. That is to say, they are seduced and hoodwinked by writing.

The Mother Matrix

Now, we must conjure with a potent symbol that animates the whole of Western discourse, for it is both the mother of the idea of structure and structure itself. Like writing, its congener, it begins and ends with lines marked on or in some surface, or it is the lines that constitute the surface itself. Thus already from this beginning that we can only imagine, there is an interplay and ambiguity between marked and marking that involves not just lines and the idea of linearity and marking, but the idea of intersecting lines that make figures, of figuration in its literal sense as the making of images whose intersecting lines and planes mirror the intersecting forces and harmonies that make the structure of the universe. Writing and the texts produced by writing are, from the first, expressions of a metaphor of figuration as "weaving." The word "text" itself derives from Latin *texere* ("to weave") and we still speak of weaving or "stitching together" (cf. *rhapsode*, "stitch together") a discourse in which the "seams" are not obvious, or one that makes a "seamless web." This weaving metaphor occurs in story after story as a symbol of order, and order itself is another weaving metaphor, derived from Latin *ōrdō*, a technical term for the arrangement of threads in the warp and woof of a fabric. And, do we not still speak of the "fabric" of a tale, the "thread of discourse," of words as the "clothing of thought," of the "network" of ideas in a text, and of "spinning a yarn," which others may "unravel"?

The essential idea here is replicative (< IE *plek-, "to intertwine," "plait") order, the "plan" of something, its secret scheme or plot flattened out in order to emulate Plato and explain by making visible (cf. IE * pla-, "flat"; > G Plato; E "plan," "plane," "explain," "plot," and "flat"). In its most literal sense, it is lines or planes laid down, placed (also IE *pla-) in an arrangement (< IE *krengh-, "circle") of circles, squares, and triangles, a pattern (< IE *pat-, "father") fathered by an original or source that it copies. As the word "text" itself reminds us, all this is connected with technique (G *technē*, "manual skill"), with what is skillfully built (cf. G *arkhitectōn*, "master builder"), of all that is articulated (< L *artus*, "joint"), reticulated (< L *rēte*, "net"), connected

(< IE *nedh- "bind," "knot"), bound, and regulated (< IE *reg-, "set straight > L *rex* "king") by the Au, the king of the text, the "au-thor's" "au-thority," "au-gust" "au-gury," and "au-gmentation."

The text is the power of lines that connect. It is akin to drawing sacred, potent, magical figures, like mandala, which are always figurations in both senses—as things and metaphors. The point of figuration, of writing and text is to capture the power (kinesis) of an exterior order through the techne of mimesis, and to defeat time by transforming motion into structure.

Here we must contemplate the connections within the series temper, temporal, temple, template, and tense (< IE *tem-, *ten-, "to cut," "cut out"). Whether we make strong by proportional compounding, or are being reasonable, or being seasonable, or constructing a religious edifice, or laying out a plan or design or being grammatical, we are engaged in building a temple of thought, a division of space and time made by lines that intersect (< IE *sek-, "to cut") and "cut out" time, trapping it in a network of interlocking spaces, subduing it, and forcing it to do as we will by our authority. Such is the alchemy of writing whose source is the mother matrix (< IE *mat-, "producer," "mother"; > L *matrix*, "womb"), the womb of created being. In this figure of the matrix, of

we capture the whole mimetic episteme of writing. The matrix is the telos and essential techne of the text, for it is the ultimate thought picture of Western desire, of the magical net that captures its own source in the creation of time, of the lust for the completion of the shroud Penelope weaves as she "passes the time" that her suitors seek to ordinate, to measure in the augmentation of rows and lines of thread that fashion the thread of this story. It is also the mark of the cultivator, of cultivation, of the field plowed in cross-cutting boustrophedon furrows and measured by the tax collector who thus marks the agency of civilization in the setting of limits and boundaries that oppress the earth, and it is the mark of the grid of the city on the face of the land.

The Cartesian grid, its coordinates and points on a line are the means of the mytheme of calculation and measure, of ratio as the proportional relation of points within the grid, and of point-to-point correspondence between external objects and the grid. Together they make the mythos of the mechanical and are the instruments of the calculus that confirms the mechanistic order that created it. The Cartesian matrix is the web of space that entraps time.

The matrix presupposes lines, intersection, points, point-to-point correspondence between image and object. Its parts are autonomous elements and its order is the regular arrangement of discrete objects in intersecting rows and columns. In it, all change is merely the difference in position and orientation of a rigid body, and all movement is continuous connection between discontinuous points. The matrix figures a vision of the universe as an array of arrays in which each column and row contains elements that can be manipulated by the rules that govern the formation of figures within matrices. The matrix is the idea of the computer before the computer, and the computer itself is only a matrix. Its programs and switching circuits are nothing more than networks of matrices, matrices of matrices (cf. Hartog 1985). Thus, the combination of analytic elements creates a figure that figures and is a figuration of a figure. The matrix makes the shape that has shaped Western thought since the beginning of writing.

The matrix is the hierogram of the logogram of the *gramme* and the hieroglyphic lust of the alphabet. The difference between the hierogram and the hieroglyph is that the hierogram cannot go beyond the units and means that constitute it, and must therefore forever repeat that structure. Whatever we seek to know by means of it will only recapitulate what we know of it and so what we come to know is endless, self-confirming repetition of the same. The hieroglyph is the symbol of the desire for transgression, for another means of writing that will enable us to transcend the limits of the alpha-matrix. It is the desire for what is beyond the matrix, for something neither created by it not represented in it as a point correspondence nor capable of being transformed into a corresponding point, but still somehow accessible to the means of the matrix, emergent within it even though it cannot be implicated by it. It is the desire for the whole that cannot be represented nor known analytically nor described. It is the lust for what is outside of *de-scribere*, for what is out of "writing," but not "out of" writing.

Derrida struggles to escape from the net of the alpha-matrix, but fails because the rebus principle, the dual coding of sound and sight, of homophone and simulacrum in the hieroglyph privileges images over sound. It is not a duality of equals. Despite all of his attempts to revolutionize the literal-figurative/letter-figure relationship of the alpha-matrix, the rebus principle merely reinstates the priority of the literal/letter. Even though images are literal/figuratives rather than figurative/literals, the rebus does not overcome the literal-figurative distinction, it inscribes it. The rebus is still marks on a surface that make images both on that surface and on the psyche. It continues the whole "co-lection" of tropes "co-nected" with the matrix, conjuring the phantoms that take shape between the lines; it remains within the language of lines, strata, impressions, images and cut-outs, and still speaks of space, mimesis and representation. So, too, Derrida's language continues the trope of the network. His images of writing are of the "system of connections," the "fabric of the trace," the "assemblage," the "interlocking," "interweaving" "web" of "threads" and "lines" that "bind together," and what is the image of the chiasmus itself, but the crossing of lines? "Isn't it a weaver's movement," of _la navette_ ("shuttle"), of _grille_ ("grid"), of stitching, of interlacing, of the _moiré_ effect of flickering produced by the to and fro of two superimposed grids (1974:223–35). Isn't it the loom of fate _(moira)_?

The idea of the rebus has all the defects long associated with images in the mind. Can we say that images have a grammar, a set of constraints on their succession and cooccurrence, or do they somehow transcend grammar, freeing us at last from succession, sequence, and time? Perhaps they do free us, but the consequence of this freedom is total arbitrariness where anything can combine with anything, and this promiscuity is, of course, what Derrida's dissemination of dream analysis suggests, as does his invocation of the principle of collage. Both are celebrations of the accidental juxtapositions of fragments that carry with them into each chance encounter memories and residues of their past associations and contexts—a karmic burden that creates the ideational and emotional equivalent of the halation of adjacent colors in an abstract painting. They are understood by a kind of cryptanalysis that recapitulates their former contacts in the manner of an epidemiological study of a virus, or of the dissemination of a gene pool, or of a set of chain reactions that make a chemical compound. (Derrida 1981:129–30). This is not surprising since the grammar of imagery is always the grammar of contact and contiguity. It is neither action at a distance as in gravitation nor discontinuous as in the case of light. It is the logic of the "chain" or "chain complex," in effect, a chance mechanism whose derivable history of chance associations has allegorical determinations.

The fragments of a collage or rebus are never what they seem; they are not direct representations of a prior totality and they are not simply substitutions of appearances for realities in the usual sense of mimesis. They are instead simulacra, appearances that make realities. They are real/models, not models of the real, for they are not approximations of some reality, they are the only reality we know. Like models of the universe they are not copies of the universe but are the means of talking about a universe that can neither be presented or represented.

The universe has only an allegorical interpretation within the fairytale of science, and its model is the means of further allegoresis.

In his own way, Derrida continues the dominant tradition of Western thought that has always tried to break down the relation between words and things (*verba* and *res*) by transforming the former into the latter. He is writing a chapter in the book of the suspicion of the word even as he glorifies the signifier and celebrates the dispersal of the transcendental signified, for his desire to write by means of things (*rebus*) rather than words is a kind of latterday positivism. The only difference is that things today are not what they once were.

Though it may at first seem perverse, we can also understand his freeing of the signifier from the transcendental signified as a move already implicated in the positivist program. To put it differently, freeing the signifier is the consequence of the deconstruction of the transcendental signified, of the exterior reality, the "real things" the signifier mirrored. In positivism this is the failure of the theory of reference. It was paradoxically associated with the rise of formalism and not so paradoxically with the gradual abandonment of an empirical program. The meaning of these two complementary consequences is that the failure of referential theories of meaning reflected a failure of the referent and not of the referential means of language. The Heisenbergian decomposition of referents, or things that made them reflexes of means of measurement, was not a failure of reference, it was the consequence of the cannibalization of things by their means of measurement. In effect, the world disappeared into our word of it. The signifier no longer refers to anything but itself and is free to construct whatever pictures of the world are given in the potentiality of its internal combinations of signs as recapitulations of its own systematicity. That is the essence of formalism, and it is also the essence of the rebus.

The rebus is not about the transcendental signified (things as they are) anymore than mathematics is. Like mathematics, it is the formalism of the transcendental signifier, and the patterns of its collocations are reflexes of its own systemic character. The features of the rebus are precisely akin to the arbitrariness of "let x equal _____," where "x" may be any "thing" that performs roles given by "equal" and the combinatory possibilities of what follows "equal," that is to say, in both senses of "follow." The rebus, in other words, is a formalism in disguise, for it is "by things" that are simulacra and not things at all. It is as if, following Derrida, we were to write r̶e̶bus, cancelling "things," and leaving only the idea of instrumentality.

One problem with this reduction, and it is equally a problem for images in the mind and for formalism, is an inherent solipsism. Who says, "let x equal _____," and by what authority? The problem with both images and formalism has always been their subjectivity. On one hand, images seem to solve the problem by being reflections of the given—of things as they are—but, on the other hand, being reflected in the mind of a subject they are contingent on his/her experience. In the case of formalism, there can be no justification or legitimation of the prescriptive "let" within the formal system itself. Justification and legitimation have to be provided by a framing allegory that is not derivable from the formal system. The formal system can neither constitute itself by itself nor by directly implicating an exterior source of its own rules. Its authority is thus compromised.

Neither images nor formalism can appeal to consensus. For formalism, there is only a single, transcendental ego whom we can hardly imagine "consensing" with himself without wondering "how?" and "why?" As for images, what means of consensus would not involve something other than images themselves? What is the source of the agreement that says: "such and such an image is an image of such and such"? What image "tells" us it is itself or that it compares in such and such a way with other images when we cannot have two distinct images in mind at once? This always leads those who think in images to think of "superimposing," as if the mind were a palimpsest or collage—as it may be—but the problem here is that the whole language for talking about images in the mind is based either on how we think we operate with images in the visual field outside the mind, or on how we think when we talk about them. We have no images about images imaging, though we might imagine it.

The solution for both images and formalism is to deny intentionality, and both deny that they are intentionally motivated. They are not the project of a conscious ego or self; the cogito is their project, not the other way around. Both claim authority by denying author-ity in the same way that God's authority is guaranteed by his unauthorizability. By thus making the system of signs independent of any subject, the whole troublesome set of questions concerning intentionality and consciousness, of language and writing as projects of active cognition disappears into the mind of the transcendental signifier called writing or the *system* of signs.

The transcendental signifier is the unconscious as a transcendental id, and the aim is for writing to mirror—not nature, the transcendental signified—but itself, as the transcendental signifier. It is to be the mirror that reflects itself endlessly, where writing and the world merge indistinguishably into a single whole and the gap between world and word closes as they are enclosed in the womb of their common matrix, and enfolded into the wo(r(l)d)mb.

Since writing is its own project, it has no need of external authors who write as autonomous actors outside the system of the transcendental signifier. The author is already inside, is already part of the play of the signifier and does not control the discourse; she is only its instrument and facilitator. This, of course, calls to mind the idea of automatic writing, the transcendental unconscious manifesting itself through the hand of the scribe who neither translates from the system of the unconscious nor even transcribes, but "scribes" without willing it. She neither "brings forth" nor "calls out," neither produces nor creates, she is the ductus, the passive conduit of the ejaculating unconscious. The master is the slave of the androgynous transcendental signifier/muse who mistresses him, and the pen is the invaginated penis inseminated/disseminator, the impregnated/impregnating dyaus/pṛthivi and śiva/śakti whose impassioned dance across the page impassionately consumes person, ego, cogito, author, creator, and will.

But why is it then, that those who most seek to abdicate, to give up their authority—Bataille, Blanchot, Derrida—are also the ones whose texts bear the clearest signature of their authorship, of conscious manipulations of structure and meaning, of bending the rules to their individual wills? It is as if the desire to write as an automaton makes writing less automatic and creates an individual style marked by that desire itself so that those who will their voices into silence leave an identifying echo in every line. And what are we to make of the idea of the author as the censor of the unconscious (Derrida 1974:157–64)? What is this censor but the will of the author constructing a text as a cognitive utopia?

Even if, as Derrida says, his texts are interesting only in what they tell us apart from his intentions, by what is written through him but not by him, what we enjoy in that is catching the poor fish in the toils of the net he has woven and cast over himself—to impale him on the point of his own pen, to land him wriggling and squirming, to squeeze out his innards, to fillet him, and serve him up roasted and sauced in his own juices. We are fishing for the unintended consequences of authorial intentions. Derrida knows this, and the wily trout tries to throw the hook by flipping onto his back, mooning us with his derrière, and making a run for the reeds, the papyrus of other texts oscillating in the inky current of the transcendental signifier. Reading is a contest of wills, a contest between the will of the reader and the occulted will of the author. The author is the game of the reader and the text is the snare they share. Even when he says "it is written by me for myself" we set the hook with a twist of the wrist that writes "Solipsism!" "Who here presumes to write in the name of the transcendental id?"

Is this not another aspect of Derrida's positivism? The appearance of authorlessness is, after all, the aim of all scientific writing. Repression of subjectivity in the name of an objective style that speaks the language of things, the scientist as the mouthpiece of the authority of nature, the author behind the author that guarantees his authority only if he signifies his objectivity by the rhetoric of his absence. The text is an uncreated object, a thing of nature, a natural object that mirrors other natural objects and its rhetoric is the unconscious structure of things.

Like the scientist and the Navajo weaver, Derrida does not weave a perfect net but leaves openings, exits, transfers to other lines, and enfolds himself in a tissue of gaps and imperfections that always needs mending or calls for more weaving. His imperfections are the equivalent of the scientist's equivocation, of "further research is needed," "available data show," "the results of these experiments are inconclusive but. . . ." The clear call for supplementation, for more of the same that makes a difference is the message thrown back over their shoulders as they escape through the holes in their own nets.

Here too is the clue to Derrida's advocacy of the rebus. The rebus is a "picto-ideo-phonographic" writing. It is a picture of something whose name is the homophone of another idea and thus combines the sensory modalities of sight and sound with the ideational and associative means of understanding. Consider the following: $\Delta = k\bar{o}$ (sound) = "mountain" (meaning) = $k\bar{o}$ (sound) = "king," "palace," "temple" (meaning). The pyramid is a pictorial image of a mountain; its name is pronounced $k\bar{o}$, which is homophonous with $k\bar{o}$, the sound of the name for "king," etc. Like dream images, rebus writing is a collage of superimposed images, associated ideas, and sounds. It is nonlinear, nonsuccessive, atemporal, pluridimensional, and it neutralizes or represses phonic substance. As a synesthetic condensation it is an organization of space that mimics the "synchronic causality" of the unconscious. A different kind of mimesis, it is neither strictly sensorial nor a sensible plenitude, for it does not represent an exterior world translated into the language of the imagination by the senses but is instead the figure of nonsensible thought. Not just the language of the dream, it is the dream of all scientific writing that pretends to universal signification through repression of the voice. It is the dream of a timeless structure of concepts, and of the complete spatialization of time and thought.

What, after all, is a scientific text but a conturbation of diagrams, pictures, dephoneticized mathematical formulae, and occasional remnants of formulaic phrases from ordinary language supplemented by acronyms, Latin words, and disseminated Greco-Latin neologisms? It has all the character of something pointed to and looked at but never read, or read only in bits of condensed acronymical jargon. Derrida's call for a new writing based on the principle of the rebus is more an acknowledgement of what already is than a call for something new.

Derrida repeats here the language of immortality that has always been written as the hope of writing, of writing as the domination of time by space, of the triumph of permanence over decay and death, of remembering over forgetting. Thinking to write against the metaphysics of presence as speech, he gives us the metaphysics of the pluridimensional past that hides itself in words like "space," "dimension," "nonlinear," "nonsuccessive," "repression," and "unconscious."

In common with other modernists and surrealists, Derrida is a crypto-positivist. He has matriculated in the matrix and he reads the message of the suppressed and dominated "oral" tradition of Western philosophy that runs from Heraclitus to Heidegger and Wittgenstein, proclaims it the reality of Western philosophical desire and then refutes it by reasserting the themes of the dominant, scientific, "ocular," objective tradition in the guise of a new dispensation, a new form of writing, as if changing the form of writing would itself eradicate metaphysics. He thus continues, in his own idiosyncratic way, to assert the tired themes of modernism, but in a way that undermines modernism's worship of science and technology. He opens the way to postmodernism by showing us that the way that can be written is not the way.

The key to his thought is indeed the threefold of the rebus. What is picto-ideo-phonographic writing but the first three components of the Aristotelian order of representation as things → thought → speech → writing written without the arrows (→) to indicate time, sequence, causal connection, and origin as in thought picture 1.4. This figure is the "history" of writing in the timeless, ahistorical, nondialectical structure of thought, of the trace within the cartouche signed by "graphy," the rebus of the transcendental signifier whose anaglyphic backside is the Picassoesque face of the sensorium superimposed on its own nose, and whose name is "icon-index-symbol." Behind the mask of the rebus is thought picture 1.5.

Despite his Egyptian fantasies, Derrida still speaks the language of mimesis, of representation, for he writes as mirror of the unconscious, and even though the unconscious is equivalent to the transcendental signifier and the mirror itself, there yet remains intact the mirror mirroring. Indeed, the new writing he sometimes writes cannot be judged on the grounds of its reflective capability since it only reflects itself,

Epode

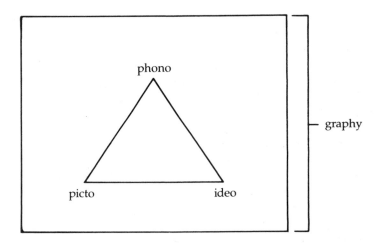

Thought picture 1.4. The "tomb" of speech. The "three-fold" of "picto-ideo-phono-graphic" writing. The exteriority of "graphy" reveals the transcendence of the "mark," just as the placement of "picto-" at the head of this macaronic compound shows the priority of visual representation in the rebus.

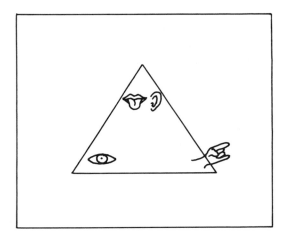

Thought picture 1.5. The rebus of the sensorial semiotic behind the mask of "picto-idea-phonography." "See," "point," and "speak/hear" are the sensorial correlates of "eye-con," "in-dex," "mouthear" or icon, index, and sym-bol.

but this does not inhibit the claim that it surpasses lineal, alphabetic writing if for no other reason than that the latter can give only a distorted reflection of itself owing to the phonological flaws in its surface. So there is a claim of better representation, and there is also a claim that representation takes precedence over communication since the latter is only the idea of speech, of one voice speaking to another and is thus bound up in the metaphysics of presence and phonocentrism.

Despite his deconstruction of the transcendental signified, Derrida still writes within the Aristotelian episteme of representation of "impressions" that make *pathēmata* (emotions) that make phantasms (representations) that make both thought and emotion which are in turn represented and expressed as in thought picture 1.6. Impressions of the outer world are represented as thoughts and emotions in the psyche which are then re-represented in expressions. Derrida changes this order by erasing "impression" and its arrow (the transcendental signifier), but he does not alter the foundational role of representation, and he retains communication ("expression") as something that derives from prior representation. Expressions express representations. Postmodernism erases this whole thought picture of thought pictured—including the inner-outer distinction and the separation of thought and emotion and writes instead: "thought/emotion/expression," or just "communication."

Derrida's relegation of communication to the derivative status of "expression" reflects more than just the glorification of representation, it is part of a larger rejection—the rejection of the idea of *communis*, which the idea of communication embodies not only lexicographi-

Thought picture 1.6. The episteme of representation.

cally in its root but symbolically, as the means of civil life. No accident led Vico and Rousseau to their tripartite understanding of writing where alphabetical writing correlated with the emergence of true civil society and all other forms of writing correlated with pastoral society, and the absence of writing correlated with savagery and barbarism. Nor is it just chance that the sensorium reflects this same idea of "agreement in judgements" in the *sensus communis*, the "higher," "civilized," "urban," "lawful," "written" "realm" of consciousness. The mind reflects the history of man and reflects the history of writing. The urban landscape of the higher, conscious mind reflects the wordly city.

Thus, Derrida continues the tale of the dominant scientific tradition. Rationalism and empiricism, whatever the disagreements that have marked them, have agreed in their pursuit of this will-o-the-wisp of undifferentiated communication, of a means of representation so accurate that men could no longer disagree. All would automatically come to the same conclusions if their means of thought and expression were not defective, and there would then be no need for communication, for all would, as it were, know one another's minds without saying anything, and all the jabbering, disputatious voices would be stilled in the telepathic silence. The whole problem of agreement in judgements and the myth of the community of scientists coming to agreement would be dissolved as each happy, interchangeable monad went surely and silently to its work, ensuring the harmony of the whole already flawless reflected in its own purified mind.

Though he writes of the fragmented *communis*, and only from the margins of what is left of civilization, Derrida still writes in the rhythms of the enlightenment dream of human utopia constructed on the model of the ant colony. True, he solves the problem of distorted communication by absolving us of the need for any kind of communication—if we but write right we can't be wrong—but in this he reaffirms the ideology of bureaucratic science and confirms its suspicion of *elocutio* and *pronunciatio* as the agonistic means of discourse that deliberately mislead. Is not suspicion of speech the very essence of the totalitarian state? Repress communication and suppress dispute, that is the maxim of every tyrant, and what tyrant has not suspended truth in the interests of the totality of signifiers? Derrida evades responsibility in the manner of the bureaucrat, propagandist, and scientist whose truth is in the text dictated by an autocratic signifier, by the "I" who does not write here.

In this, too, the arche-Derrida is an arch conservative. His return to rhetoric is a return to a truncated rhetoric which has a hand but no voice and consists of *inventio, memoria,* and *dispositio*—in itself as odd as the differently distorted rhetoric of Ramus. *Inventio* and *memoria* are the means for the production and justification of simulcra, for the science of models and simulations that legitimizes itself within itself. It is no accident that Derrida, like Ramus before him, eliminates all enunciation from his rhetoric and focuses instead on *topoi, inventio,* and *dispositio,* for these are all allegories of space, of the arrangement of elements in places, and they are fully consistent with the kind of associationism that underlies the rebus principle. *Inventio, topoi,* and *dispositio* exploit and enable the visual allegory that has been the dominant tradition in Western philosophy and science. Derrida's rhetoric is conservative, scientized, visualized, and spatialized. So, too, his use of language, his lists of juxtaposed nouns, reveals a bias for the visual, for the subject rather than the predicate. Here the contrast with Heidegger is most apparent. Heidegger's infamous verbalized nouns, as in "the world worlds" or "nothing noths," express a preference for the predicate, for the verbal aspects of the predication, but Derrida's juxtaposed nouns are like so many juxtaposed pictures, predications without predicates, collocations (co-locations) of things corresponding to the notion of "places" in the rhetorical handbooks on memory, reflexes of the idea of the matrix. It is part of the Western lust for the noun, the *res* that the idea of the predicate, the verb, *verba* has always challenged. In the end, the rebus principle is fully consistent with the dominant scientific ideas of space and local motion symbolized by the matrix and effected through it.

Here I confess to reading Derrida "against the grain," for he intends (if one may use that notion in writing of Derrida's supposedly "intentionless" writing) to "destabilize" the noun. Like Whorf and Bohm, he seeks to shake, or in his word, to "solicit" (< *sollus,* "whole" + *citare,* "excite," "put in motion") the whole structure of Indo-European predication: its emphasis on the categorematic noun as the name of a stable, concrete entity whose variable qualities and attributes are expressed by the verb or adjective; its focus on the priority of the "given" over the "new," of the *thema* (the known, the thing placed) over the *rhema* (the unknown, the thing said, catachrestically derived here both from *rheo-,* "to flow" and IE *weiro-, "to say"); of "thing" over what is "said" of the thing, and of anaphora over cataphora. His shaking of the Indo-European noun and predication thus parallels his interest in the catabolized metaphor whose figurative meaning precedes its literal meaning. Inasmuch as the rebus principle breaks down the lineal

trajectory of discourse, the whole economy of discourse could resemble a paratactic or catenated list, or an onomantic catalogue instead of a hypotactic structure of dialectical sublation.

The rebus principle similarly involves cataclasm; it breaks the cataphracted noun apart, decomposing it into elements that have no independent reference to the thing the catagmatic noun refers to, as in the
elements that comprise the Aztec name, "teocaltitlan" (< _tentli_, "lips,"
otlim, "road," _calli_, "house," _tlantli_, "touch") cited in _Of Grammatology_
(1974b:90). In all, Derrida aims to give priority to the verb, to the flow
of cataphoresis over the uncatastasized nouns suspended in it. His interests thus parallel Whorf's concern for the "vibratile" aspects of
Hopi (1936), and Bohm's desire for a language of motion and activity,
as expressed in the idea of the rheomode (cf. pp. 26–28). We would
anticipate, then, that he would consequently emphasize kinesis over
mimesis, especially since he recognizes that the other of _eidos_ is "force,"
but he does not. He remains trapped in the catacombs of mimesis,
partly because he is somewhat misled by the rebus principle, but
mostly because of his catatonia, his suspicion of speech, which has
always been an immanent image of the flow, of the cataract, of the impermanent, of the changeable, and of motion and kinesis. His speechlessness thus cuts him off from this potent symbol of kinesis.

In the case of the rebus, it is correct to say that it can catalyze some
kinds of nouns, but the elements thus catalyzed are catadioptric before they are catacoustic; they are first visual images and reflections of
things before they are reflections of sounds. The visible marks and
traces that make writing also make it impossible to overcome the priority of the visual image and its mimetic bias. It might be possible to
stay within the domain of the visual without the prejudice of the visual image if writing were entirely gestural, as in deaf signing. That
would be the ideal Derridean writing, for it erases itself in making itself, and leaves behind neither bothersome visual residues nor echo-
ing voices, but even gesture cannot escape the net of mimesis, for its
kinesis, too, is derivative, and relies on the substitution of appearances in the gesture that mimics the thing.

In this catasterism of the verb there lingers some residue of the displacement of the subject in symbolic logic, where the relation or function (the logical equivalents of the verb) are placed in front of their
arguments and variables as in R (a,b) where "R" is a relation and "a"
and "b" are arguments (= nouns), giving a predicational order of
verb, object, object rather than the normal Indo-European order of
subject, object, verb. So, too, logic's dislodgement of the copula, its
removal of it from the center of the proposition and placement outside

the proposition as an "existential operator," a "there is some x" ($\exists$x), mirrors the marginalization of being. In logic, being and the subject are both misplaced, extruded and catapulted to the margins of thought as parenthesized hangers-on of relations. Yet, despite these marginating movements, this cataphysis of noun and verb, the foundational structure of Indo-European predication remains as unaffected in logic as it is in Derrida's catallactics.

This connection with the *solve et coagula* of logical analytics is apparent too in Derrida's emphasis on deconstruction and decomposition. Like analysis (< G *ana*, "above" + *lys*, "to loosen"), they are breaking down, a taking apart, a reduction to elementary, differential units themselves without meaning or stripped of meaning. This seemingly unlikely resemblance to logical atomism is the direct consequence of Derrida's disdain for dialectics, and especially for the Hegelian *aufhebung*, the upward movement from the sensible to the conceptual, from the concrete to the abstract. Against this upward movement toward the light of reason, the sun of thought, the motionless hyperspace of abstractions consciously constructed, Derrida proposes a downward, decompositional movement toward the dark, energic, pathematic, passionate realm of the moonlike aleatory unconscious. He opposes the hyper-celestial realm of the Platonic other of union with the catacombs of the other of difference. His opposition to dialectic leads him down the gyring path to the underworld where science has preceded him into the sunset of the modern age, into the postmodern umbra broken only by the anaclastic light of distant, already dead stars.

Ⓢ : Placed Together

Another myth is abroad in the land. Its name is "system" (< IE *sta- "to stand" > G *sunistanai* > *sustema* "place together," *histos* "loom," "web," "tissue," "statue," "idol"; L. *stamen*, "warp threads"). It is a synonym for the network of parts that make the loom that makes the tissue of this tale. Invoked to evoke some sense of the whole that could be constituted analytically if we but knew all the details of its "con-position," it names the ultimate possibility of holistic synthesis at the same time as it confesses the absence of its analysis. The hope of holistic synthesis is the name of its lack. We invoke "system" whenever we wish to convey some intimation of collectivities that transcend individual experience but are still in principle knowable by individuals. Thus we speak knowingly of the "system of signs" or of the "system of languages," or of the "system of the universe" as if we had given a full account of their details and composition. This is our way of integrating the fragmentary orders we think we know and understand with what we do not yet know and understand but suppose we could some day.

The myth of system has many versions, but all have in common the model of the alphabet as their constitutive means. Just as the signs of the alphabet constitute language, so other systems are constituted by their elementary signs. A system then, always consists of elementary units combined into larger units by fixed rules. These larger units may then interact with the elementary units that constitute them or with one another to form still larger units that repeat the pattern of the lower units from which they have emerged. As we already know from the mother structure of language, there are really only two features here: signs and their combinatory possibilities. This is both language as the limit and the limit of language.

The rudiments that make systems can be apprehended graphically as follows:

     o   = elementary unit

     ➤   = combinatory property of units of the same order

     --➤   = combinatory property of units of different orders

     o‿o = combination of elementary units

     o‿o ➤ = production of a higher order unit

 = higher order unit consisting of two combined elements

= combinatory relation between units of different orders

With these simple operations we can constitute systems representing whatever contingency we want. Consider, for example, the generalized system of thought picture 1.7.

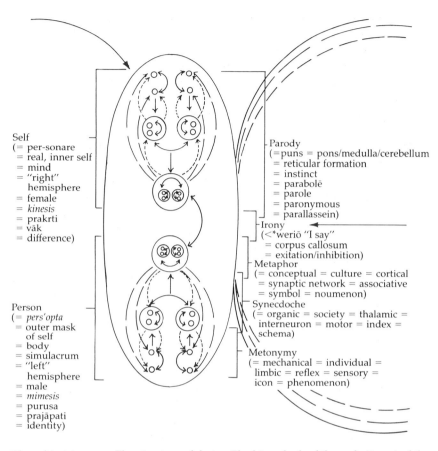

Self
(= *per-sonare*
= real, inner self
= mind
= "right"
hemisphere
= female
= *kinesis*
= prakrti
= vāk
= difference)

Parody
(=puns = pons/medulla/cerebellum
= reticular formation
= instinct
= parabolē
= parole
= paronymous
= parallassein)

Irony
(<*weriō "I say"
= corpus callosum
= exitation/inhibition)

Metaphor
(= conceptual = culture = cortical
= synaptic network = associative
= symbol = noumenon)

Synecdoche
(= organic = society = thalamic =
interneuron = motor = index =
schema)

Person
(= *pers'opta*
= outer mask
of self
= body
= simulacrum
= "left"
hemisphere
= male
= *mimesis*
= purusa
= prajāpati
= identity)

Metonymy
(= mechanical = individual =
limbic = reflex = sensory =
icon = phenomenon)

Thought picture 1.7: The structure of desire: The hieroglyph of the emboîtment of the hylomorphic "wonam," the Peirce-*opta* invaginated with and "structurally coupled" in autopoetic desire to its other within the Cosmic Egg. With apologies to the Koyas. This selvage says: "svanāmi or sva nāmi or svan am I."

Thought picture 1.7 is the image of a hylomorphic system whose component ideas are ancient in Indo-European languages. It is the image of man as a microcosm of the cosmos. We can "read" it either in its "completed" form as a myth, a timeless structure of interacting parts, or as a narrative that tells of its origin and evolution from primitive, primordial elements (o, →) whose combination (o_o) produce larger units (o_o → (o/o)) whose combinations in turn produce still larger, more complex organ-izations, and so on. We ascend from level to level as an order of perception or as an order of growth from simple to complex by a series of connected, repetitive operations. So-called higher levels are only more complex organizations of simple "mechanisms." All change, mutation, growth, decay, and metamorphosis are produced in the same way by some form of local motion. The whole is produced mechanically and has no emergent character—except for a lingering mystery about the inseminating and the inseminated $\rightarrow$ and $O\_,O \rightarrow$ which resist reduction to something like an "additive" property.

This epicene image repeats Aristotle's hylomorphic characterization of the three forms of *anima* (vegetable, animal, and man) as tropes of textualization (metonymy, synecdoche, and metaphor), as general tropes of conceptualization (mechanical, organic, and conceptual), as tropes of the nervous system (reflex, interneuron, and synaptic network), as tropes of the regions of the cerebrum (limbic, thalamic, cortical), as tropes of the functions of the cortex (sensory, motor, associative), as tropes of the order of perception (sensation, perception, conception), as tropes of the order of social life (person, society, and culture), as tropes of the order of signs (icon, index, and symbol), as tropes of the order of thought (phenomenon, schema, noumenon—in its Kantian version), and as tropes of the means of thought (abduction, induction, deduction, á la Peirce, or thesis, antithesis, synthesis, according to Hegel). In all, it is a tiresome metaleptic repetition of the ancient Indo-European mythos of the tripartite order of earth, sky, and sun, but it is a telling ordered now by the analytic means of the alphabet, which mechanizes the whole tale, and the tale itself becomes the trope of the alphabet as the order of understanding that makes the effigy of man caught in the web/womb of the mother matrix (see thought picture 1.8).

The duality of inner/outer is the duality of reality/appearance, mind/body, time/space, and speech/writing in which the first is always a parodic mimesis of the second created by the ironic means of the second. The inner of the self is the outer of the other, and the shadow of its substance, which guarantees that the reality of the real, inner self will always be compromised by its insubstantiality. So too will it always seem occult even though its very innerness grants us direct access to it and a way of knowing it as an image before the mind's inner eye, inner speech, or feelings, that knowing is always private and cannot be made wholly public. Incommunicability, which is the consequence of its givenness and direct accessibility, makes the self suspect, incomplete, disorderly, defective, secret, magical, occult, phantasmic, dark, shadowy, primitive, potent, and profound. Its compelling monody guarantees its parody even as it ensures its private potency. And the other, the "person," must consequently be incom-

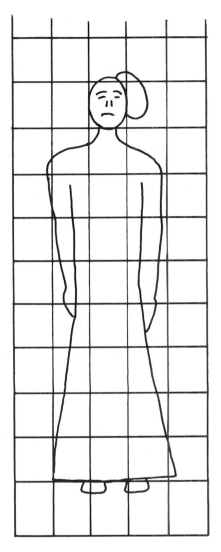

Thought picture 1.8. The sorcerer's victim. Koya sorcerers draw this image on the ground by dribbling rice powder through their fingers while chanting in a low, almost inaudible voice. They thus bind their victims, and that is why they are called kaṭṭubōtu, "animal who ties."

plete, defective, apparent, unreal, surface, the mask that hides the true self.

This idea of a system, then, is only the latest lamentation in the threnody of lost wholeness. Though the system is only a simulacrum of wholeness—a presentation of itself pretending to be a representation of the unrepresentable unknown—it still portends an implicit order whose every part repeats the order of the whole, much as Leibnitz's monads reflected the order of the universe to the best of their ability, or the way the fragments of a hologram contain the image of the whole. In other words, it pretends to present the whole it cannot represent by means of a fragment or part bearing the imprint of the whole without being in point-to-point correspondence with the whole. In thought picture 1.7, this would be tantamount to erasing all the solid, straight arrows (→) and thinking of each element (0) as if it were a slightly

defective $\left(\begin{smallmatrix} 0 \\ \mathit{7} \\ 0 \end{smallmatrix} \right)$, a monad doing its best to reflect the whole but not

quite measuring up.

Apart from the complications of the visual metaphor, what disappears here is the idea of smooth, unbroken movement from simple to complex in which each transformation derives analytically from prior transformations. It recognizes in other words, the peculiar "leap" of 0 ⌣ 0 →, and allows for the possibility of simultaneous orders not derived from lower, more primitive levels of order. Different orders are copresent possibilities whose histories are divergent and unconnected except in some greater, unspeakable whole. It is as if they are disconnected narratives told by different voices that sometimes develop, harmonize, or even speak contrapuntally as in:

> Once upon a time there was . . .
> . . . forced, as that time she . . .
> Time was when . . .
> . . . in that time, in that place . . .
> . . . make time the poet.
> . . . even though the time time telling . . .

Without the transcendental ego, these voices make no matrix. They are akin to the parallel times of Borges, or the parallel lives of different people who meet only once, whose paths cross but remain parallel in the aleatory poem of time.

In the end, the idea of system is only nostalgia for the wholeness analysis has killed and thinks to resuscitate by reinfecting the corpse with the germ that killed it. "System" is another name for the great spider goddess.

Sensus/Communis

The fundamental paradox of all mimetic writing is that every gain in mimetic power is paid for in decreased communicability. The better the mimicry, the less it is understood. Mimesis does not ensure automatic communication; it fosters idiosyncrasy. The idea of mimesis harbors an inherent contradiction. While it provides the means of knowing whatever it mimics—even if that is only itself—it reveals itself as a trick, a sleight-of-hand; it gives and takes away at the same time. The history of the word tells its duplicitous tale. It derives from the Indo-European root *mei-, which means "a deception," "a magical trick," "an illusory appearance," and its sense is best revealed in the Sanskrit word *māya*, derived from this same Indo-European root and meaning "the illusoriness of the phenomenal world." A better mimesis then, is a better trick, a better piece of illusory play that points to the mastery of magical means by a trickster, sorcerer, demon, a knowing consciousness. The master of tricks is the one who plays tricks best, whose technique and style produce illusions so brilliant and captivating that they are valued above the reality they both obscure and reveal, not because they are understood but because they seem to be just beyond the limit of understanding at the same time as they are within it. This is the source of the idiosyncrasy that gets in the way of communication, and it makes the circumstance of augury, the need for interpretation. Its autopoetic mystery creates a community of mandarin interpretants who co-opt and routinize the illusion. From Pound to Derrida the fate of the ideogram is the idiogram. It is the [ay] that makes [ay], for the hand that writes "[ay]" is quicker than the [ay] that reads. The all-seeing [ay] insinuates the "sign us" of the matrix it makes.

Surely this is a misreading of Derrida. Does he not decry the hegemony of the eye and exalt other senses as sources of sense at the limit of the letter even as he seeks to make us hear with the eyes? Does he not propose taste and smell as alternative models for thought and writing because their nonobjectivity and nonrepresentationalism recommend them as better allegories of the nonrepresentational signifier? Is not the Western tradition's reduction of value to "taste" the circumstance that ensures the degradation of value? And is this degradation of *aisthesis* not also at the same time the elevation of episteme, so that knowing always precedes and grounds valuing? Is valuing then, anything more than the pathology of the subject, ultimately reducible to the unreason of "feelings," to "*I* like it," "*I* don't like it"? After all, what object does taste produce or represent? Does it not instead decompose objects? What object does an aroma, an odor, or a stink constitute? And who can remember the smell of fresh-baked bread in the absence of the aroma itself? We remember only the smelling but not the smell, and why is memory the final test here?

This catechism of the teaching of the nonobjective senses reminds us that they are always in our thought connected less with knowledge than with feelings. They do not so much represent the world by direct reproduction of its appearances as they remind us of our response to it and symbolize our feeling-judgements about it. They are the *pathēmata*, the feelings of the subject engendered by contact with the nonobjective, attributional, qualitative characteristics of the world. They cannot have the objective, referential character of visual signs because they are consigned to function only within the lower gyre of the brain called the limbic system where they are cutoff from direct contact with higher cortical functions. At least that is the story told by the associative cortex that acquired its hegemony over the rest of the brain by cannibalizing and repressing the tissue of the olfactory system during man's evolution from lower, more primitive beings driven largely by the smell and taste of the world. Thus the myth of the structure and evolution of the human brain is a metalepsis of the metaphysics it validates by its recapitulation. It guarantees that whatever we feel is good, bad, beautiful, and ugly can only be feelings and passionate ravings that index our bestial past.

Values are both just "feelings" and "just" feelings, the fancies bodies make by invisible means, and the means made visible by fantasy. They thus symbolize at once what is beneath reason and language and beyond them, what is behind them, and what is before them. They symbolize the conjunction of upper and lower, inner and outer, the duplicity of the "sub-lime," that lower limit, that illimitable upper and sub-limation of the limbic system.

It is no surprise, then, that we think our "true," "inner" feelings are not fully communicable, that they are deeply private, innermost to ourselves, and beyond language. Language cannot plumb their depths for they are the unrepresentable true self that precedes the social. They are behind the mask of the persona, the *per's-opta*, the "for seeing." Like the cataphracted noun, they are the armored/amour, the "am-our" of the self.

The *coincidentia oppositorum* of putrefaction/congellation symbolizes the antonomasia of feelings as sensation and sense sensibility. Derrida seeks to escape the subjectivity and incommuncability of feelings by endowing them with the properties of the transcendental signifier which has no need of referents but has yet an inner structure of chance that is neither the product of a subject nor of the objects that make the subject's experience. Since the transcendental signifier is both the means of the subject's experience and the object of it, Derrida attempts to redress the balance of the sensorium by means of tropes and allegories of taste and smell, the nonrepresentational senses. This maneuver both undercuts the *eidos* as representation and short-cuts the dialectical movement from nonrepresentation to representation in the representation of nonrepresentational feelings in representational language. Instead of the compositional, synthesizing upward movement from sensation to concept, from concrete to abstract, from literal to figurative, from unconscious to conscious, from particular to universal, from sense to sensibility there is a decompositional, downward movement that does not end in the particular or the neutralized subjective, but is universalized in the unconscious itself.

Here Derrida at last breaks with the tonic theme of representation. Like Gadamer, he attempts to transgress the devaluation of value accomplished by the Kantian afterthought of the third critique. He challenges the whole mode of representational discourse that makes devaluation the automatic consequence of the irrepresentationalism of values. If discourse is not representational even in its most representational guise of scientific fact and demonstration—if the *apophantic* fact-stating proposition has no more representational foundation than the impassioned outcry of the *euchē,* then the domination of episteme and representational knowing over *doxa* is ended, and the reasons of the heart, the feelings, and e-motion are at last the allegorical equals of *ratio.* No thing any longer provides exterior justification for either heart or head and no boundary separates them. By asking what the nose knows we sniff out the rat named epistemology and snuff him out.

Absent from Derrida's text, though, is the Gadamerian turn to dialogue. Derrida's distaste for sound, his suspicion of communication, his speechlessness, his affair with the unspeakable chokes off dialogue. He soundlessly gags at the thought of the subject who comes up as the emetic consequence of communication. He cannot swallow the specter of the speaker and he retches at the prospect of the hearer. He is nauseated by all this effluent of the "sayn-us," by the disembogued, recongellated conscious subject, the transcendental ego and the metaphysics of self-presence that dialogue seemingly implicates. But the idea of dialogue, as Bakhtin (1984), Gadamer (1976), Rorty (1979), and others have already foretold, evokes a subject who is neither a self-constituted center of perceptual experience nor the sole author of its experience and identity. The subject emergent in the flow of dialogue is not a fully autonomous ego, an all-knowing indutive monad, for its autonomy is fully realized in the situation of "saying" by means of the saying to and saying of another. The name of the self is not an "auto-nomy"; it is the name spoken antinomously by an other. It is the emicant [ay] of the emanent other.

Dialogue, not writing, is the ineluctable source of the difference that makes identity. It dispenses with the language of visible marks, gouges, scratches, traces, and engraved engrams of signs and accomplishes the dissilience of the ego not in its dissolution but in "co-opera." Dialogue is not the work of the emmetropic [ay], and fashions no illusory permanences; it is the work that makes no works and leaves no traces.

Like Lao Tzu, Derrida wakens from the slumber of the [ay doz], of the eyed entity and finds only the speechless id-entity of the dream. So we must ask what we have gained from this metamorphosis, this transubstantiation of the transcendental ego into the transcendental id, and the transfiguration of the transcendental signified as the transcendental signifier. Is it just that the transcendence of the one can be sustained only in the repression of the other, or is it perhaps that their correlativity marks no transcendence at all but an immanent mutuality where no one dominates the other? Do we free ourselves from the tyranny of the autonomous signified only to become helots of the autonomous signifier and sign away our emancipation from the autonomous ego in exchange for the limes of the autonomous id? Wouldn't a real postmodernism reject the whole idea of absolute autonomy in favor of discourse-negotiated limits that are only provisionally autonomous for present purposes and pertinent understandings? And why not reject outright the whole idea of the sensorium, of representation, of the correspondence between inner and outer signifiers whether known as mind and body, thought and language, words and things, or any of the "othering" dualisms that have trapped us (cf. Rorty 1979)? Why not break the spell of higher and lower, of conscious and unconscious, of civilized and primitive, of light and dark, or male and female, and so to end the narrative of the journey from the sense of the outer world to the sense of inner thought. Let us, too, seek to think without the emplecton of the succoring matrix, without the plectrum plying to and fro implicating the multiplying matrix miming the interweaving breaths, the pneuma/prāṇa of the Indo-European universe. And if representation is immanent in communication, does that not mean that we no longer need the comfort of the harmonious whole, the one in the many, the consensus of the *communis*, the totalitarian lure of undistorted communication, the resolution of all dissonances in the lost chord, the closure of the borromean knot, the essentializing ideas of individual, society, and culture as systems of complementary parts straining to replicate themselves in a parody of capitalist lust? And why not, at last, rid ourselves of the fetishims of space whose only teachings are separation, displacement, and alienation? When men shall roll up space as if it were a piece of paper, then there will be an end to evil, and we shall know the magician who creates the illusion of the universe. And the Great Noun, the thing called language, the *māya* of the gram, that plicate creature of the grammarian and grammatologist—let all speak of it as the unspeakable plexiform illusion it is, and turn to discourse without the metaphors of space and light, of *potentia* and *actus*. Discourse is being time without the and, honey without the honeycomb or the bee. And this might be the postmodernism whose coming has been foretold and whose arrival is still awaited.

Beneath the glimmering boreal light, mirrored polar ice groans and heaves, the flame flickers feebly on the altar hearth, in the alter heart, into the holy, breathing darkness of the antipodeal night.

PART ONE

MEMORIAE ET REMINISCENTIA

2

WORDS FOR DEEDS AND THE

DOCTRINE OF THE SECRET

WORLD

TESTIMONY TO A CHANCE

ENCOUNTER SOMEWHERE

IN THE INDIAN JUNGLE

Proem

Words and deeds in that commonplace world of our daily lives constitute a context of mutual implication that is the background of our awareness and, when they fly apart in deception, dishonesty, and error, the object of it. Little wonder then, that when Plato seeks to illustrate in the *Lysis* the Doric harmony of word (*logos*) and deed (*ergon*) he evokes the image of the household (*oikos*), that concrete locus of familiar reality where reciprocal expectations—and their failures—are expressed in the words and deeds of ordinary life.

With this image of the social in mind nothing seems more obvious than the mutuality of word and deed which it so effectively symbolizes, yet in Plato's attacks on the poets and Sophists, in his emphasis on dialectic at the expense of rhetoric, and by his location of the real in the *logos*—in all these he destroys that harmony of word and deed expressed in the concrete affairs of everyday life and conjures in its stead an abstract and hidden world where words only imply other words. Plato's condemnation of rhetoric and poetry, and his flight from the concrete social world may have been motivated, as he claims, by moral necessity and the inexorable workings of dialectical reason, but they were also consequences of the transition from oral to written discourse—a transition which his texts both accomplish and symbolize (Havelock 1963).

Words for Deeds and the Doctrine of the Secret World

Plato's flight from the oral traditions of the poets and rhetoricians symbolizes a movement from speech to writing, from the concrete to the abstract, from the social to the conceptual, from deeds to words, and, finally, from action in the world to contemplation of what word we have of it. This textualization places primary emphasis on the text itself, thereby deemphasizing the speaker's role, effacing the relation of the speaker to the hearer, and obscuring the relation of text to reader. *Ethos*, the speaker's intent and character, and *pathos*, the character of the audience, are both subordinated to *logos*, the structure of the text. The consequence of this movement from *ethos* to *logos* was to replace honesty with truth, for the former is an evaluation of the speaker's character derived from the harmony of his words and deeds, while the latter is only a relation of words to words.

The relation of words to deeds or of words to things becomes problematical in the text because the text only re-presents deeds and things and is not itself a harmony of them. To repair this disjunction between the world and its representation the Greeks pressed into service the dramaturgical notion of mimesis. The text mimics or copies the world, in a relation that we now understand as the correspondence theory of truth. Here there is no reflexivity between word and world but only a correspondence—a relation between two independent orders of existence, which confounds the texts' aim to order its representations logically, for correspondence as a mode of representation is ultimately not logical, but tropological. Metonymy, metaphor, and synecdoche are the means by which signs substitute for both words and the world. They, not mimesis, are the real modes of representation, and when we understand aright this double function of substitution we also understand why Aristotle sought to make tropes functions of the text alone, and we see too how the whole structure of opposition expressed in the separation of logic and rhetoric, of truth and honesty, of demonstration and persuasion, and ultimately of speech and language is an illusion.

It is not without significance that linguists and ethnographers seek to accomplish this same movement by means of written texts. Their grammars, dictionaries, and ethnographies are all re-presentations of speech and behavior, textualizations of oral traditions, of concrete deeds and acts of speaking. They too destroy the harmony of word and deed, and erect in its place a timeless structure of words alone. Like Plato, linguists and anthropologists seek to constitute an idealized world of necessary facts—of mutually implicated concepts. The merely possible and probable—those worlds of poetry and rhetoric originally given in experience—are transformed into necessity, that hidden world conceived in the union of logic and dialectic which, though it transcends all experience, yet pretends to represent and explain it in some still mysterious way.

It is one of the paradoxes of Western thought, and the essential problem of our time, that this world of abstraction can represent only by destroying what it seeks to represent, and though it may seem odd, if not perverse, to think of writing a grammar or an ethnography as an act of violence, that is how these seemingly humane, scholarly ventures are now seen by many of those from whom grammars and ethnographies have been "expropriated" (Said 1978). Though we may deny colonial intent, there is a clear parallel here between Plato and the poets, and the anthropologist and his people, for just as Plato took his inspiration from the poets and rhetoricians while banning them from his Republic, so too does the anthropologist and linguist take inspiration from his people while denying them any place in the kingdom of his text. It may be, as Nietzsche claimed, that all representation is violent, but it seems more reasonable to suspect the modes and purposes of representation rather than representation itself, for it is these elements of the rhetorical context which the text must obscure or falsify in order to be a text. If we look, then, at the moment of textualization, at that process by which a text becomes a text we may discover there the source of the problem and some hint of its remedy.

Here I seek to accomplish a double movement of representation and textualization. Though the two movements are separate in time, they are nevertheless juxtaposed here in the timeless world of written form. The first movement is one of deed to word, captured in a Koya text about a festival. The second movement is another text, a translation and commentary on the first. The second movement, often misunderstood as a movement from words to words, is here accomplished by means of two other discourses; one is the original dialogue between myself and Pūsem Laksmayya, which enabled the first movement from deed to word. The other is part of another kind of dialogue between myself and that unwieldy body of discourse I have unwillingly inherited from several disciplines. There is a sense in which this text is not really about a Koya text at all, but about our received understanding of certain Greek texts, such as Plato's *Phaedrus* and Aristotle's *Rhetoric*, or at least of such Greek terms as *ergon, logos, grammata, rhetoric, dialectic, enthymeme, pathos, ethos,* and *topos*. The original dialogue from which the Koya text emerged is not reproduced here, only its rhetorical function in establishing a context of textual interpretation is made explicit at several points.

Those who would make that dialogue the focus of ethnography are

Words for Deeds and the Doctrine of the Secret World

in a sense correct, for dialogue *is* the source of the text, but dialogue rendered as text, which must be the consequence, is no longer dialogue, but a text masquerading as a dialogue, a mere monologue about a dialogue since the informant's appearances in the dialogue are at best mediated through the ethnographer's dominant authorial role. While it is laudable to include the native, his position is not thereby improved, for his words are still only instruments of the ethnographer's will. And if the dialogue is intended to protect the ethnographer's authority by shifting the burden of truth from the ethnographer's words to the natives' it is even more reprehensible, for no amount of invoking the "other" can establish *him* as the agent of the words and deeds attributed to him in a record of dialogue unless he too is free to reinterpret it and flesh it out with caveats, apologies, footnotes, and explanatory detail (*per contra* Crapanzano 1980). These, then, are not dialogues, but sophistic texts like those pretenses at dialogue perpetrated by Plato. The test of true dialogue is that when it is captured in text or recording it is almost incomprehensible, a thing of irruptions and interruptions, of fits and starts, thoughts strangled halfway to expression, dead ends, wild shifts, and sudden inexplicable returns to dead and discarded topics. No, the meaning of the dialogue is not in the dialogue any more than it is in the clever text of a dialogue; it is instead in what the participants make of it separately and in concert, at that time and on later reflection. What follows in the form of a text and its commentary is some of what I have made of a dialogue with Pūsem Laksmayya. What he made of it, I cannot say, but I hope that on reflection it caused him some laughter and no pain.

Narrative

This text was composed and written in Telugu character by my principal Koya informant Pūsem Laksmayya. It was dictated, tape recorded, transcribed, and translated on May 15–17, 1963. The text is obviously based on Laksmayya's general knowledge, but more importantly, it is his account of what he saw in the village of Kāsinagaram on May 12–14, 1963, during a performance of the "Hill Festival."

Kāsinagaram, a village of mixed population (Koyas, Naykulus, Hindus, and Christians), is in Bhadrachallam Taluk on the banks of the Godavari River, approximately two miles upstream from Dummagudem in Andhra Pradesh, India.

The content and meaning of Laksmayya's text was supplemented by

Words for Deeds and the Doctrine of the Secret World

direct questioning in the process of translating, by comments elicited from other informants, and by my own observation notes made during the festival. The text itself, however, is unaltered, merely transcribed here from the text as it was originally written by Laksmayya.

THE TEXT

1. koṇḍāla   kolupu   tunganaddu
   mountains   festival   doing it

2. iddu   kōya   nāykurku[1]   tungāni   paṇḍum
   it   kōya   Naykus   doing   festival

3. dīnini   pāṇḍrājurkīnki[2]   kolusāni   kolupu   intōru
   it   Pāṇḍava Kings for   worship   festival   they say

1. A distinct section of the Koyas, many of whom no longer speak Koya. Also known as Naikpods, they inhabit villages in Andhra in the vicinity of Bhadrachallam, Kāsinagaram, Kottagudem, and Cherla, and near the Bastar-Andhra border. Their separateness from the Koyas is marked by their reputed vegetarianism and by restricted intermarriage with Koyas. They no longer give wives to Koyas and though they are said to accept wives from them, no case of such intermarriage occurred in the genealogies collected by me in 1962–63. Several pan-Indian themes are manifest here. Hypergamy is expressed first of all in the intermarriage between Bhīma and a tribal woman, and also in the Naikpods' refusal to give wives to Koyas, who are symbolically lower because of their nonvegetarianism. The principles of caste separation and division are explicit in these practices. Possession of a common ritual, on the other hand, still unites Koyas and Naikpods as a single group having not only a common origin, but a shared right to a common territory. This latter fact is symbolized in their worship of the Pāṇḍavas not only as genitors, but as Kings of the mountains. The mountains are at once symbols of territory and origin, and thus of rights to exploit a territory. The mountain symbol is highly complex and figures prominently in a number of myths and tales, not only in Koya, but in Dravidian and Indo-Aryan culture as well. Even the name Koya is derived from *ku, "hill, mountain," as are the names of the majority of other Dravidian tribes. So, too, the names of each of the exogamous divisions of Koya society contain the word "gaṭṭa," "mountain". For further discussion of this theme, see notes 3, 4, and 6.

2. Though the Koyas are not Hindus they consider themselves to be descendants of Bhīma, one of the Pāṇḍava brothers in the Mahābharata. Both Koyas and Naikpods trace their descent from Bhīma and his Koya wife. Significantly, all of the Pāṇḍavas are worshipped in this festival. Hypergamous marriage between a tribal woman and a Hindu god, sage, or king is a common theme in many castes and tribes. It is one of the commonest means by which non-Hindus establish a character of legitimacy and justify their position and rank in Hindu society. It symbolizes, through the female link, the subordination of tribal society to Hindu society, and indexes the movement from tribe to caste, the incorporation of the tribes as just another caste in the system of castes. Hypergamous marriage, mythical or factual, is both the symbol and the means of dominance/subordination and of inclusion/exclusion, primary processes in the caste system (cf. Dumont 1970: 109–25).

Words for Deeds and the Doctrine of the Secret World

4.

kōitōru	vāṇṭi	valla	vīrki	bātanna	sāyam
Kōyas	them	by	to them	whatever	help

itku	vāṇṭi	peddērṭe	bātanna	gaṇḍam
if said	their	in name	whatever	difficulties

tīrku	vāṇṭīni	moḍikitōru
if relieve	them	they worship

5.

vāṇṭīni	nammi	vāṇṭīni	nāykīni	aggāṭikunci
them	having faith	them	Naykus	near from

tahci		vīru	vāṇṭīki	kolupu	tungitōru
having brought		they	to them	festival	they will do

6.

tungāni	tiru	bēla	itku	vāṇṭi	peddērṭe
doing	method	what way	if said	their	in name

ēṇḍatki	orro	dammu	erra	jēṇḍa[3]	tohci
year for	one	time	red	flag	having tied

nāhkīne	nembāḍi	sannāy	mēlakīntōnṭe	sambaram
villages	through	clarinets	drums with	festival

tungōre	jōngu	talapitōru
doing	collection	they will ask

7.

ā	jōngu	talapta	dabbīne	tōnṭe	bēdō
that	collection	asked	money	with	whichever

orro	rōju	nirku		tungi	ā	nāṇḍu
one	day	arrangement		having made	that	day

itku	ādivārāte	nālo	gaṇṭāni	vēlāte		marte
if said	in Sunday	fourth	hour	in evening		tree

porro	mandāni	goḍuguku[4]	ḍippitōru
on	being	umbrellas	they will take down

---

3. The flag and the flag staff are symbols of power and authority. In southern India a flag staff is erected in front of the entrance to the garbha gṛha, the sanctuary where the deity is kept. Flying a red flag from a pole located near a village shrine is common practice among Hindu castes in Andhra Pradesh (cf. Whitehead 1916:96).

4. The "umbrellas" referred to are nine silver umbrellas approximately six inches in diameter with small bells dangling from the bottom edge. They are arranged in tiers on a tripod. They are the symbols of state of the Pāṇḍava "Kings of the Hills". Like the flag staff, the umbrella is a pan-Indian symbol of power and authority; it represents the dome of heaven, its shaft the axis of the universe. The tiered effect here is like that of the tiers of umbrellas above the Buddhist stupa. Each umbrella represents a heaven, and the many heavens rise above one another in tiers. They may also be likened to the chakras of yogic physiology. The mountain, the shaft of the umbrella, and the flag staff are all symbols of the axis mundi, the center around which the cosmos rotates. These symbols are, of course, appropriate to the designation of the Pāṇḍavas as "Kings," and imply their control over cosmic order.

8. | vāṇṭīni | orro | paḷḷete | vāṭi | | orro | vedduru |
|---|---|---|---|---|---|---|
| them | one | on plate | having put | | on | bamboo |

pullāni	gummatam[5]	pēysi		nālungu
of sticks	basket	having taken hold of		green gram

piṇḍi	pasupu	kumkum	orro	gobber kāya
flour	turmeric	decorations	one	coconut

orro	ravike pīṭi		orro	korupīse[6]
one	woman's jacket cloth		one	chick

pēysi		godātki		ohsi
having taken hold of		to Godavari River		having taken

vāṇṭiki	itku	goḍugukīnki	nālungu
to them	if said	to umbrellas	green gram (flour)

vāṭi		ēruputitōru[7]
having put		they will bathe

9. | ā | gummaṭāte | goḍukini | gaḍḍāsolam |
|---|---|---|---|
| that | basket in | umbrellas of | shaft |

ḍippi		erraguḍḍa	gummaṭatki	singarisitōru[8]
having taken down		red cloth	basket to	they decorate

10. | erraguḍḍāte | porro | pisirkāya | selāku | singarisitōru |
|---|---|---|---|---|
| red cloth | on | silk | upper cloth | they decorate |

11. | ī | goḍugu | peydanōṇḍu | erpundi | | gummaṭāte |
|---|---|---|---|---|---|
| this | umbrella | took he | having bathed | | basket |

lopāle	ningi		pēysi
inside	having entered		having taken hold of

5. Actually "basket, dome, or cupola."

6. With the exception of the chick and coconut, which are sacrificial objects, these are all components out of which the symbolic representation of the cosmos is constructed. It consists of a bamboo frame, roughly basket-shaped, draped with cloth, and nine silver bells mounted on an inverted silver tripod—three bells to each arm of the tripod. The basket is inverted and the center rod of the tripod, longer than the others, is inserted through its upturned bottom. The man who carries the image in the procession wears the draped basket over his head and shoulders and carries the image by grasping the center rod. The whole assemblage resembles the stupa, and like it is an icon of the cosmos. The basket represents the mountain at the center of the universe, the umbrella shaft, the axis of the universe, the umbrellas the many heavens, and the man inside is the power of the king who grasps and upholds the universe, maintaining its order.

7. Laving the implements of the ritual with nalungu and flowing water is a common purificatory procedure in Hinduism. The Godavari River itself is sacred, being known as the "Ganges of the South." Like its northern counterpart, its waters have great purifying power.

8. That is, they drape the cloth around the basket, covering it.

Words for Deeds and the Doctrine of the Secret World

    nicci   mantō
    having stood up   he will be

12. aske   gavaridēvi[9]   gaḍḍe[10]   inji   iskete
       then   gavari goddess   throne   having said   with sand

       gaḍḍe   tohtitōru
       throne   they build

13. dāniki   pasupu   kumkum[11]   boṭku   vāṭitōru
       to it   tumeric   kumkum   spots   they put

14. dāni   munne   nūkān   tōsi
       it   before   cracked rice   having sprinkled

       korupīsetīni   īlā   moḍiki
       a chick   in this way   having worshipped

       muttisitōru[12]
       they cause to peck

15. sāmi   talli   gavari   dēvi   (n)āsi[13]
       honored   mother   goddess   having become

       manji   māku   sāyam   āsi
       having been   to us   help   having become

       mandavālinji   modakaminnōmu
       must be having said   worship we are

16. pagu   vāṇḍu   cuṭṭam   āsi   ārekālde
       enemy   male   relative   having become   in sole of foot

       koyyēn   gittukunta   sāyam   mantāninji
       thorns   without piercing   help   I will give having said

9. More commonly, Gauri. A Hindu rather than Koya goddess, she is one of the consorts of the god Śiva, but in the peasant villages in Andhra is often worshipped as one among many mother goddesses. She is especially the object of vows (vratas) undertaken by women to avert widowhood and to procure children and the affection of husbands (cf. Iyer 1935, vol. 1:348–55).

10. Actually a flattened mound of sand which functions as the dais for the representation of the goddess. The throne or plinth is another symbol of authority. The sophisticated and village varieties of Hindu deities are either installed on an elaborate throne or a simple raised plinth of stone or wood.

11. A red powder used in decorating various objects, again a common Hindu practice.

12. They are taking an omen. If the chick pecks the grain it is a sign that the sacrifice is acceptable to the goddess. This is a common practice in tribal and peasant India, see, for other Gondi groups, Fürer Haimendorf (1979:476).

13. The name of a deity in invocation always has this standard form: name + (n)asi + manji. Calling the deity's name calls that deity into being in the representation designated. The deity "comes into" its icon. See also footnote 14.

ī	korupīse	muttavāle	mā	talli	inji
this	chick	must peck	our	mother	having said

korupīsetīni	nūkān	koṭṭisitōru			
chick	cracked rice	they will make to strike			

17.
korupīse	nūkān	koṭṭapayya	pān	dāttōṇṭe[14]
chick	cracked rice	after pecking	life	gift with

korupīse	ravike	pīti	gobberkāya	pahci
chick	bodice	cloth piece	coconut	having broken

ā	ēru	bōdeteporro[15]	vaḍipi
that	(coconut) water	tree trunk on	having made to flow

nāluvūru	manusūrku	nālu	mūlān	bodetīni
four human	men	four	corners	tree trunk

etti	eddurumkīni	ēte	ōsi
having lifted	to chests	in water	having carried

gangāte	kalipitōru
in Godavari River	they mix, combine

18.
goḍugu	pēysi	sambaram	tungōre
umbrella	having taken hold of	festival	while doing

nāṭeniki	vayitōru[16]
to villages	they come

19.
bajārte	vāsomatku	lōhtki	orro
in bazaar	while going	to house (each)	one

gobberkāya	tahci	dēvaṭimunne
coconut	having brought	goddess before

kundedēru	vāra	tōsi	gobberkāyān
clay pot full of water	over	having poured	coconuts

14. Skt. *prāṇa*, "breath, life." The expression is a Skt. borrowing with Koya inflection and phonology (dāt- Skt. dāti "a gift"). The phonological process here is: dāti + tōṇṭe (with) dāttōṇṭe. The borrowing is probably via Telugu. The idea expressed in pāndāttōṇṭe is both metaphorical and metonymical. Metaphorically, it parallels the English expression "the gift of life," but the metaphor is made concrete by sprinkling the slain chick's blood over the icon. Animating the icon by means of the gift of life (literally breath) is a common practice among Hindu icon makers at such temple sites as Pūri, though the actual ceremonies differ from that reported here. The practice is related to prāṇa doctrines in Hindu esoteric physiology (cf. Eliade 1958:240).

15. Again, a pan-Indian practice. Libations of coconut milk are part of many ritual performances, not only in village Hinduism, but in the pūjas of the great temples as well. The log is cut from the trunk of a tree and is an icon of the goddess.

16. The initial phase of the ceremony is complete here and consists in the sanctification of the icon.

pahcōre | dēvatīni | peytōniki | pasupu
while breaking | goddess | to one who held | turmeric

kumkum | rāsōre | | gaddetagga | itku
kumkum | while writing (drawing) | | throne near | if said

āru | mōgarān | mundu | dūlān | vātta | pandite[17] | rendu
six | logs | three | beams | put | in pandal | two

gadi | tohci | | mattagga | tahci
rooms | having built | | being near | having brought

dēvatīni | ī | pandite | tohtōrro | gadite | vātitōru
goddess | this | pandal | built one | in room | they put

20. dāni | cuttu | bōde | tohci[18]
it | around | log (icon) | having tied (set up)

ākipaccā | nallā | pasupū | tellā | mugu | tōsitōru[19]
leaf green | black | yellow | white | diagram | they pour

21. dānini | ā | gadite | dippi | | ā | manasōndu
it | that | room in | having set down | | that | man

bāydiki | vayitō
to outside | he comes

22. ā | dēvāti | munne | gudda | terra | tohtitōru
that | goddess | before | cloth | curtain | they tie

23. pūjāri | gannasāri | iruvūru
priest | oracle, shaman | both (together)

pulungam | | sēru
rice boiled with green gram | | two pound measure

17. A covered porch or awning in front of a house or temple entrance. In the latter form it is a "rustic" parallel to the mandapam of a Hindu temple, which itself originated from this more primitive version.

18. This expression is used for any kind of fabricating.

19. The verb tos- ("to pour") used here refers to the fact that these drawings are made by "pouring" colored powders from the hand to form lines and auspicious designs. In Hinduism these designs (mandala) represent the cosmos. As here, the deity is at the center of the design as the energizing principle of the universe. The lines of the diagram are radiant energy, their intersections create the structures and levels of the cosmos. This notion of cosmic structure as a network or web of intersecting lines is, of course, widespread (cf. Eliade 1958:200). In the West it is homologized to the idea of weaving (ordos) and symbolized in the labyrinth, but among the Koyas it is homologized with the idea of a cultivated field. A field is plowed north-south, east-west, creating an intersection of furrows. In Koya mythology "heaven" is the intersection of "lines" (furrows, rows) of boys with lines of girls, known as "row boys" and "row girls". There is here an interesting clue to the origin of the name of Rama's wife Sīta ("furrow"). The "row boys" and "row girls" are connected with the idea of human sacrifice in the cult of the mother goddess.

giddedu[20]　　　　　noka
one-eighth full　　　cracked rice

pesali　　　　　　　　　　　　　　pappīni[21]
green lentils (*Phaseolus radiatus*)　split lentil seeds with

bellam　pulungam[22]　　　　　　atti
jaggery　rice boiled with green gram　having boiled

sambaram　tungōre　　　　dāniki
festival　while doing　　　to it

nāyjam　　　　　　　　　　　tungitōru
sacrifice, offering, obeisance　they do

24. andōrukanna　munne　pūjāri　gannasāri
　　everyone else　before　priest　shaman

　　sēri　　　　　　　　　mundu　mudda　tinji
　　having joined (jointly)　three　pieces　having eaten

　　takkina　pulungam　　　　　　　　agge　mannāni
　　remaining　rice boiled with green gram　then　being

　　andōrki　palāram[23]　tungitōru
　　all to　sweet　　　　they make

25. īlā　　　　ādi　　　somma　mangala　buddavāram　ī
　　in this way　Sunday　Monday　Tuesday　Wednesday　these

　　nālugu　nārkān　nālugu　pāyalīn　sambaram　tungitōru
　　four　nights　four　days　festival　they do

26. lacivāram　pāyale　mūndu　cendra　　　　marku
　　Thursday　daytime in　three　sandalwood　trees

　　sambarakintonte　　　　　　adivitki　anji
　　for the purpose of the festival　to forest　having gone

　　dēvi　　　　pīki　　　　　　nāten(i)　gattīnki[24]
　　having dug　having plucked out　village　boundaries to

20. That is, a full one and one-eighth of a sēru, gidda (one-eighth of a sēru) + edu ("-ful").

21. Pappu denotes anything from which the shell or outer husk has been removed, but here refers to the fact that the lentil seed is split, similar to the English distinction between "whole" peas and "split" peas.

22. Pulungam (Telugu pulugam) is the name of the whole dish made from these ingredients boiled together. In this sentence, everything between ". . . iruvūru pulungam . . . pulungam atti . . ." is parenthetical, a recipe for pulungam. Parentheticals are usually indexed by itku ("that is," literally, "if said").

23. Telugu Phalāhāramu "vegetarian diet", Skt. *phal-*, "fruit" + āharam, "food".

24. Another symbol of authority and order. The village boundaries, marked with boundary stones or menhirs commemorating some heroic personage, delimit the re-

teyitōru
they bring

27. | tahtapayya | mūṇḍu | nālugu | vandāni | manasūrkintōṇṭe |
    |---|---|---|---|---|
    | after bringing | three | four | hundreds | (with) of people |

mālāvu	sambaram	tungōre	nāten(i)	cuṭṭu	orro
great	festival	while doing	village	around	one

cuṭṭu	uḍḍi	gaḍḍetagga	tahci
circuit	having circled	throne near	having brought

pandite	porro	mōḍolīn	vāṭitōru[25]
pandal	on	tree stumps	they put

TRANSLATION

1. The doing of the festival of the mountains. 2. It is a festival done by the Koya Nāykus. 3. They say it is a festival in worship of the Pāṇḍava Kings. 4. They worship in the name of the Pāṇḍavas if they need help from them to relieve their difficulties. 5. Having faith in them, they bring them from the Nāykus and do the festival. 6. The method of doing the festival is in their name once a year to tie a red flag (to a stick), and with clarinets and drums, go through the villages and take up a collection. 7. With the money asked for, they will arrange some day for the festival, for example, Sunday at four o'clock in the evening, and take from the tree the "umbrellas" which were there. 8. They put them on a plate, and along with a bamboo "basket" decorated with auspicious marks, a coconut, the cloth for a woman's jacket, and a chick, take them to the Godavari River, mark them with green gram flour, and give them a ritual bath. 9. They take down the umbrella shaft (that was) in the basket and decorate the basket (with) a red cloth. 10. They drape an upper cloth over the red cloth. 11. The one who took the umbrella bathes (ritually), gets under the basket and stands up (inside it) holding the shaft of the umbrella. 12. Then,

gion of protected order, beyond which is an unsafe, unprotected region inhabited by demons, wild animals, and other uncontrolled elemental forces. It is significant that the villagers go into this region—the forest—in order to procure the tree stumps which play an important role in the next phase of the ritual.

25. After several intermediate rituals devoted now to the worship and sanctification of the tree stumps, which are icons of the forest King, a pit is dug, the stumps are cut up and put in the pit. The wood is fired and after it has formed a bed of coals, the shaman walks on the hot coals, followed by all those who have made special vows. This is the climax of the festival. It culminates with a feast and ceremonies involving the return of the ritual's paraphernalia to their keeping places.

saying "Gavari goddess' throne" they build a throne out of sand. 13. They decorate it with red and yellow spots. 14. They sprinkle some cracked rice before it, and worship by causing a chick to peck (at the rice). 15. "Oh honored mother goddess Gavari we must have help, we are worshipping (you)." 16. Saying "make (our) enemies as relatives and prevent thorns from piercing the foot, (if you) say 'I will help', this chick will peck", they make the chick peck. 17. After the chick pecks, they smear the chick's blood (on the icon) with the piece of jacket cloth, they break a coconut, pour its water over the icon (then) four men (at) four corners of the icon lift it up, carry it chest deep into the Godavari River and let it combine with the water. 18. They take the umbrella, and doing the festival, come to villages. 19. Before the goddess is installed the man who carries her into the temple is decorated with yellow and red markings, and the householders, each of whom having brought coconuts from the bazaar, break their coconuts before the idol, and pour a clay pot full of water over it. The goddess (the icon) is brought to the temple porch and placed on a throne made of six logs and three beams and located in one of the two rooms of the temple porch. 20. Around the icon set up (on its throne) they draw green, black, yellow, and white diagrams. 21. Having installed the idol the man who carried her in comes out. 22. They place a cloth curtain in front of the goddess. 23. The priest and the shaman together make pulungam and offer it to the goddess. 24. Before all the others the priest and shaman each eat three portions of pulungam. The remainder is distributed among the participants who consume it. 25. For four days and four nights they do this festival in this way. 26. On the fifth day in the daytime they go to the forest for three sandalwood trees, dig them up and bring their stumps to the boundaries of the village (that is, to the boundary markers). 27. Then three or four hundred people make a great festival, circling the whole village with the stumps which they then bring to the temple porch and put in place on its roof.

Commentary

In many ways this text is rhetorically anomalous. Unlike most of the texts collected from the Koyas it is a true written text, not just a transcription of an oral performance. Consequently, it has a "literary" structure quite unlike that of a text transcribed from an oral performance. Compared to oral discourse it is far less rambling, less repetitious, and less redundant. It has few fillers, no false starts, no backtracking and spontaneous reformulation, and no sentence fragments. Its syntax is more complex and its sentences are longer. It is also marked by the absence of such specifically oral devices as echo words, interjections, vocatives, and other speaker interventions like "you understand?" "you know?" "listen!" "how awful!" "alas!" "enough!" "isn't it?" "just so," "fie!" "Where was I?" "What did I say?" "Now," "next," "I'm forgetting this," "I'm telling you now," and many others. Morphology, too, is different. In this text plural nouns are almost always marked by plural suffixes, and finite verbs always occur with their full pronominal endings. In oral discourse nonhuman nouns are seldom pluralized unless the context absolutely requires it, and finite verbs, particularly of the third person masculine and first person, usually occur in abbreviated forms. This text also contains a higher frequency of Telugu loan words than is generally the case for an oral text. Finally, it is highly focused, containing almost no extraneous topical departures. It reflects, in short, interesting cognitive adjustments that are partly induced by written form.

The most important adjustment to writing is reflected in its organization. Like the pseudodialogues in the *Phaedrus* the written character of this text is betrayed by its *oikonomia*—that logographic necessity expressed in the order of its parts, the artifice of its arrangement. It has an introduction, a narrative, implied arguments, and a conclusion (proem, narrative, proof, and epilogue). It is thus a real logos having that organic structure of a living animal whose parts are so disposed as to form a whole, or, in Plato's words, it has a head, body, and feet.

The introduction consists of a topic phrase or "title," which frames the interpretation by restricting it to an appropriate topical context, a series of statements intended to reveal the reasonableness of what follows, references to a wider mythological context (a context of belief), and notices of personnel. These lines in the introduction evoke the "rational" basis of action as a means to an end. Line four provides the motive: "whenever they need help, they worship in the name of the Pāṇḍavas." The reasonableness of worship is an enthymeme evoked in a general way without specific argumentation, but it establishes that the narrative to follow is not just an account of what happened, but why it happened at all. The argument here is something like: (1) "worship brings help from the gods," (2) "when people need help they worship the gods." Only the second argument appears in the text. Line two implicates a myth not given in this text—the myth of the common descent of Koyas and Naikpods from Bhīma, one of the Pāṇḍavas. It is a topical index in the Aristotelian sense of a topic as commonplace knowledge which can be used to found or justify a line of argumentation. Topical mention alone is sufficient for the hearer's location of the discourse within a background of commonplace knowledge.

The narrative mimics the organization of the festival—its sequential order of topics corresponds to the temporal sequence of episodes in the festival. Part of its structure is given by what it seeks to describe so that the order of words mirrors the order of deeds. It departs from this strict temporal order in only two respects; changes of voice, and descriptive asides. The voice of the text is primarily that of the narrator with only an occasional use of direct discourse in the form of quotation, as in the direct quotes of the shaman's ritual formulae and the prayer in lines 5 and 16. These are formed with the standard syntactic devices "quotation + inji (having said)" or "itku (if said) + quotation." Descriptive asides are used to fill in details about artifacts, locations, procedures, and personnel mentioned in the text. After their initial mention in the text, they are referenced usually in the sentence immediately following with the formula, "thing mentioned itku ("if said") what it is". Arguments and proofs are vaguely prefigured in the form of enthymemes, but are not overtly expressed. Apart from justification—the reason for the festival given in line 3—Laksmayya makes no judgments on what he reports and thus has no need of explicit arguments beyond those of enthymeme, topic, and example. His purpose is epideictic rather than apodeictic. The text, in other words, does not achieve a dialectical movement in the form of a commentary on the narrative or its implications. The narrative does not become the object of reflection in the text itself and the discourse moves directly from narration to conclusion. The conclusion is a terse paraphrase of the title: "This is the way of doing the hill festival." Its only function is to provide closure. There are no recapitulations of content, implied arguments, evaluations, or references to other information or authority. As Aristotle observes, a discourse that makes no arguments needs no epilogue.

Laksmayya makes no judgements about the narrative in part because that seems not to be his purpose—he intends to describe, but there are other reasons, the most important of which is that the "meaning" of the festival is not an object of discursive knowledge apart from contexts involving its proper execution and instrumental efficacy. It is a normal object of interpretation only with respect to questions about past and future performances—when and where to do it, how to do it properly and whether it produces an appropriate result. Its meaning is in its usages and outcomes and not in its supposedly underlying symbols. Concrete instrumentality, not the abstract structure of concepts is the focus of commonsense interest here. The festival is not yet transformed into a demythologized metaphysical object, nor has it yet become only a metaphor of deeds in the manner of the purificatory rites in the *Apology.*

In the text, Laksmayya reveals nothing of his ethos, of his intentions or of his reasons for writing this description. He appears to practice an image making art that attends only to the details of what the image represents, constructing an imitation that omits the perspective of the observer. His account is seemingly that of an objective reporter who communicates what he sees without judging it. It looks like the sort of thing an ethnographer might produce as primary data, but in fact there is a deception here analogous to the deception practiced by the ethnographer, for just as the ethnographer is a scientist and a thrall of that ideology, Laksmayya was a Christian, and that is the unspoken part of his intention and character, that rhetorical ethos which helps to explain—apart from being in my pay—why he would be motivated to describe at all. Though his judgments are formally absent from his text, they are there in the act of constructing a text. Moreover, his condescending attitude toward the festival was expressed in response to my questions on points of translation. He would, for example, aver that Koyas did the things they did in the ritual because they were ignorant and uncivilized, venturing not only the opinion of Telugu-speaking Hindus and Christians resident in the Koya area, but an opinion which he also supposed was consonant with mine.

This last observation serves as a reminder that Laksmayya's text was composed with a specific audience in mind. For both its form and content flow from Laksmayya's judgment of what I liked to hear. The rhetorical pathos of his text, its accommodation to the soul of its hearer, was based on his previous experience as my informant and translator. He knew the sort of thing that was likely to interest me, that nothing pleased me more than descriptive details, and when he was sulky over some real or imaginary slight would withhold them, retreating into mumbled "I don't knows" in response to my queries, or in serious cases disappearing for a day or two on some pretext or other, only to reappear, bringing with him some ethnographic treasure he was sure would delight me as a way of patching things up between us—all the while expanding on it with a happy deluge of explanations and interpretations. A small contretemps in fact precipitated the text on the Hill Festival. It was spawned by a minor dispute over the meaning of the shaman's speech as recorded in my notes, and occurred one afternoon during the festival as we sat in the shade of a

Tamarind tree near the God shed where we had sought refuge outside the village from the heat, dust, and noise of the feasting going on there.

By focusing on this larger dialogue between Laksmayya and me in which this text emerged, I am implicating Laksmayya's motives not to impugn them, but to expose those presuppositions which we bring to the text as part of our interpretive practices, and in particular to question our presupposition of the descriptive purpose that motivates the text. The text seems to be a description of a series of events, their order, participants, related artifacts and purposes, which seeks to communicate who did what to whom when, where, why, and how. We think it is a description because it seems to do what a description ought to do, and since it does, it must have the structure and rhetorical functions of a description. Namely, the person making the description intends to describe something describable to someone for some reason by adequate means. To put it differently, if something is a description it is for whatever descriptions are for. We move easily then from the identification of form to the implication of function, and it is this recognition of a familiar use of words which facilitates our interpretation. We understand describing and accord it a high place in our inventory of the uses of words, but it is just this easy recognition of a familiar task which misleads us at the same time as it enables us to interpret.

We are all acquainted with mundane descriptions in the everyday world such as "bring me the brown boots with top stitching and a two inch heel"; they are among our means of directing someone to attend to relevant features of some object or circumstance in order, among other things, to help him act upon them appropriately. In this we make no distinction between objects and events; whether we substitute words for things or words for deeds is not a particularly important difference, our tendency being to think of deeds as slightly infirm things, but things nonetheless. Just as we describe objects by listing their particulars we ought to describe events by lists of episodes, of particular happenings, and imagine that in both cases we create a similar sort of image.

In Koya one commonly describes objects similarly even though there is no comparable metaphysical category "thing," but to describe an event this way would be unusual, for deeds are occasioned by motives and governed by conventions. If asked to describe an object a Koya will often respond with a list of salient features, but if asked to describe an event, he begins to tell a story. There is an obvious difference between telling about something and telling a story about something, for a story is not just a list of episodes nor even an hyponymous ordering of them. It is a whole whose episodes are ordered by temporality and governed by purpose. The Koyas thus remind us that there are two kinds of descriptions—those which provide details without much attention to their integrative sequence and those for which the sequence is the integration.

It is a commonplace though many-named fact that there are two modes of integration, one a metaphor of space, the other a metaphor of time. The former is a static image of simultaneously coordinated parts, an objectlike structure, while the latter is a dynamic sequential relation of parts. Since Plato, at least, these modes of integration have been correlated with different modes of discourse, the sequential with narration and the simultaneous with argument or exposition. Plato's distinction between rhetoric and dialectic reflects this correlation, for dialectic in discriminating genera and species creates a taxonomy, a static and spatial image of reason which the syllogism merely recapitulates. In modern discourse analysis we have a similar contrast between the sequential and temporal formalisms of Propp and the simultaneous and spatial formalisms of Lévi-Strauss. Significantly, both Plato and Lévi-Strauss subordinate sequence to simultaneity. The indices of time—sequence, cause, consequence, and result are dominated by images of space—inclusion, exclusion, hyponymy, and the syllogism.

This same transformation is accomplished in the movement from description to explanation in our noncommonsense use of description, and it is just this movement that Laksmayya's text lacks. By itself it neither contains nor implies exposition, dialectic, or explanation. It is merely itself, and we can infer a movement beyond the narrative only if we ground the text in a concrete dialogical context where it has purposes which express its author's intentions, but this is contrary to the movement of dialectic which seeks the abstract and universal rather than the concrete and particular. It is not a return to the rhetorical context, but a movement away from it.

We can now understand what is bothersome about Laksmayya's text as a description—it does not implicate an exposition that goes beyond the rhetorical circumstances of its performance. There is no movement from narration to exposition, from rhetoric to dialectic, or from description to explanation. At best it is a description in response to a commonplace problem like that of describing brown boots, except that we do not know what problematic circumstances evoked it.

This description seems odd because it has no commonplace purpose in our scheme of commonplaces, and odder still because it has no dialectical function. It is given neither as a means of solving a mundane problem nor as an objective report of facts for the purpose of future comparison and generalization. Moreover, it has no commonplace purpose among the Koyas, for it arose in that peculiar dialogical context of ethnographer and informant, that unique circumstance of juxtaposed commonplaces. Nor does it have a dialectical function in the context of Koya life. Not that Koyas do not describe, for they do, but they do not engage in descriptive discourse as we do for all the reasons we do. Koyas resort to descriptive discourse mainly when something has gone awry in communication or social relations. Description is evoked when the context is problematical, when someone misunderstands, is ignorant, or commits a misdeed. It is one means of clearing up a muddle. Koyas do not normally describe in the hope of constituting a body of irrefragable facts which can be woven into a fabric of propositions purporting to explain the nature of nature; they describe in order to mend a rent in that web of mutual understanding which is both constituted in communication and makes communication possible. They neither hope to universalize a local problem by projecting its rhetorical means onto the nature of knowledge in a quest for "pure reason" nor do they seek out problems solely for their synecdochical or metaphoric value as microcosmic representations of the unrepresentable. Though, like us, they see problems as metaphors, problems themselves are not metaphors of the cosmos but are metaphors of a cosmic problem. Their divinitory function is consequently symbolic rather than mimetic. And so a seemingly ordinary problematic event, such as the death of a cow, may point to supernatural interference, and though the manner of death may similarly implicate the motive, neither fact nor manner of death are microcosmic copies of a macrocosmic enactment. The cow's death then is the symbol of a problem in which cows are only incidental artifacts, and even though we and the Koyas might agree in the locution, "the cow died because _____," we neither agree in what comes after "because" nor that the cow's death is the real focus of the sentence. If the cow died because of the wrath of a goddess, for example, that fact "explains" the cow's death, but that is not the point, for the cow's demise is no longer the issue. The real problem is "why is the goddess angry?" and "what can we do about it?" One of the things to do about it is to appease the goddess by participating in a festival like the "Hill Festival," but that does not precipitate a description of the festival though it might create the conditions for it to become a dialectical topic or commonplace in deliberations about the feasibility of participating.

Because the festival is a part of common knowledge and can be a means of practical action it is a dialectical topic and can be used to deduce future facts ("If one performs the festival, the goddess will be appeased"), or as an enthymeme topic of cause and effect either in the past or future ("The sacrifice pleased the goddess"), or it may function inductively by reference to historical examples ("The people of Pedda Nallaballi performed the sacrifice two years ago and have not lost a cow since"). It may function as a special topic with reference to good and evil ("The goddess is angry because evil deeds have been committed here"), or even of politics ("The goddess has come here and visited destruction on us because our relatives performed the sacrifice in their village and drove her here"). Finally, it may serve inductively as a fictive example in the form of a parable or myth. In short, it may serve all the Aristotelian forms of dialectic. This dialectic, however, is neither directed toward universal truths and the formulation of esoteric theoretical knowledge nor is it explanation derived from prior description. Its purposes are practical; it is concerned with the means and ends of action, and with its possible and probable consequences. It is the dialectic of common sense which finds its arguments in the commonplaces of everyday life.

This conclusion points to yet another difference, for it collapses the Aristotelian distinctions between demonstration and dialectic, and between dialectic and rhetoric into a single category. Since the Koyas normally pursue reason neither for itself nor for the sake of the universal truths of theoretical knowledge it might reveal, demonstrations are meant to persuade someone of an appropriate action, they are merely one of the ways in which words coerce deeds, and there is no commonplace context created by written discourse where a demonstration might function in protected isolation from its persuasive purposes. Now it may be that writing can create the illusion of a separate *topos* for demonstration, but it seems to me that it is the Koyas, not we, who are correct here, for I can conceive of few demonstrations which are not also intended as persuasions. A demonstration, for all its pretense of universalized context, is entrained in order to convince someone of something. It is not then a separate genus of reason but a species of persuasion, and there are consequently no grounds for separating logic and rhetoric in their communicative intent.

As for the distinction between probable and necessary which supposedly separated dialectic from logic, the one reflects certitude of evidence, the other certitude of language, and both are corruptions of the notion of "likelihood," which motivates behavior in the common-sense world. In any event, it is certain that the gradients of possibility are not restricted to forms of discourse; we make use of the possible, the probable, and the necessary in logic, dialectic, and rhetoric. To put it another way, commonplaces or topics may be the source of the possible, but they are also the source of what counts as evidence, and we cannot separate enthymemes of evidence from the commonplaces which articulate them. In the Koya example the cow's death is evidence of the goddesses' anger, for goddesses kill cows when they are angered. Evidence is evidence only if it fits into a scheme of commonplaces, and that is the source of its relative certitude, whether we have in mind the commonplaces of common sense or of scientific theory. The necessary is only probable in the realm of the possible.

Apart from Aristotle's formal definition of rhetoric as continuous discourse and dialectic as debate, most of the other differences between them are insubstantial, and in fact Aristotle tends to reduce rhetoric to dialectic. Here the arrow of reduction points in the wrong direction. Historically, dialectic emerges from rhetoric, and logic from dialectic. Moreover, dialectic is already immanent in the narrative, just as logic is immanent in the exposition. The articulation of parts in the narrative constitutes a dialectical movement, for the movement of the narrative from initial conditions to complications to resolution exactly parallels the dialectical movement thesis, antithesis, and synthesis, and both movements merely universalize the systematic alternation of voices in dialogue. The narrative is an internalization of the exterior voices of the dialogue in which the parts of narrative speak to one another much as speakers do in dialogue (cf. Vygotsky 1962). Dialectic is the abstraction and formalization of narrative as a structure of argument, the parts of narrative having been reinterpreted as parts of argument. The next stage in this development occurs when dialectic is attached as a now separate part of the narrative in the form of exposition, proof, or argument. Narrative and dialectic, having been separated from one another are rejoined to create a new discourse form which is fully accomplished when the epilogue is attached to the speech as a third level of commentary. Each part now having become a commentary on the preceding part(s), the stage is set for the emergence of logic, which has as its principal concern the division and arrangement of parts in wholes. Logic is a reflection on the order of parts in discourse which takes as its object the whole discourse, just as the epilogue does. Logic emerges from the epilogue as an abstraction of its function, and eventually establishes itself as the external judge of the discourse, thus arrogating to itself the function of those real judges to whom the discourse was addressed. We may visualize this movement as an organic evolution, as in thought picture 2.1, or as a structure, as in thought picture 2.2.

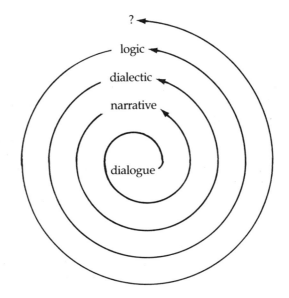

Thought picture 2.1. The sequence of stages in the growth and differentiation of discourse. Each stage grows out of the preceding one, incorporates it, but does not replace it. This narrative sequence of stages is apprehended by logic not as a sequence, but as a simultaneous structure of parts or kinds of discourse ordered by inclusion according to their power of abstraction and role as arbiter of truth, as in thought picture 2.2.

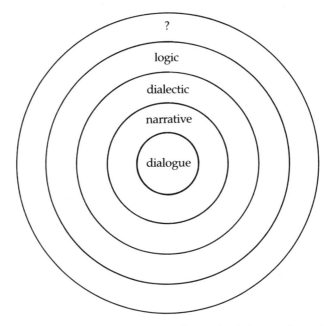

Thought picture 2.2. Simultaneous structure of parts. Logic is most abstract and is the final arbiter of truth.

Taken together these two diagrams are simplified representations of the process by which each succeeding stage is a differentiation of the preceding one and at the same time a whole constituted by the new stage and the one or ones out of which it came. In the mythology of modern science the evolution of the human brain exemplifies this process, and in Hindu mythology it is the process by which the whole cosmos grows and develops, commonly symbolized in the spiral form of Viṣṇu's conch. All are, of course, analogues of the way we comprehend discourse, that original synthesis of the sequential and simultaneous expressed in dialogue.

The sequence of development from dialogue to logic is accomplished by means of the discourse taking itself as its object, and by this progressively abstract reflection on itself, it eventually disjoins the world of words from the world of deeds. The final stage in this movement is facilitated by writing, that necessary supplement to memory which keeps track of the discourse as a sequential order of parts and as levels of simultaneous reflexivity. It makes, in other words, a more complex integration of the sequential and simultaneous orders of information which constitute all discourse. In our time these orders have become the objects of our reflection, presaging yet another synthesis, still unformulated, but the signs of whose struggle into being beyond logic are apparent in all of the so-called modern movements in literature, even in those which reject language or writing altogether, seeing in them no longer the means by which expression moves to ever more complex levels, but as the very obstacle to that movement. One of the possibilities for the future then is not another still more abstract mode of discourse, but of a return to the world of living speech, in a reversal of the process of differentiation comparable to a degenerative phase of the cosmic cycle in Hinduism, as if all of language had become entropic.

But to return to an earlier time by means of another topic, consider again Laksmayya's text. When we remember that narrative is its own dialogue and its own dialectic, then Laksmayya's text seems no longer to need an exposition, for its dialectic is immanent in its narration and dialogical context. Its argument is an enthymeme of its commonplace, its source in common knowledge, which includes the reasons for and consequences of rituals. That it lacks a formal exposition merely confirms its partial and recent emergence from orality into literature, and stresses by its absence the taken-for-granted, unproblematic character of the commonplaces themselves. Consequently, the deed itself is the whole aim of the narrative, not the structure of concepts which enable it.

Words for Deeds and the Doctrine of the Secret World

If Laksmayya's text has an immanent dialectic does it also have a hidden logic, an underlying structure of symbols which constitute the real argument of the text? In the footnotes to the text some effort was expended in identifying the pervasive Hindu symbols which appear to constitute the "hidden" meaning of the text. Now it is undeniable that those symbols are in the text, nor can it be denied that they form a nexus of interpretation at a deeper level, but what is questionable is for whom are the symbols there and for whom do they have this meaning function? Remember that this text is about a festival which, even though Koyas participate in it and know about it, we cannot wholly attribute to them. This is not just a question of who, so to speak, owns the ritual; instead it is a question about the Koya context of the symbols that are seemingly articulated within the text.

Nothing suggests that the Koyas have any real understanding of these symbols either as symbols or even less as symbolizing what they are supposed to symbolize in the context of Hinduism. Do we then conclude that the Koyas mindlessly participate in a ritual that sur-passes their understanding? From an objective viewpoint, the answer is yes, since this condition is scarcely different from any laity's faulty grasp of the subtleties of esoteric knowledge. But the real answer is no; the Koyas do not worship in ignorance of what they worship, for no real, objective realm of esoteric knowledge exists in the context of this ritual. Esoteric knowledge must be, after all, someone's knowl-edge, but that is just the condition that is not met here. The analogy of the Christian or Hindu ignorant of the esoteric foundations of his faith is inappropriate, for neither the Koya religious functionaries nor even less the Naikpod participant has any fuller knowledge of the fes-tival's underlying symbols than the Koya onlooker. No priesthood possesses these esoteric meanings nor busies itself with their inter-pretation and elaboration. It is only the ethnographer who arrogates to himself the doxological function and weaves together the strands of an unknown cosmos.

In some sense, then, these symbols which we so easily recognize in the text are not really symbols since their symbolic function is re-stricted to the ethnographer's imagination. Except there, they are not objective, abstract, collocatable forms whose meanings are indepen-dent of the ritual in which they occur. For the Koya, wearing a deco-rated basket and carrying a set of umbrellas does not symbolize the cosmos; it is part of what one does when one performs the Hill Fes-tival. The significance of that act and those artifacts is the part they play in the ritual as a whole. Their sign function, then, is indexical

rather than symbolic. They do not portend a secret world of underlying meanings nor even less a structure of esoteric knowledge.

Even though the words and deeds of the Hill Festival are not part of
a structure of theoretical knowledge or even the objects of casual
speculation, they, or their likenesses, can be found in contexts outside
this ritual, a fact which dialectical reason would take as sufficient
grounds for inferring that they have a wider symbolic function, but
the condition of independent existence does not by itself imply symbolic function. When we see, for example, that objects are often
bathed as part of a ritual or that the same form of incantation or exhortation occurs in several different rituals that does not mean that these
standardized acts and verbal formulae are symbols which can be combined and recombined to produce endless ritual variations whose
meanings are different only because their pattern of combination is
different. They are not, in short, variables in some syntactic structure
like those envisioned in Lévi-Strauss' *Mythologiques* or in Chomsky's
Syntactic Structures. The same words and deeds occurring in different
contexts of other words and deeds need not entail analytic reason,
that combination of fixed elements by means of fixed rules. It suggests
instead the existence of rather fixed schemata, combinations of words
and deeds that may function in many contexts as the appropriate way
or standard method of doing something. They have a function similar
to that of making a roux in preparing a sauce, or of making a sauce for
a meat dish. They are whole routines whose presence and combination in some order or sequence produces some larger whole such as
ris de veau à la financière or "The Hill Festival." As such they are neither
products nor objects of theoretical knowledge. They are not means of
knowing what it means, but means of knowing how to do it, which is
only part of what it means. Consequently, they portend no separation
of words and deeds, but are instead the means of their harmony.

Epilogue

Having denied that Laksmayya's text has meaning as
actual discourse in the context of Koya culture, or even as an uninten-
tioned collocation of underlying symbols, I seem to have established
its meaninglessness, but surely that is too extreme a form of deconstruction to have made of it only testimony to a chance encounter
somewhere in the Indian jungle, so perhaps this conclusion goes too
far. My original intention was to reveal the meaning of Laksmayya's

text by making its contents an index of some unspecified whole like "Koya Culture" or "Koya Discourse," but in working through the translation the text became more of an index to discourse about discourse, and so the focus of my meditation shifted from the strange familiarity of Laksmayya's text to others as familiar but less strange in their familiarity where I might find some useful analogue with which to make his text similarly familiar. I found instead that those texts were made unfamiliar, as if Laksmayya's text had in some mysterious way infected them with its strangeness, and it was not until I perceived the oddity of description unsolicited by an appropriate commonplace that I began to understand why Laksmayya's text was at one and the same time familiar yet strange. Though Laksmayya's description fitted perfectly into my ethnographer's commonplaces, it was by that fact made mute about its own, and I came to see how objective description could be a means of alienation, a means of making strange the commonplace implied by its narrative. Without its own commonplace Laksmayya's description was also made odd in that ethnographer's commonplace it had seemed to fit so well, and there it remains, dangling somewhere between Laksmayya's world and mine, but at home in neither. Laksmayya's text did not yield up its hidden meaning—if it has one, but by making them less familiar it opened up those other texts with which I had sought to pry his open, and revealed the germ of discourse in that movement from the familiar to the unfamiliar which makes the unfamiliar familiar and the familiar unfamiliar.

3

ETHNOGRAPHY,

INTERTEXTUALITY, AND THE

END OF DESCRIPTION

And in fact we are always under the influence of some narrative, things have always been told us already, and we ourselves have always already been told.
Lyotard 1977

What could be less intertextual than an ethnography, that factual description of culture and mirror of social reality? What mirage of other texts does it evoke, what prior text transform?[1] Its representation of native life gives the appearance of a direct confrontation of mind and nature, word and thing, subject and object, of clear referential meaning. Its appearance of objectivity seems to deny intertextuality, yet it is just that appearance and that denial that signifies its intertextuality, for they index an ideological interest in setting literature aside by concealing the literary artifice that produces the appearance of objectivity. That ideological interest stems, of course, from the discourse of science, which though undeniably textual, claims to be more than "merely" textual. Its intertextuality appears in the guise of "theory" and "method," where some part of method includes practices of textualization, and theory takes the form of invocations of other texts.

In this respect, the most obvious intertextual practice in ethnography is its relation to ethnological theory and the comparative method.

1. This chapter is part of a longer meditation motivated by the strong, but partly contrapuntal voices of W. Ong and J. Derrida. It does not attempt to reconcile them in a "free voice," it only adds a different voice to the fugue of the written word. The paper makes use of discussions on ethnographic writing held in a recent seminar at the School of American Research in Santa Fe. Papers from that seminar have been published under the editorship of James Clifford and George Marcus (1986). Readers looking for extended discussion of the relation between ethnographic writing and current issues in semiotics, such as the one here on intertextuality, will find there reflections on what George Marcus, one of the seminar organizers, has called an "experimental moment" in the writing of ethnographies.

Ethnography, Intertextuality, and the End of Description

The latter consists in the intercomparison of ethnographic texts in the interest of genetic or structural explanation and aesthetic understanding. Intertextual comparison is the basis for the historical reconstruction of defunct cultures and languages, for the study of transformations of myths and other customs either historically within a single tradition or structurally without reference to time or tradition, and for tracing the diffusion and dispersion of culture traits and complexes. It is also both the source of, and test for generalizations about human capability, character, and conduct. This kind of intertextuality has always been the focus of theory and method and needs no discussion here except to point out its role in constituting a community of discourse defining itself, and being defined by interpretations of an emergent body of texts. Less obvious, and much less the object of theoretical interest, is the practice of intertextuality involved in producing an ethnography. This form of intertextuality has been easily ignored, for an ethnography is, after all, a description or an account, not of other texts, but of other people, and involves, moreover, as an essential part of its ideology, the valorization of fieldwork, of the direct experience of seeing and observing, and an open contempt for "arm chair" ethnography, a practice defined negatively by reading and writing.

One could say that an ethnography is a textual practice intended to obscure its textual practices in order to present a factual description of "the way things are" as if they had not been written and as if an ethnography really were a "picture" of another way of life. Ethnographers have pretended to ignore the constitutive implications of the suffix "-graphy," except in the interest of objective reporting, the achievement of a distanced, objective voice intoning "just the facts," and thus betraying by this interest the ethnography's intertextuality, for this interest itself indexes an orientation to ideology defined in other texts. The desire for objective description grounds the ethnography intertextually within the discourse of science.

Despite its ideology of description, its pose of being a writing about something that is fully external to other texts, the ethnography is actually a complex intertextual practice, ranging from overt citation of other texts to allusion by failure to mention what ought to be mentioned, noting in the first instance by presence and in the second by absence. In between these two extremes are numerous means of implicating other texts and textual traditions, either by direct comparison or indirectly through presuppositions, genre conventions, common tropes, key concepts, and the set of commonplaces that constitute the so-called theory and method of a community of discourse.

Easiest to isolate, though seldom discussed, are the genre conventions that identify ethnography as ethnography (rather than biography, for example) and comprise a set of uncodified practices for writing ethnographies (Marcus and Cushman 1982). Apart from the fact that every ethnography is modeled on and is the potential model of another ethnography, and the general scholarly conventions governing citation, quotation, and bibliographic reference, so little is explicit in this tradition that one might think that each ethnographer would be free to write in whatever manner best suits his purposes or most felicitously represents "her people," but, in fact, ethnographers most often use some version of "natural history," tricking out their ethnographies in the form of objective descriptions of natural objects. Faceless abstractions like "The Neur" or "The Koya man" are puppeteered through their "social structures" and "religious systems," and this rhetoric of distanced description signifies that larger discourse of scientific writing into which ethnography insinuates itself.

The guiding dogma consistent with this rhetoric is the fable of the ethnographer as "participant-observer," she who effects the stance of an "outsider/insider" and describes what she sees by a kind of curious double vision in which one eye sees as observer, the other as participant. This may conjure an image of the ethnographer as cross-eyed, "one who sees with a forked eye," but it also indexes the visual bias of science itself, the empiricism of "being there" and "seeing with one's own eyes."

Though the rhetoric of description and referential discourse make it seem that the ethnographer's words refer to a world beyond his text, that world is actually built up by the textual conventions that govern the writing of an ethnography and with the connivance of the reader, for in the end, readers must take the ethnographer's word for that external reality or judge it by comparison with other texts of other realities whose externality is determined by yet other texts in an infinite or cyclical profusion of texts (cf. Pratt 1986, Thornton 1984a). As Nietzsche remarks, this is how the world becomes a fable, for a fable is something told, having no existence outside the tale (1968:24).

Part of the ethnographic genre are other, subordinate rhetorics, hidden, or perhaps fleetingly revealed, behind the dominant rhetoric, and seldom explicitly acknowledged. These are the rhetorics of power and poetry, of provocation and evocation, for much ethnography is reflexive—a message to the world, an ill-disguised tract for social reform and cultural criticism, or the romanticized evocation of the exotic and libidinal, of a preindustrial past, of noble savages in a pastoral eden, a kind of escapist fiction (cf. Clifford 1986). Then too,

Ethnography, Intertextuality, and the End of Description

ethnographies are enabled not only by the ideology of science, but by the political and economic hegemony of Western culture which transforms all cultures into objects of exchange and establishes the conditions for their reduction to objects of scientific scrutiny (Said 1978).

Ethnography is a genre that discredits or discourages narrative, subjectivity, confessional, personal anecdote, or accounts of the ethnographers' or anyone else's experience. Its objectivity ensures its intertextuality, for it can make no direct and legitimate appeal to the reader's subjectivity by way of the author's experience. The reader is confronted by a text that might have been written by no one or everyone, a condition that guides her interpretation away from her own experience and leads it safely in the direction of other texts. There is in the end, neither author nor reader, only an endless play of text upon text.

Constellations of key concepts and hagiography comprise the commonplaces that pass for theory and method in the community of discourse called anthropology. Every ethnography is organized around or by means of these commonplaces, for they serve as loci for arguments, as frameworks for organizing and interpreting facts, and as orientations for observation. They are both the instrument and the structure of knowledge, just as were the commonplaces of rhetoric (cf. Ong 1982, Yates 1966). Words like "social structure," "culture," "kinship," "religion," "marriage," "tribe," "pastoralism," "role," "status," "clan," "taboo," "interaction," and "group" are among the congeries of concepts that articulate in the multiform patterns that constitute ethnographies.

Appellations like "Kroberian," "Malinowskian," "Boasian," "Lévi-Straussian," and "Geertzian," often found in the introduction or "theoretical orientation" chapters of modern ethnographies, eponymously index differing patterns of dominance, schematization, and classification of key concepts. Such words as "structuralism," "functionalism," "symbolic anthropology," and others are part of this litany of indexicality in which a single word is a synecdoche for a whole body of literature and evokes it by mere mention. The hagiography or invocation of "ancestors" justifies, either by exhortation or exorcism, attitudes or orientations toward the influence of one or another of these "strong" authors (Bloom 1973), and words like "structuralism" or "functionalism" index an attitude toward a more or less anonymous constellation of concepts fulfilled not so much in the texts of a single author, but in a larger discourse consisting of a collection of texts and their commentaries. Many key words name the content of chapters and provide the major headings of ethnographies. A common collection of chapter headings might be : "material culture," "economic organization," "kinship and social structure," "religion and ritual," "art and dance," "language."

Whatever their attribution, these key concepts function synecdochically as indexical particulars. Ethnographers invoke them, presuming that readers can make the appropriate connections by filling in the absent details from their general knowledge of the literature. The use of key terms thus depends upon the presupposition of an intertextual practice that constitutes an imagined community of discourse, a fictitious group of engaged and knowledgeable readers.

Less evident, because unnamed and often not consciously known to the ethnographer—and the more powerful for that—are tropological conventions derived from the whole tradition of Western literature or from certain strong texts in that tradition which form the largely unconscious source of any author's sense of how discourse is organized, concepts linked, coherence achieved, and an illusion of completion or resolution created. Consider, for example, the movement from "concrete to abstract," "material to spiritual," hidden in the innocuous looking sequence of chapters given earlier as: "material culture," "economic organization," "kinship and social structure," "religion and ritual." Here is an explicit, but unacknowledged convention reflecting the trope of perfective movement of spirit or intelligence from the natural to the supernatural, from the gross, material aspects of the world to those of spiritual or aesthetic understanding which has informed the whole of theological, philosophical, and scientific discourse in the West (cf. Derrida 1976:85–87). The order of chapters recapitulates the evolution of man from nature to culture.

For similar reasons, descriptions of rituals assume dramaturgic or narrative forms, despite the general repression of these forms in ethnography (cf. Turner 1974). Rituals become sequences of acts or episodes which unfold like some Proppian folktale, not because that is how they are but because the ethnographer imposes upon them the single perspective of the observer or narrator, or ritual specialist for whom some acts, persons, sayings, or episodes are central and others peripheral. When deeds become words they commonly assume some form of narrative sequence which suppresses parallel, simultaneous, or multiple perspectives. The ethnographer suppresses the experience of ritual, its fits and starts, movements from center to periphery, its plurivocalism, and substitutes for it the smooth, uninterrupted flow of a univocal narrative in which the sequentialized action builds logically to its climax and moves unfalteringly to its conclusion. Both ethnographer and reader suppress their experience of ritual and know it only as literature, as a text of a ritual which can be understood only by comparing it to texts of other rituals, seeing it finally as part of the ultimate "how to" book of magic, or as a preliminary, though hesitant, step on the road to science.

Ethnographers use such tropes because they must tell an exotic tale that can only be told and understood as if it were another story already told and understood (Clifford 1986, Thornton 1984b). Thus, our understanding of ritual as narrative stems in part from our prior acquaintance with the already allegorized story form of textualized Christian ritual. Other allegories such as "origin," "comparison," "quest," and "pastoral" are story forms similarly already given in the tradition of Western literature (Clifford 1984). By means of these allegories, different cultural worlds are understood not by their differences but by a similitude conveyed through implicit or explicit comparison to stories already known. This is how contemporary primitives are deprived of their contemporaneity and become "relics of the stone age" (Fabian 1983), how we imagine the origin of social customs can be found among still living peoples who have not yet ascended the higher rungs of the ladder of social evolution, or conversely, how we atone for the sins of civilization in a fable of loss and alienation in which the wholeness of primitive culture stands in didactic contrast to the fragmentary character of contemporary life, or lacerate our consciences with tales of the "vanishing Indian," whose disappearance marks not just his passing, but a nostalgia for all the past before corruption.

Such allegories are complex encodings of critical oppositions in Western thought: the past and the present; primitive and civilized; East vs. West; whole and fragment; integration and disintegration; growth and decay; oral and literate; holistic and analytic; libidinal and rational; rural and urban; *communitas* and *civitas*; microcosm and macrocosm; subject and object; master and slave; self and other; identify and difference; mythos and logos; left brain and right brain; developed and underdeveloped; male and female; and the complexes blood, earth, and kin vs. machine, city, and bureaucracy. These, and many others, are all part of the ethnographer's storytelling repertory.

But all is not storytelling, a tissue of dramaturgy and narrative, for ethnographies are more commonly organized in their totality by metaphors of space rather than time. Natural history writing, which is neither natural nor history, is the premier spatial model of ethnography, and this accounts for the rather "Linnean" structure of ethnography, though some recent ethnographies, inspired by the binary oppositions of computer flow charts, seem to owe more to Ramus than to Linnaeus. Nonetheless, the rhetorical form of ethnography exploits "classification" as a textual formula or trope that projects an imaginary whole consisting of logically implicated parts (Thornton 1984a).

Ethnographers project their fragmentary and incomplete experience of exotic cultures onto a rhetorical form that creates the illusion of a comprehensive and coherent whole, and readers, by prior acquaintance with this form, fill in missing parts, creating in their imaginations what is not given but must be there by implications drawn from the form itself.

One of the commonest tropes in ethnographic writing is the trope of "translation." It has two variants, one iconic and one symbolic. The iconic version consists in the actual translation of real texts which are written transcriptions of various kinds of spoken native accounts, myths, tales, life histories, and conversations. Apart from the complicating fact that it is usually the ethnographer who accomplishes the textualizing move from the oral to written word—itself a complex and highly metaphoric act—the ethnographer plays here the relatively humble role of scribe. His importance emerges, of course, in the translation and commentary which relativizes the text to the intertextual discourse of ethnology. Thus, the Pārēḍu Gaṭṭa Gōtram Pūrbam ("'History' of the Pārēḍu Mountain Sib"), is not just a text of a tribal account, but becomes an instance of a "myth of origin" to be compared with other myths, dissected, classified, and filed away in the greater encyclopedia of exotic customs, and the ethnographer is promoted from scribe to savant. Except for some notable revisions of this technique (cf. Crapanzano 1980, Tedlock 1983, and Hymes 1981), few ethnographers now practice this honorable craft. More common, by far, is translation in the symbolic mode.

The transit to the symbolic is actually accomplished by separating language from culture and making the thing to be translated no longer a language or anything so crude as a real text; culture or "modes of thought" are the objects of translation (Asad 1986). Something so amorphous is capable of being practiced in a great many ways, but the main differences have to do with how far culture is separated from language, and how far the latter is removed from native utterances. For ethnoscientists, language is the chief index of culture, and their practice of translation is akin to structural lexicography, the translation of the implicational patterns of native word sets—uttered for unreported reasons—which have rather clear referential uses. Others, of a more symbolic and interpretive persuasion, limit language to a few "key words"—uttered under unreported circumstances—which are

Ethnography, Intertextuality, and the End of Description

the foci of cultural themes and sources of the foundational metaphors whose exegesis constitutes the sense of "translation."

In either case, it is clear that the idea of translation is itself a metaphor based on the notion of making the meanings of one way of life comprehensible in the language of another. What is not clear is the intertextual practice involved in this translation, for both forms adopt a practice justified in theoretical and methodological texts and are primarily oriented toward that ideology, despite all the brave talk about understanding the native point of view in its own terms or of representing native cognition. It all begs the question of the source of the authority that enables the ethnographer to speak for the native, no matter how it is done. Moreover, it makes explicit the motivation of ethnography, which, like the metaphor of translation itself, seeks to dominate difference by means of identities or equivalences which make native life fit the civilized contours of our own discourse, make it palatable to our sapience, and amenable to our interests. Even when ethnographers disagree, as in the recent Mead-Freeman controversy, the disagreement is not really about native life, it is about rhetorical strategy and allegorical choice, for both reduce the significance of the Samoan to an identity with our interests and ensure that the meaning of native life is only its meaning "for us."

Among other tropological conventions is one that reveals not only intertextuality, but indexes the troublesome nature of that intertextuality. Some texts are, after all, better left unacknowledged. "The arrival scene" that often chronicles the ethnographer's first glimpse of the natives is a personal narrative establishing the ethnographer's authority, the "I was there" that founds the description in the ethnographer's firsthand experience (Pratt 1984). This convention was already established in travel literature by the sixteenth century, from which it was borrowed by ethnographers. Travel literature and ethnography share common interests in the description of exotic places, both are grounded in personal experience, and both are combinations of narrative and description. Ethnography, however, distances itself from travel literature (although the two sometimes overlap) by repressing personal narrative, relegating it to the functions of "setting the scene" and establishing the author's authority by means of his "presence" (Pratt 1986).

Apart from travel literature and the related "manners and customs" literature (Pratt 1984), the "anxiety of influence" for ethnographers can be traced to two other broad literary traditions: missionary accounts of native religion and colonial administrator's reports of native customs. Both often deployed the rhetoric of natural history, and both founded their descriptions on incontestable narrative presence based sometimes on more intimate and enduring contact with native life than that of most ethnographers. Both traditions have also produced fine ethnographies. Consequently, these two communities of discourse were, and still are, highly problematic for ethnographers, for they infringe upon their claim to representational hegemony. Ethnographers had to distance themselves from missionaries and colonial administrators by impugning their motives, even as they used their information and relied on their good offices for help in the field.

This distancing was achieved in two related ways. Ethnographers disclaimed any self-interest connected with Christianity or colonialism. They succeeded in convincing themselves, but not the natives or hardly anyone else, that they were not part of a civilizing or dominating mission, that they did not interfere in native life, that they were champions of the native, opposed to changes that would destroy the integrity of a way of life. This stance, though it succeeded in separating missionaries and ethnographers, had the unfortunate result of allying ethnographers and colonial administrators, for both had an interest in maintaining the status quo. This identity of interest facilitated the ethnographer's access to the native, especially as compared to the missionary, whom political officers often suspected of fomenting change, even though unwittingly.

The ethnographers' second move was to disentangle themselves from too close an identification with administration. In places like India this was especially difficult because ethnography, and archaeology too, were actually branches of the government, staffed by members of the prestigious Indian Civil Service who were often as well-trained as their academic counterparts. Nonetheless, ethnographers eventually succeeded in establishing their claim of political disinterest, a move unavailable to their compromised competitors, by asserting a superordinate interest that transcended both politics and religion—scientific theory! Ultimately their claim to higher knowledge and academic credentials established the rhetoric of their ethnography as the true doctrine, for their ethnographies were not contaminated instruments contingent on the rhetoric of power; they were pure instruments in the dominating rhetoric of universal science.

That historical perspective has made all these claims bogus is not the point here. What is interesting in this context is the invocation of theory as a rhetorical strategy, for theory gives direct access to the *logos,* and is thus the ultimate justifying intertextual move, establish-

Ethnography, Intertextuality, and the End of Description

ing a connection not only with regional or topical theories, but with the whole of that larger, intertextual enterprise known later as the "unity of science."

This self-aggrandizement was paid for later in the coin of self-deception, not only in the sense of a repressed rhetoric of power and political domination, but more importantly in the suppression of another rhetoric which could not be tolerated by that political rhetoric nor accommodated to the need for a dominating scientific authorial voice (Clifford 1983). I speak here of the suppression of the voice of the native, of the dark twin of Socrates, of "she who does not speak" in the ethnography, the trace of whose voice is only its absence.

The fable of participant observation both reveals and obscures the presence of the native, for participation implies a "doing together" which might include speaking together, and though ethnographers make claims of fluency in the native language those claims are seldom documented by examples of dialogue. This absence of dialogue signifies the subordination of participating to observing and the use of participation as a deception, as a means of establishing a position from which to observe. That is why the native is muted, or speaks only through the voice of the ethnographer in "language," in the form of a grammar, or in a translated tale or myth relegated to the appendix. But, even this trace, this faint and garbled whisper of the native's voice is only a means of hiding the fact that ethnographers spend more time talking and writing than in strict observation unmediated by talk. Yet this talk, which is the enabling condition for observing, is nowhere reported because it would contaminate the image of pure, unmediated, objective observation as the ground of description. It would jeopardize the scientific status of the description by complicating its vision with the merely oral and auditory.

There is, then, another rhetoric and another text, unacknowledged and hidden by a form of writing. It is the dialogue between the ethnographer and his native participants (Clifford 1983). It is, in a sense, an originating text, and that may explain its silence, for it is like the originating voice of God, whose only trace we now understand is its silence (cf. Lyotard 1954:45). It is as if native dialogue were not discourse, as if it were part of an originating antepredicative world of pure but dumb experience. The ethnographer thus gives voice to that which does not know how to speak, but cannot give an account of dialogue because, like all originary experience, it cannot be reconstructed or made explicit and still be what it originally was. Properly speaking, nothing may be said of it, it is the allegory of an original past that was never present but nonetheless coincided with the movement from a personal subject to an impersonal and anonymous subject, a movement from the ethnographer's perceptual experience, which founds his account in science, to a writing of that experience which must obscure that experience as the experience of a personal subject, not only because it cannot do otherwise, but must obscure it in the interest of science. The native and the personal subject vanish together in the penumbra surrounding the absolute subject for whom alone the native has a meaning.

Then, too, dialogical textualization, despite its honorable association with philosophical tradition, is unfashionable in sciences where the object of observation "talks back" only in visual patterns. It is, besides, subjective, and properly a fictionalizing trope best left to novelists, yarn spinners, or other tellers of tales and jokes. It carries, so to speak, the oral taint of self-reflexivity, of suspect truth and fiction, of "gossip," "rumor," "hearsay," and of "talk is cheap." It is what is only heard but not seen (cf. Tyler 1984).

Thus, the ethnographer's text reveals a vision of a way of life only inasmuch as it takes away the living dialogue, for the letter of ethnography killeth. The ethnographer is a symbol of doom. His appearance among the natives is the surest sign of their disappearance, a disappearance that is effected as much by the textualization that purports to record and save their way of life, not for them, but for the good of science or the implicit moral lesson it has for the West, as it is brought about by the political and economic domination that enables the ethnographer's presence and which his presence symbolizes.

Even when dialogue becomes the focus of ethnography, as it has in recent times, it appears in the text only as a means of verisimilitude in the interest of empirical verification, or as an object of linguistic analysis, and always under the authorial control of the ethnographer. Thus, the now old "new ethnography" reported dialogue between ethnographer and native not as such, but as "controlled elicitation," of "evidence" for the ethnographer's interpretation of native categories, as a "public record" of the "facts" out of which he inductively built his "descriptions," his folk taxonomies and systems of social classification (cf. Tyler 1969: 12–13). So, too, did the so-called ethnography of speaking transform native discourse into an object of analysis, into "data" to be manipulated in the interest of sociolinguistic theory (cf. Gumperz and Hymes 1972). Even "dialogical anthropology," which seems to acknowledge some sense of polyphony, and allows the native to direct the dialogue, does so for reasons of theory and analysis. The tape-recorded dialogue is "evidence" for ethnopoetic structure, if nothing else, and of course the ethnographer relinquishes none of his

Ethnography, Intertextuality, and the End of Description

final authorial control (cf. Tedlock 1983, Crapanzano 1980, Hymes 1981, Rothenberg and Rothenberg 1983). The basso of the ethnographer still speaks for the falsetto of the native.

There is not yet in ethnography a real "effacement of an enunciating" subject, of an authorial presence. Even the absence of *an* ethnographer's narrative voice in the interest of objectivity, marks not just the absence of a personal subject, but reveals the presence of an impersonal subject whose text is its cognitive utopia. So, too, photographs of natives reveal not the native, the ethnographic object, but the presence of this same impersonal subject. In avoiding the solipsism of the personal subject ethnography only succeeds in displacing solipsism onto a transcendental, impersonal ego. Seeking to control its subjectivity, the ethnography represses its object but does not thereby overcome the subject.

An ethnography is a compromised and problematic genre whose message and possibility are founded in a dilemma. It must be grounded in perception, in the "I have seen," but it must at the same time eliminate from its text the "I" who sees and speaks (cf. Clifford 1983). It must put it "under erasure," as Derrida would say. Moreover, in order to be a description it necessarily obscures description by denying the constitutive act of writing.

Because the role of the subject is compromised by the demand for objectivity—the demand for its erasure—an ethnography cannot be an account of the originary experience of the ethnographer of the sort attempted by Rabinow (1977) and Fischer (1986), for apart from its impossibility, that would be to admit that the subject of the ethnography is the subject, an account of the ethnographer's subjectivity rather than a description of the native as object. The native would recede into the background, becoming only the means of the ethnographer's biography in the manner of peripheral bit players, the local color in a movie whose hero and central figure is the ethnographer.

Then, too, what can be made of the claim to originary experience, experience that happens before the text, which the text encodes and is an account of? We must believe that no part of that experience was mediated by writing, either in the form of preparatory texts—the ethnographer's field notes—or by other texts from the discourse of anthropology. This is a mythology of the ethnographer as a "tabula rasa." The ethnographer's fieldnotes, which he claims to "write-up," attest to the historical stratification of that ethnography, for the final account is preceded by other writing, by another text, a subtext which does not appear in the final text. Moreover, are those notes accounts of the ethnographer's experience, or are they the means by which that experience becomes experience? Is the writing of ethnographic notes not already part of the ethnographer's experience, and the chief means by which he comes to construe that experience? What could possibly count as unconstrued, "raw" experience?

It is commonplace knowledge that field work and the writing of ethnographies are situated both within the history of anthropological discourse and within the context of other discourses (Marcus 1980, 1986). Every ethnographer is a child of her time and comes to the field informed by contemporary significances; the meaningful events of her generation and the consensus of theory and practice are the landmarks and boundaries of her imagination. This guarantees that what she sees and writes is not likely to be what Haddon or Rivers or Evans-Pritchard or even Lévi-Strauss would have seen or written, and this difference has nothing to do with anything that may have happened to the people ethnographers study, though that too is part of the historical context, but is simply the result of all these other ethnographers having written before, of their having contributed to a discourse which is always emergent, always being interpreted, which the ethnographer enters at a unique point, and which is as much the object of her enterprise as the natives themselves.

The professional training of the ethnographer—her acquaintance with the discourse of anthropology—becomes the means by which the occultation of the native is ensured. She is ". . . blinded by the visible, dazzled by writing" (Derrida 1976b:37). She sees the natives through eyes bandaged with texts, and would not see them otherwise, for the natives are not just signified by these texts, they are their signs, signifiers of them, and because they signify the discourse that signifies them, they are unities of signified and signifier, living arguments against the arbitrariness of the relation between signs and objects, for they have always been caught up in a discourse that has a history but no origin to establish the condition of their original textual separation, and no moment in which sign and object were first arbitrarily joined in a ". . . and God said . . ." (cf. Derrida 1976:36).

And because they too have now read Kroeber and Boas, they are the ethnographer's interpretants, not of themselves in the sense of an interpreter, but of the ethnographer's texts, displacing her from that directive position within the triad of signification. Their intertextuality exemplifies the Peircean intersubstitutability or reflexivity of sign, object, and interpretant, and signifies that so long as ethnography pretends to describe, it can only be a subject seeming to inscribe an object which is itself, and can at most evoke only the possibility of a cycle of permutation which is an identity that makes no differ-

Ethnography, Intertextuality, and the End of Description

ence, but whose meaning is the end of description, the possibility of direct intuition, and the return to evocation (cf. Tyler 1978:459–65; Tyler 1986).

Ethnography is the endorphin of culture, an intertextual practice which, by means of an allegorizing identity, anaesthetizes us to the other's difference. Its other is a same, made so by a process of double occultation, for the ethnographic text can represent the other as difference only inasmuch as it makes itself occult, and can only reveal itself inasmuch as it makes the other occult, which is the condition of modernism. Postmodern ethnography must be another kind of intertextuality whose project is not to reveal the other in univocal descriptions which allegorically identify the other's difference as our interest. It must be instead, a fantasy of identities, a plurivocal evocation of difference making a unity in fantasy that mimics on every page the rationalism that seems to inform it, and reveals between every line the difference it conceals in every word, that it might speak not for the other "for us," but let the other's voice be heard, too, and not just "for us," but "for us both."

MEMORY AND DISCOURSE

4

*. . . an immediate conclusion is seen in the premises by
the light of common sense, and where that is wanting, no
kind of reasoning will supply its place.*

Reid (1895:701)

In his *Confessions,* St. Augustine tells us that human knowing is only synecdochic, for human speech occurs in time.[1] God's word is timeless and could not be a linear sequence of sound. It is a whole and eternal. Linear temporality cannot comprise the whole, and that is why the word became flesh, for we could not otherwise understand it (*Confessions* XI:7). In speaking of speech Aristotle observes that ". . . none of its parts has an abiding existence, when once a syllable has been pronounced it is not possible to retain it, so naturally as the parts do not abide, they cannot have position" (*Categoria* 5). Speech is not a proper whole, but in *Categoria* 13–15 he speaks of simultaneity as reciprocal dependence where each part involves the other whether the other is actually present or not, as in such terms as x is double of y, x is half of y, or of species of the same genus distinguished by the same method of division. These are all wholes whose parts do not abide in the present, are not present in the present, but are nonetheless wholes whose parts interrelate, not lineally but simultaneously. In his commentary on Aristotle, Hamilton adds that a whole once constituted, though it be constituted sequentially, may be simultaneous in memory (1895:912).

I invoke these ancients here as a means of drawing attention to the interplay among time, sequence, simultaneity, parts, wholes, dis-

---

The original version of this chapter was a paper given at the Second Rice University Department of Linguistics and Semiotics Seminar February 10–14, 1984.

1. Conventions used in this analysis are as follows:

. . short pause	‖ B ‖ breath at end of a phrase
. . . long pause	f forte
. . . . deletion	acc. accelerated speech
´ primary stress	dec. decreasing speech rate
˘ secondary stress	[ ] overlapping speech, two people talking
⌐ raised pitch on phrase	at once
⌐ lowered pitch on phrase	⌐ second speaker attaches utterance to
‖ end of phrase	first speaker's uncompleted utterance
ǀ B ǀ breath in middle of a phrase	

course, and memory as topics intimately involved in the discourse about discourse. The ancients are conjured for another reason—to remind readers that much of what we now call discourse analysis is little more than a rediscovery of what these ancients called rhetoric. Discourse structure, like the *dispositio* of rhetoric, is concerned with the arrangement of parts relative to a larger whole; semantic memory is clearly the modern equivalent of *memoria,* one of the principal parts of rhetoric; and the current interest in inference and implication is obviously paralleled by the concepts "argument" and "demonstration" in the rhetorical tradition. Even something so modern sounding as "conversational implicature" has its ancient equivalent in the concepts *ethos* and *pathos* which had to do with the speaker's judgments about the hearer's participation.

Some things are, of course, omitted. Significantly, modern studies have no equivalent of the *inventio,* the speaker's means of finding ideas to talk about. Its absence in contemporary discourse analysis signifies the fact that modern work is reader/hearer oriented. It reflects the contemporary bias toward written forms which provide linguists with visual objects to analyze. It also reflects their long-standing prejudice against intentionality. Writing made it possible for authors to control and manipulate their intentions in a way that speakers in oral dialogue could not. Authors could sustain occult or ambiguous intentions through irony or by shifts of voice without the accountability of hearer intervention. Flight from intentionality as a source of interpretation derives from the reader's suspicion of the author's "true" intentions and marks the recognition of the author as a kind of "trickster." Obscurity of authorial intention has been the justification for the necessity of interpretation and consequently for the enhancement of the reader's role at least since Aristotle's *De Interpretatione,* and reflects, as does that work, the problematic character of writing.

Writing made it possible for the reader to dispense with the author's intentions in another way. Because texts always say both more or less than authors intend, authors do not have full control over their texts. They are dupes of the text. Readers arrogate to themselves an understanding of a text superior to that of its authors, an understanding which the author has only limited rights to contradict.

We come, then, to a paradox at the heart of contemporary discourse analysis. One cannot *analyze* oral discourse as discourse, for in order for analysis to work, it must have an object that can be dismantled and reassembled. Discourse analysis consequently first transforms all oral discourse into written text in order to analyze it. It must first destroy what it seeks to analyze. A written transcription of oral discourse is no longer oral discourse as it was created and understood by participants; it is an object created to be analyzed by nonparticipants for reasons that are remote from those that usually motivate participants. What relation this object and its analysis has to the understanding of participants is problematic at best. This is not to say that analysis must recreate the understanding of participants, for that would entail an explication of common sense that is neither possible nor necessary. What need would it fulfill? If participants are able to understand oral discourse without the benefit of linguistic analysis, what need could they have of analysis? Analysis seeks its justification, then, not in practical application, but in the loftier *telos* of theory. Here is another contrast with the ancients, who though often as singular in their pursuit of abstract knowledge as any contemporary linguist, yet grounded rhetoric in the real world of practical action.

Schemata: **Discourse Ready-mades**

Scheme, schema, schemata, frames, or words to that effect, have joined the list of hegemonic invocations in cognitive and linguistic studies, replacing the former rule of "rule" in our conceptual kingdom. The terms scheme, schema, and schemata are usually attributed to Bartlett (1932), but actually derive from rhetoric, where *schemae* and *figurae* referred to the making of tropes by fixed formulae. Apart from attesting once again to the unacknowledged rhetorical tradition, these terms signify a general retreat from grammar as an axiomatic deductive system. Interest in schemata points to a concern for preformed units of comprehension and production that are not entirely fixed and that are not just names for syntactic categories, such as "noun," "verb," and "phrase," nor single words. Schemata are "ready-mades" with "options" rather in the way a Cadillac is a Chevy with all the trimmings. They are, in other words, constituted wholes whose parts interact with one another by means of the whole of which they are parts. As signs, their representational mode is indexical and their colligational mode is synecdochic (see thought picture 4.2, p. 124).

In the past, linguists have treated this group of collocations under the general rubric of "idioms," or "frozen expressions," as forms of fixed multilexical construction whose meanings are not mechanically predictable by part-part summation. Such forms, however, are merely one kind of schematic ordering. They are of the type whose parts and their relations are fixed, such as: "I mean . . . ," "gimme a break . . ." "take a break . . . ," "break a leg . . . ," "stick 'em up . . . ," "get off

my back . . . ," "he went 'n . . . ," and so on. Some are complete utterances, but by far the greater number are parts of larger utterances.
Though they are fixed, even the most frozen expression has the as yet
unrealized possibility of optionality, of deletion or expansion, and it is
this capability that characterizes the majority of schemata.

Some schemata are indexed by a key term or terms, all other terms
being optional. Who does not immediately recognize "if _____ then,"
"_____ is to _____ as _____ is to _____," "_____ as _____ as _____," "the
more _____ the less _____," "the _____-er, _____ the _____-er _____."
Key-term schemata are so predictable that they enable hearers to anticipate what is coming and at the same time economize the speaker's
effort in hanging together the bits and pieces that eventually make up
his utterance. It is as if, when in talk we come to a schema, the rocky
road of discourse opens into a broad, smooth highway which we speed
along with ease, and that is why most talk—and writing, too—is not
novel, but consists of long stretches of freeway interspersed with construction detours. Easy idioms bridge the gaps and comfortable metaphors ease us through the traffic.

From this point of view (a nicely built, but much used bridge), discourse is not so much a matter of grammatical constraint—at least in
the usual sense of grammar—but of the stitching together of schemata
into a rhapsody in very much the way the rhapsodists of oral traditions have always done, and for the same reasons; schemata are much
closer to the form of inner speech and thought than are sentences and
propositions (cf. Ong 1982, Lord 1960). Oral discourse, and thought
too, are orders of schemata to which grammatical conventions are attached. Grammar is an optional add-on.

Key-term schemata need not have the quasi-sequential or part-
propositional ordering of the previous examples, but may be thought
of instead as instances with simultaneous possibilities of realization.
This is not so much a key word as such, but an index to a family
of possible schemata. This, in fact, is a very common form of what I
call the "family scheme" as illustrated by the "nice" and "problem"
families.

> "nice":   "it's nice"
>   "it's kinda nice"
>   "it's real nice"
>   "it's sorta nice"
>   "it's quite nice"
>   "it's so nice here"
>   "it's so nice of you to _____."

"how nice."
"whata nice _____."
"hava nice _____."
"thatsa nice _____."
"thats not nice"
"it's not nice to _____."
"wouldn't it be nice if _____."
etc.

"problem": "whatcher problem?"
"gotta little problem?"
"_____ gotta little problem with _____."
"_____ have a problem."
"_____having a problem with _____."
"_____ having problems."
"the problem (with that) is _____"
"there's only one little problem _____."
"that's one helluva problem."

"that's a $\left\{\begin{array}{l}\text{real hard}\\\text{big}\\\text{bad}\end{array}\right\}$ problem"

"whatsiz problem?"
"is that ever a problem!"
"is it ever a problem for you to _____?"
etc.

Some of these are relatively fixed, but most have optional expansions or transformations of one sort or another. The point is, though, that the key terms "nice" and "problem" are foci. Around each is a cluster of common expressions which the focal terms index but do not themselves represent. "Nice" and "problem" are synecdoches of the expressions in which they commonly function as focal parts.

Other key-word schemata are more directly "keyed" to parts of discourse than to situations. Consider, for example, discourse "openers" such as "what I would like to find out more about is your operation," Susan's opening line in the Susan/Karen interview (see appendix). This is a prominent member of a family of openers. Some of its more commonly used congeners are:

"what I intend to talk about is _____"
"what I would like to try to explain is _____"
"what I have in mind is _____"
"what I am going to speak about is _____"

> "what interests me is _____"
> "what I want to ask you about is _____"
> "what I mean to explain is _____"
> "what I wanted to speak to you about was _____"
> etc.

These are all keyed to the opening of one or another kind of speech event, some to speeches or talks, others to chats, and still others to conversations. Some can be used almost universally in any kind of speech situation ranging from opening an interview to seizing an opening in a conversation, discussion, argument, or debate. All, however, are indexed by the "what I _____" key term and have the effect of providing reasonable context for what is to follow.

Consider, too, the schema "_____ for example," in the paragraph preceding the examples above. "For example" is a phrase that indexes exemplification and ties what is to follow with what has gone before as illustrative instances of a general case. It was known in the books of rhetoric as the *exemplum,* and was tied to the argument part of the *dispositio.* "The following _____" has a similar linking function and may also be used argumentatively. "Follow" itself indexes another set of bridges—consequential ones. The most common of these in the Susan/Karen discourse is "so" (about 30 instances), as in "so I thought _____," "so I said _____," "so I figured _____."

"So _____" and other schemata may function as conclusions or summary paraphrases of what has preceded. They may also be used as "turn-keepers," indexing no inferential connections between what has gone before and what is now to come, as in "so, well listen _____," or even as openers in "so tell me what you _____." In all of these cases they have a common function of giving the appearance of connectedness of discourse either within the discourse itself or by means of the distribution of speaker/hearer roles, but they also alert us *to the fact that* schemata share an important feature with words—they are context dependent at the same time as they are makers of contexts. They mean different contexts and their different contexts mean differently. "So I thought X" need not mean that my thinking "X" is actually directly the conclusion or consequence of whatever preceeded "so I thought X," it may only index *the fact that* I've got more to say and am using this schema *to hold the floor* until I *figure out* what, or how to, or if I should say next.

Contrast this situation with "empty schemata" which are "meaningless" and whose function is to give the appearance of meaningful grammatical connection between parts of a sentence. In the preceding paragraph I used, in addition to the tired but useful schemata "to hold the floor" and "figure out," an empty schema—"the fact that ____" schema. In the sentence "this alerts us to the fact that etc.," "the fact that" is there not because there is a fact, but because one has to be alerted *to* something, and in the sentence "it may only index the fact that ____," "the fact that" is there because an index indexes something. Not all "fact thats" are so empty, for they may signify "evidence of consequence," as in "the fact that he fell means he slipped," but most "fact thats" are as empty as "at this point in time" of Watergate infamy, signifying flabby speech and insipid prose. Other examples of "format" (Goodman 1971) abound in speech and prose. Consider, "the thing is that ____," "in terms of ____," "from the point of view of ____," "well maybe I ____," "to sorta ," "n' those sortsa things____," and those other wretched members of the "fact family": "in fact ____," "fact is ____," "the fact of the matter is ____," "the true facts ____," "factually speaking ____," "from a factual point of view ____".

These are not far removed from pure "gap fillers," meaningless phonation meant to exclude other speakers as in : "you know ?" or "I mean ____," or "you know what I mean?," or "like," "like well," or— in a paroxysm of gap filler—"you know what I mean, like well ____." In a more charitable mood we interpret these as the speaker's urgent plea for us to complete in thought or speech what neither of us knows or can say as an index of the known but ineffable.

(Well) I think that, it seems to me that, I believe that I should have thought that this discussion is sufficient introduction to the use of schemata in the Susan/Karen discourse. It remains to say only that schemata—even of the gap filler type—are part of the poetry of oral discourse. They have rhythmical functions either in the words and phrases of utterances themselves or as means of "making time" for the harmony that is expressed in the speaker's and hearer's synchronous coordination of gesture, body position, body tension, and gaze (cf. Tannen 1984 : 152–59). I suggest, then, that the list that follows be read in the manner of a poem, aloud and perhaps polyphonically with different readers starting at different intervals, as in singing rounds. This will as closely as possible approximate to our sense of different voices clamoring for our attention as we speak and listen. Following is a list of schemata used in the Karen/Susan interview/conversation.

    what I would like to find out about
    that you are having done
    you see

find out what happens to
find out more about
I have a similar problem
you've got a real problem
the problem is
having tremendous problems
I don't have a problem
going to do something about it
well, maybe I
so, tell me what
my friend who
that was great
does that mean
everyone going like this
someone else pay for it
didn't you notice
(well) I mean
(n') every thing else
and stuff
and stuff like that
and all sortsa stuff
and all that other stuff
and all that kinda stuff
you can't even
there are other things
like (I, maybe, well)
it's like
can you like
just time and money
just not even
I just
let's just
I always wanted
I only wanted
get this thing fixed
someone told me that
you really should get
I am sort of
I sort of
sort of
Those sort of
(n') that sort of

That's a real sort of
It's all sort of
It sort of
(n') all sorts of
_____ sort of like _____
to figure out how
They may have to, they may not (maybe yes, maybe no)
I got around it
if that's all straight
gonna look real funny
straighten that up
an that's all
be put asleep
that's nothing
I don't know
able to breathe out of
a lot
right
yeah, right
that's right
they're right
(and) you know
I'm tired of
I was tired of
in fact
the fact that
get rid of
(even) went in for
to see what
or something
(or) something like that
this way
the real good stuff
I swear
it was when
I wish I could
go in and get a total overhaul
(and) things like that
instead of saying
it seems to me
I don't like (it)
but luckily

I've got a great reason
it happens to be
in an automobile accident
I really didn't realize
what (a) state I was in
but, had I known
(know(n)) what he was doing
I hadn't thought (of it like that)
it's a good thing
I'm thinking ahead
whole outlook on life
and things
and everything
who knows
we heard a story
couple weeks ago
difficult child
always getting in trouble
long lost relative
I learnt right off
would last in
and then I'd
whip it off
I just couldn't stand it
I've thought about this for awhile
it's all in your head
(I know) it sounds like
really stay with you
long enough for
out of the blue
Do you know what
to move over
so that it
torn away from
I must be totally
basically its like
the reason
the thing is that
Imagine this
all those years
all at once
way to go

and besides
This better be a _____ that's all I can say
That's all I can say
This better be a
maybe you should
they do feel
gonna feel like
what's wrong with you
drop the subject
be real rational about this
that's about the only
(I mean) other than
(he said) just—forget it
and at least
I'm not gonna admit to that
I haven't been able to breathe for years
ah that's a shame
it's gonna be a new experience
for the first time (in your memory)
I was hoping that
go really low
or whatever
where _____ comes from
what they figure is
going to surface
now that
have you ever
it's an OK book
I wouldn't use it
open up a whole new world
all make sense
I didn't do it
you are the person in charge
whatever you punch in
it has a mind of its own
its magic
that's nice
sort of nice
its nice for
see, so its nice
gave up on me
can't do anything

taken care of
life can be OK (beautiful)
black and blue
when I came out of
up for

Inventio: Where Do Topics Come From?

Discourse also indexes action schemata. These may be represented in the mind not just in propositional agent/patient form, but as visual images, sensorimotor patterns, or in a rebus combining elements of verbal, visual, and motor patterns. Consider, for example, what we might call the central topic of the Susan/Karen discourse—Karen's nose and what is to happen to it. The conversation uses the "nose rebus" as a base schema which establishes and maintains discourse coherence. The nose is Karen's; it's to be changed, to be broken, to be operated on, to be straightened, to be made handsome. All of this, and more besides, is commonplace knowledge about noses and what can be done to them. These are mostly agent/patient schemata in which the nose is the recipient of some action. They are the basis for much of Susan's questioning. She makes inferences from the nose rebus about problems with noses, who fixes problem noses, how it is done, what it means to be a patient, the subject of an operation, and who performs the operation. These, and others, provide the content of her questions and comments. For example: (22) "You couldn't breathe through the . . . ;" (45) "Do they have to break your nose . . . ;" (58) "Are they going to put you to sleep . . . ;" (70) "Are you going to be black and blue . . . ;" and (115) ". . . probably pretty swollen. . . . " All of these are based less on what Karen says, though that is also part of the condition for saying them, than on what Susan knows about noses; you breathe through them, they get broken, operations are performed on them, broken noses are accompanied by bruises and swelling, and so on. There is, in other words, a readily available account of reasonable action relative to noses that Susan uses as the *inventio* for her questions. Here the concept "nose" functions as a "topic" in exactly the same way as the *topoi* of classical rhetoric. It is a commonplace (*locus, topos*) in memory which is capable of suggesting a collection of indexical particulars. Consequently, we can say that it is this topical structure, this nose schema, that already provides the possibility of a coherent conversation. Its principle of organization is that of a substance (noun) and its accidents (attributes) or, in other words, the qualities and relations of a subject. This is the underlying conception of a semantic network (Quillian 1966), but it was first worked out in detail by Aristotle in *De Memoria*, and later by Hamilton (1895:899–900) among others. The essential idea is that there is a concept ("nose") and what may be predicated of it. The predications (what may be said of noses) are the accidents or qualities, functions, characteristics, and attributes of noses in general. These constitute what one can say about noses and thus are not only the source of information about noses that speakers and hearers use in saying things about noses, they are also, at least in part, the structure of what can be said.

In this same way Karen uses other schemata to organize her account. First of all, her narration has the predictable overall narrative structure of setting, complication, and resolution. Within this larger structure she uses various related episodes. Line 213, for example, introduces a story within a story (cf. Sacks and Schegloff 1974). Susan, too, uses the story schema at 199: "There's some guy . . . we heard a story. . . ." Karen also shifts frequently from narrative voice to dramatic dialogue: (13) ". . . my friend who is a nurse said, 'listen . . .'"; (16) "I said, . . ."; (35) ". . . sure you've got a real problem . . ."; (38) "so I said, well . . ."; (50) "well, listen, is it . . ."; (53) "he said, 'Well, OK.'"

Apart from such narrative and story schemata, the first part of the discourse is organized by another schema, that of the interview. The interview schema is a type of exchange between speakers where one is in the role of interviewer, the other in the role of interviewee. The interviewer asks questions, the interviewee responds with answers that are supposed to be relevant to the question asked or to its presuppositions. In addition to asking questions, the interviewer has rights of summation, supplementation, clarification, emphasis, and overall direction, as well as the duty to assess the quality of cooperation, relevance, quantity, and general quality of the interviewer's contributions, though all of these may be shared with or challenged by the interviewee. The interviewee's questioning rights are largely limited to clarification and challenge, in the fullest sense of "What do you mean by that question?"

Interviews fall into two broad types with respect to these characteristics: friendly and cooperative, and hostile and adversative, rather like the different roles of defense and prosecution in forensic discourse. Cutting across these distinctions are two other characteristics: an interview may have an agreed-upon agenda that both speakers more-or-less adhere to, or it may have no specific agenda apart from a rather broad and undefined topic that both speakers agree to explore

Memory and Discourse

together. The first part of the Susan/Karen discourse is a cooperative and explorative interview. Finally, the interview has a fairly rigid pattern of turn-taking. Overlapping turns are less prevalent than in a conversation (cf. Sacks and Schegloff 1974). The general expectation is that one person asks a question relevant to the agenda, then the other answers that question with relevant and sufficient information (cf. Grice 1971). This can take the form of a direct response, a clarification, a reinterpretation of the question, a challenge to the interviewer's rights to and reasons for asking, or a parry in which the interviewee declares the question improper or unanswerable without saying so. The interviewer's next question must then be relevant to the answer or to the agenda, and so on.

At approximately line 188 a different form of exchange emerges. Here the discourse shifts from interview format to the looser organization of a conversation. The question/answer schema breaks down and Susan takes a more active role as contributor who does more than just ask questions. Susan begins to build on, amplify, and complete Karen's utterances. As, for example:

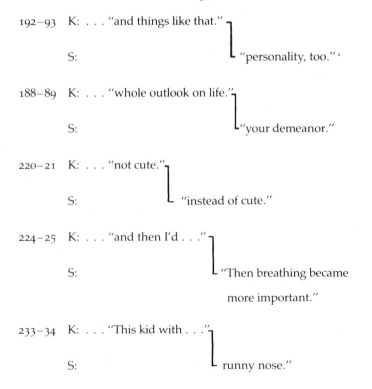

192–93   K: . . . "and things like that."

S: "personality, too."[2]

188–89   K: . . . "whole outlook on life."

S: "your demeanor."

220–21   K: . . . "not cute."

S: "instead of cute."

224–25   K: . . . "and then I'd . . ."

S: "Then breathing became

more important."

233–34   K: . . . "This kid with . . ."

S: runny nose."

273–78   K: . . . "die because you've got

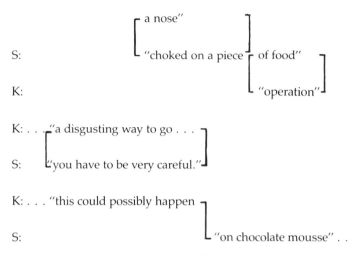

S:

K:

In jazz parlance, Susan takes off on a "riff," a thematic variation on what Karen is saying. In common speech, we might observe here that they are "getting it on," "getting into it," or "relaxing into it" as each picks up a piece of the theme and creates a virtuoso improvisation in harmony or contrapuntally with the other's utterance.

All of this signals that the discourse has moved from the style and structure of the interview to that of a conversation. It is now marked by freer and partly overlapping turn-taking, looser topical coordination between speakers, and flights of interpretive play on both meanings and implications. Cohesion is no longer a function of thematic exploration of the literal content of the nose schema, but is one of figural transformations of that content. This is a move from what might be called the central area of the nose schema to its periphery where "looser" associations predominate, where breath and nose are no longer linked by the "serious implications" of "nose is what you breathe with" and "obstructions in the nose cause problems of breathing," but are linked instead by "breathing through different nostrils is a Yogic technique that effects the mind" (199–210, 327–78), and the humorous implications that flow from that. That is, instead of being something that needs blowing, the nose blows the mind.

Coherence is also accomplished by a kind of associative chaining rather than by repetition of previous content as the old information to be built on. The patterning of thematic repetition is replaced by associative novelty. Note, too, that utterances here are characterized by hyperbole (264–68), conceits (327–78), and parables (199–210) in place of description or of exposition by argument and example. Each speaker also makes fuller use of enthymemes rather than the material implications and presuppositions which were the predominant inferential means in the interview part of the discourse. In sum, both speakers rely less on the *inventio* of the nose rebus and more on the possibilities of verbal play created by the discourse itself.

De Memoria

Contemporary linguists, like their ancient counterparts, the rhetoricians, invoke memory or knowledge structures as part of the system of discourse comprehension. Here, too, linguists and psychologists have largely reinvented much that was already fully established within the rhetorical tradition (cf. Yates 1966, Ong 1958). There are, of course, interesting differences. The rhetorical tradition, for example, understood memory as a source of information for speech production; contemporary linguists understand it primarily in its role in comprehension. This difference in perspective—production on one hand, comprehension on the other—is a shift in focus from the speaker/writer to the hearer/reader, and signifies the transition from a context of oral discourse to one of writing. This contemporary emphasis on the passive consumer of print is the consequence of having an object in the form of a written text and has the effect of displacing the speaking subject as the creator of discourse in favor of the autonomous text itself or of the omniscient interpreter. It thus expresses that antipathy toward authors/creators of all kinds that has constituted so much of the theme of alienation in Western thought. It also reflects the resistance to writing as an occult practice that reveals only inasmuch as it conceals. This ambivalence to the text as an occult document requiring interpretation is responsible for enhancing the role of the interpreter at the expense of both text and author. It is the condition that creates linguists and the condition that linguists create, the condition that Derrida (1967) both documents and exemplifies. The emergence of the interpreter, which Peirce's theory of signs so clearly signified, is part of the glorification of the role of the disengaged, objective observer that both characterizes the age of science and is its central problem.

Two dominant themes have characterized memory research from its beginnings in Greek thought to the present. They are "time" and "representation." The latter is a metaphoric implicate of "space," of objects in space, and refers to the manner of "coding" information ("memories") about objects in the world. "Time" implicates a family of concepts having to do with remembering and forgetting, with "retention" of memories or their "vividness" (Aristotle *De Memoria*, Hume 1888, 2.1.1), or "recoding" (Seamon 1980:101), or "depth of processing" (Craik and Lockhart 1972). To put it differently, "time" has to do with the qualities or accidents of an object. Memory research thus recapitulates the general Indo-European linguistic schema of predication of a noun (= real object) and what can be said of it (= its contingencies or accidence).

A third topic relating to "will" in the "act" of remembering is the source of the difference between merely having memories and remembering. This volitional aspect of remembering has always been the subject of conscious mnemonic systems or "artificial memory" in the rhetorical tradition. In its pathological form of "forgetting as repression," it has been the focus of psychoanalytic research, as the tale of volition unconsciously thwarted and repressed. We thus have the concept of will ambiguously marked, so to speak; positively as conscious remembering, but negatively as artifice and as that which obscures true, unconscious significance.

Will apart, most thinking about memory is dualistic. With respect to time, memories are either "vivid" or "faded" in older terminology and common speech, or in the less vivid language of modern research, "short-term" or "long-term," or in the somewhat less contemporary usage of James (1890), "primary" or "secondary." Short-term memory is itself sometimes divided into "working short-term memory" and peripheral or unused short-term memory, thus indexing a sense of focus that articulates with will in its contemporary reading as "awareness" or "attention span." Working short-term memory is focused attention, consciously controlled by the will; peripheral short-term memory is unwilled, unconscious, and, in some understandings at least, doomed to sudden death. There is also an unspoken bias that connects short-term memory almost exclusively to the processing of on-going external sensory stimulations, that is to say, with the present. Long-term memory, on the other hand, is only indirectly involved in the present. It is the past itself. The duality of memory research derives from an unspoken opposition in time between the present and the nonpresent. All that is nonpresent derives from the present (cf. Derrida 1967:6–26).

Representation, too, is dualistic. The rhetorical tradition distinguished between *res* ("thing") and *verba* ("word") as modes of representation, a distinction that continues today in the differences be-

Memory and Discourse

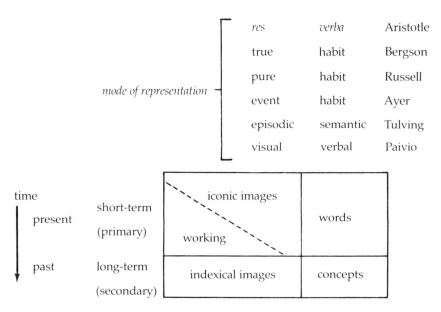

	res	verba	Aristotle
	true	habit	Bergson
mode of representation	pure	habit	Russell
	event	habit	Ayer
	episodic	semantic	Tulving
	visual	verbal	Paivio

time		iconic images	
present	short-term (primary)	working	words
past	long-term (secondary)	indexical images	concepts

Thought picture 4.1. Generalized cognitive memory model with dual coding (visual, verbal) and dual term (present, past).

tween "visual" and "verbal" images (cf. Paivio 1971), and "episodic" and "semantic" memories (Tulving 1972). These distinctions in turn reflect a deeper issue that underlies all "dual coding" theories, namely, the distinction between "contingent" knowledge and "necessary" knowledge. Both representation and time acknowledge a transformation of the present as a re-presentation that moves from more to less vivid or from short-term to long-term. The presented is coded and re-coded in successive re-presentations that move from iconic to indexical or symbolic images, in the case of visual or episodic representation, and from the sounds of words to concepts in the case of verbal or semantic memory. The transition from present to past is thus at the same time a movement from concrete to abstract representation. These conditions are illustrated in thought picture 4.1.

Among the overtly dualistic treatments of memory are those of Bergson (1912), Russell (1921:167), and Ayer (1956:134–42). Bergson distinguished between "habit memory" and "pure memory." The former was a "mere motor mechanism," the latter the remembering of an actual event in one's past. Russell kept the same distinction but called pure memory "true memory," the recalling in imagery of a personal experience. Habit memory for Russell was a kind of verbalization, as in "knowing by heart." Ayer discriminated between "habit memory" and "event memory." Habit memory he characterized as "being able to do something" or as "knowing a fact." Event memory was the remembrance of a particular occurrence. A part of the distinction involved in all of these cases is that between memories for occurrences and memories of nonoccurrences. Stated in this way the latter seem hardly to qualify as memories, hence Russell's expulsion of them from the domain of true memory. It reveals a bias in favor of personal experience. Habit memory, by contrast, is only indirectly—if at all—derived from personal experience. What basis is there in our personal experience for remembering that "cows calve," "sows farrow," and "mares foal"? Pure memory is more "real" than habit memory because the latter is only a kind of "hearsay." My memory of the world, of reality is my experience of it derived from my perceptions of it. My true memory is thus a kind of perception of a past event in the present. All of my other memories were never really presences, but are only knowing how to do something or remembering some collection of words. It is clear that the philosopher's distinction between habit memory and true memory is nothing more than the ancient distinction between *verba* and *res*. So, too, with the psychologist's distinction between episodic and semantic memory.

There is, however, a problem in the way these pairs of concepts correlate with the underlying distinction between contingency and necessity. The problem is signified by Tulving's "episode" and Ayer's "event." Episodes and events are not proper substances (*res*); they involve action and motion and are thus attributes of substances rather than substances. Nor is semantic memory a proper substance. It is only indirectly derived from experience, being instead what is given by the facts of language. Its content corresponds to analytic propositions whose meanings are functions of the structure of language rather than images of things in the world. Though semantic memory is thus *verba* and not *res*, it nonetheless has the necessity of an analytic proposition. In the case of Ayer's "event," the problem is "how can the merely contingent facts of my personal experience be necessary?" This reflects not only a different understanding of the kind of reality that is necessary, it also implicates a different interpretation of the foundational sensory allegory, suggesting in place of static "pictures" of things something more like action, movement, and change, an imagery of the motor and kinesthetic rather than the visual. In short, events, episodes, habits, and semantic memory are all *verba* and contingent, and consequently illusions rather than realia.

In the original Aristotelian distinction, only visual metaphors counted as representations of reality, and that is why philosophers and psychologists continue to speak of events and episodes as if they were visual pictures of substance rather than qualities of substance. How else are we to understand the use of the common term "representation" for all? The same is true of verbal memory. It is written about as if it were an object of some kind, though few are ready to specify the shape or locus of this *lingua mentis*. In effect, philosophers and psychologists have kept the ancient distinction between substance and accidence, but have confounded its implications. They are victims of an Indo-European linguistic bias that connects nouns, substances, reality, presence, and visual perception as mutually implicated concepts.

The underlying issue (to use another favorite piece of mythology) has to do with the conservation of objects. All memory theories speak of memories as if they were objects or substances of some sort that are conserved over time. Memory is the conservation of an object, and that is why memories can be "stored," "fade," leave "traces," and "decay." We generally understand movement and change as Aristotle did—as attributes of objects, not as objects themselves. The conservation of objects is their *identity* in *differences* of motion and time. In simple terms, we say something is the same (identity) when we see it in different times and changed circumstances. Observers apart, conservation thus entails three conditions, one of identity, and two of difference: object, motion, and time, respectively. These, in turn, are metaphoric implicates of the sensory modalities of vision, kinesthesia (proprioceptive and tactile), and verbal/auditory, respectively. Representation, then, is not dualistic, it is triadic.

This is an implication that could well have been drawn from Peirce's semiotics, but is actually worked out in other places. Consider, for example, Don Locke's (1971:47) treatment of memory as consisting of three kinds: factual memory, as "remembering that"; practical memory, or "remembering how to do"; and personal memory, or "remembering some specific person, place, thing, or incident from personal experience." These distinctions parallel Ryle's analysis of knowing, but they also recapitulate the ancient divisions of rhetoric symbolized by *verba*, *ergon* (activity, motion), and *res*, which are themselves sensory allegories of "saying," "doing," and "seeing." Factual memory, as defined by Locke, consists in remembering what is given by or in language; remembering "how to do" (practical memory) obviously refers to action; and personal memory is the remembering of things witnessed, things once really present in the rememberer's experience. In the analysis of meaning these quite obviously parallel the distinctions among sense, pragmatics, and reference.

The memory model of Atkinson and Shiffrin (1968) is similar to Locke's. It has three memory structures: a sensory register; a short-term store; and a long-term store. These are linked by rehearsal and coding. Information is transferred to the long-term store by rehearsal in the short-term store. The model has been modified in subsequent publications in response to criticism concerning the connections between "stores" and "processes," but the triadic structure has been retained and widely used in research. In the present context, it is the mode of representation in these three stores that is interesting, for it is clear that their modes of representation correspond to the representational modes of the sign types, iconic, indexical, and symbolic. The sensory register represents iconically, the short-term store represents indexically, and the long-term store represents symbolically. The model, in other words, recapitulates Peirce's semiotic categories, which are themselves allegorical recapitulations of Aristotle's three categories of *anima*.

Recoding is also triadic. The distinction between short-term memory and working memory, for example, is not just a distinction of focus and time, it is also a distinction of relative transformation. Nonfocal short-term memory consists of relatively untransformed sensory information; working memory deals with information already transformed and is not restricted to contemporary sensory information. Long-term memory is further transformed and can be independent of current sensory information. To speak of "depth of processing" (Craik and Lockhart 1972) is only another way of talking about the transformation of information as it moves from one store or level to another. It is a less interesting way of speaking of vividness. Both recoding and depth of processing are ways of talking about identities within differences in a manner analogous to Peirce's sign types. Moreover, they correspond to the antique distinctions *sensus, imaginatio,* and *intellectus.* They are also aspects of time, not just of present and past as in thought picture 4.1, but of present, past, and future. Symbolic, long-term memory is not really oriented to the past in the way we usually think memory is; it is the future, what the future is made of—reconstructions of the past.

The implication is clear; memory contains as part of itself what we would normally call thinking and sensing. The latter are neither separate from nor coordinate with memory; they are aspects of memory. Now we can perhaps understand why the Greeks made Mnemosyne the Queen of the Muses.

The intersection of the dimensions "time" and "representation" yields thought picture 4.2. At the iconic and indexical levels there are sensory-specific representations. That is, each sensory modality has

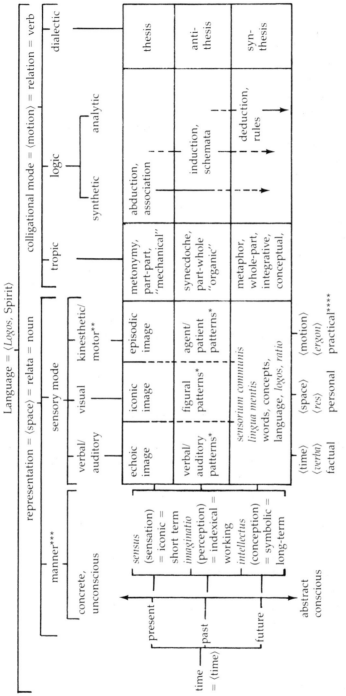

Thought picture 4.2. Triadic model of memory as a *loci communis* for metalepsis and *inventio*, or "How the World Becomes a Fable." *verbal/auditory patterns include: melody, rhythm, movement, frequency, intensity; figural patterns include: shape, dimension, orientation; agent-patient patterns include movement, orientation, rhythm, frequency, and intensity. **kinesthetic-motor includes tactile and proprioceptive sensory modes. ***manner of substituting appearances = recoding = memory stores = depth of processing = time. ****Don Locke's memory types (1971). Taste and smell are excluded because they do not make representations. Words in ⟨ ⟩ are metaphoric implicates.

its own images and patterns, but all follow a similar course of transformation. In addition, kinesthetic representations are partially integrated with visual representation at the indexical level, and both visual and kinesthetic are integrated at the symbolic level by a higher order mode of representation which represents itself and all lower modes of representation. It is a *sensorium communis,* a *lingua mentis,* a *summa essentia locutio,* an interior *locutio,* "language," the "word," the *logos.*

Each sensory modality has a metaphoric implicate. Verbal/auditory has time or *verba;* visual has space or *res* (that which has extension in space and identity in time); and kinesthetic has motion, change, action, function, work or *ergon.* Moreover, each dimension of time or manner of representation has a characteristic mode of tropic ordering. Iconic representation is metonymic, the mechanical juxtaposition of part-to-part. Indexical representation is synecdochic, the organic relation of part-to-whole. Symbolic representation is metaphoric, the relation of whole-to-part. The symbolic can recapitulate in its own form all of the sign functions of the other levels but cannot recapitulate what they transform after they have transformed it. Finally, each manner of representation has a more-or-less correspondent mode of logical ordering. Iconic has associativity; indexical has schemata; and symbolic has rules, or in Peirce's terms, abduction, induction, and deduction.

This account implies that thought picture 4.2 can be read in several different contexts. Most obviously, it is about memory, how memories are coded, transformed, and integrated, but it is as well a pictorial story of perception, of how percepts are sensorially coded, transformed, and integrated in the movement from sensation to conception, from concrete to abstract, from unconscious to conscious. It can also be read developmentally as the child's transition from kinesthetic to visual to verbal modes of thought. It is an outline of sensory integration in the development of thought, perception, and memory. Each sensory modality does not develop in isolation, but is always interacting with other modalities and that integration produces crossmodal integrative systems characteristic of each major developmental stage. So too with thought, which achieves its highest integration in the emergent symbolic system of language, of thought "properly speaking." It strongly implies that thought is immanent in this highest level of integration rather than something that precedes it or transcends it. Moreover, it does not so much reduce thought and perception to memory as to make all three different aspects of a single, unifying process. It purports to be a unified model of perception, thought, memory, and development.

Memory and Discourse

Thought picture 4.2 can also be read metaphorically in several ways. It recapitulates Reid's (1895) mental powers of man, Peirce's triadic system of signs, and McLean's (1973) concept of the triune brain, which are all, in turn, variforms of Aristotle's founding allegory of the three forms of *anima*. It is a metaphor of the three tropes, metonymy, synecdoche, and—here is its irony—of metaphor itself; and of the three modes of inference, abduction, induction, and deduction; and of the three means of sign colligation, association, schemata, and rules. It epitomizes the dialectic, both in its implication of progressive unification, sublation, abstraction, and emergence, and in its implicit ordering of the relations among sign types. Without going into detail, it understands iconic and indexical signs as inverses of one another, for an iconic signifier is determined by its signified, but an indexical signifier determines its signified. Iconic and indexical are thus related to one another as thesis to antithesis. Their opposition is neutralized in the symbol whose signifiers and signifieds are mutually constituted and reciprocally determinative. We thus have the familiar structuralist triangle of thought picture 4.3.

Just as the sign functions iconic, indexical, and symbolic are variforms of *sensus, imaginatio,* and *intellectus,* the Latinized versions of Aristotle's three forms of *anima,* so too are the sensory modalities metaphorical implicates of Aristotle's semantico-grammatical categories. Verbal/auditory is "time," and *verba,* visual is "space" and *res,* kinesthesia is "motion," "movement," "action," "function," "work" or *ergon.* These are reflexes of the underlying categorical distinctions between substance (*ens per se*), the first category, and the other nine categories which are all attributes (*ens per accidence*) of the first category.

Other metaphoric implicates can be worked out, but enough have been given to suggest the persistence of an episteme, of a structure of foundational concepts which keep getting reinvented. In that sense, the rediscovery of Aristotle in the Middle Ages is itself a sort of allegory of this whole cyclical history, so that what passes for memory functions in discourse analysis in linguistics and cognitive science today is only another rediscovery of the rhetoric of the Stagirite.

I note now a final harmony between past and present. Thought picture 4.2 is itself a memory system—at least for me. It functions as *inventio* and *topoi.* It is an organization of places (*loci*) for ideas as concepts, imitating, but poorly, the memory systems of Bruno and Lull, being like them a system of memory *loci* whose *locus* is memory itself (cf. Yates 1966: 173–230). It tells us why we persist in searching for the location of memory in the brain, as if it were a granary in a farmyard,

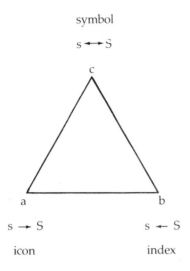

Thought picture 4.3. Dialectical relation of constitutive signs. s = signified, S = signifier. "a" is the inverse of "b," and "c" is the sublation of "a" and "b". The dialectic thus "rationalizes" the order of signs.

and each memory a needle in a haystack, and why that is as compelling as it is peculiar.

The preceding picture of memory focuses on representation, but has little to say about memory in discourse or communication. The following is a brief account of the integration of discourse from the speaker's point of view, or more appropriately, his point of speech. It is based on the musical analogy of melody and harmony, the former being a sequence of units in time, the latter the synchronous or simultaneous or nontemporal integration of different "spatial" positions. Though these correspond to what linguists have sometimes referred to as the syntagmatic and paradigmatic axes of language, they are used here not in the context of language as a whole, but with respect to some part of discourse. I omit discussion of other forms of synchrony, of the integration of unsaid thoughts or processes outside of the focal pattern, even though these contribute to the composition of utterances as surely as counterpoint and polyphony do to music.

As in music, our sense of discourse orderliness is given by theme and variation, a pattern of repetition with change, of identity with difference, corresponding more-or-less to the linguist's categories of theme and rheme, "old" information and "new information." In a related sense we can say that it is given by the integration of prospect—

what will be said—and retrospect—what was said. These, in turn, correspond respectively to long-term memory and short-term working memory. The relation of units—words, phrases, sentences, breath groups, the linguist's "beads on a string"—is metonymic, synecdochic, and metaphoric. The speaker's "saying" is informed by an emergent whole which is reconstituted in memory as "the said," and becomes the condition for the speaker's continuing to "say" or for his silence.

Consider the following simple case of someone saying the ABCs. Assume that the conditions for saying them are appropriate: the speaker can speak them, her saying them is preceded by an intention to say them, and her intention includes an apprehension of the ABCs which is complete enough for us to say: "She knows them." This apprehension is not the whole sequence of the ABCs; it is "ABC . . . go on in the same way to . . . Z." That is, it is an inchoate whole whose parts are incompletely articulated (in both senses). In saying the ABCs she articulates this whole but never makes it present as a whole, for it emerges as the metaphoric relation of a whole to its parts. We would not say, for example, that the whole was either A or Z or anything in between. Nor would we say it was the presence of the whole sequence, since that is never present in the way it might seem to be if we wrote out the sequence on paper. It is, then, an emergent whole different from its parts but it is never articulated as a whole or in one or all of its parts. Nonetheless, it can become itself a part in some other utterance, as in, for example, "say your ABCs ten times."

Moreover, the speaker's saying of each separate letter is conditioned by the context of that letter, which is the correct saying of the sequence to that point and the anticipation of some part of the sequence that is to follow. Saying "E," then, is enabled by the memory of having said A–D, with something like an echoic memory or feedback of B–C–D, the rehearsal of F–G–H, and the anticipation of I–Z. That is to say, when the speaker says "E," she has other things than "E" on her mind that make saying "E" possible. This "saying E" is illustrated in thought picture 4.4

In these senses, saying the ABCs is analogous to saying any other sentence or part of a large discourse. It is, of course, too simple and mechanistic to be like real speech. All of its units, for example, have roughly equal prominence and can thus be linked unambiguously by metonymic association, unlike the layered units of syntax which are synecdochically induced. But, even in this simple case of saying or singing the ABCs there are rhythmical and breath groups which are

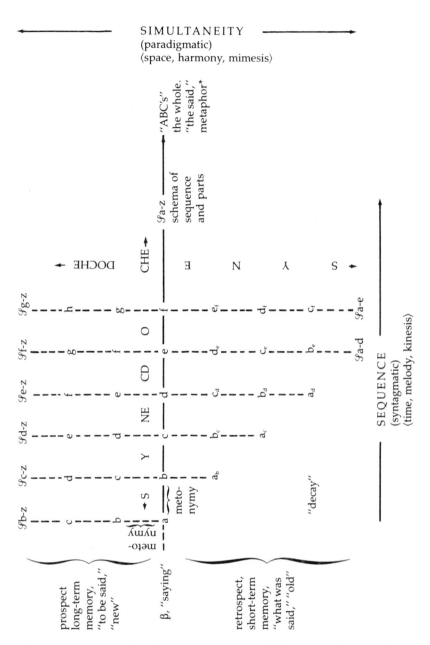

Thought picture 4.4. "Simplest case" integration of discourse. *the Aristotelian sentence as *logos*. Words in ⟨ ⟩ are metaphoric implicates. β indicates "conditions for saying."[2]

2. Note that this thought picture gives a different value to the concepts "metonym" and "metaphor" than that in Jakobson (1960). Jakobson restricts metonymy to the syntagmatic axis and metaphor to the paradigmatic axis, but there is no more reason for

synecdochic structures (cf. Halliday 1967, Ladd 1980, Thompson 1980, Liberman and Prince 1977). For example, one variant of singing the ABCs has:

	ABC	DEFG
Rhythm group	I	II
Breath group		A

	HIJK	LMNOP
Rhythm group	III	IV
Breath group		B

	QRST	UV
Rhythm group	V	VI
Breath group		C

	WXY	and Z
Rhythm group	VII	VIII
Breath group		D

"Now I know my ABCs/Aren't you proud of me?"

identifying sequence and metonymy than for equating simultaneity and metaphor. In thought picture 4.4, both metaphor and metonymy are treated as either simultaneous or sequential. Historically, the idea of metonymy—as association—was sometimes thought of as the "chain" of elements in a sentence (as, for example, in Hume) and sometimes under the name of "suggestion" as the "chain" of thoughts and memories apart from the strict lineal sequence of words in the sentence. The latter might interfere with the train of thought and expression, but the former were the train of thought and expression. The latter were also poetic and rhetorical means and were opposed to "plain style." For further discussion of this point, see chapter 1, "Epode."

Here the metonymic sequence of letters is broken into schemalike groupings which are in part imposed by the necessity of breathing, but are also arbitrary rhythms reflecting protosemantic orderings in the grouping of signs alone. Note that each rhythm group is divided into beats of accented and unaccented parts, and of prolonged and shortened sounds thus,

A-B-Ć—Ď-E-F-G—Ĥ-I-J-K—Ĺ-M-Ń-O-Ṕ—Q-Ř-S-T—Ú-V̇—W-X̂-Y-and Ź—

In these groupings we see the emergence of a kind of "protosyntax," which breaks up the lineal sequence of the letters, not just by grouping them into adjacent groups, but by bringing them together as constituents of groups that are nonadjacent. The grouping overthrows the adjacency aspect of metonymy.

Other groupings perform a similar function. In addition to breath groups and rhythm groups, this example also has a rhyme scheme and accent groups. With the exception of rhythm group III above, all rhythm groups end in a prolonged [ī] sound, as do the concluding lines. Accent groups consist of accented or stressed letters in the same breath group. In the ABCs, as outlined above, we have the syntaxlike groupings of thought picture 4.5.

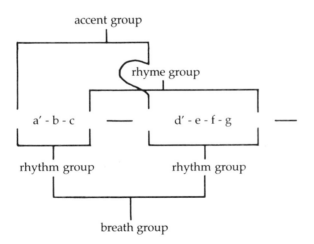

Thought picture 4.5. Prosodic groupings in the "ABC" song.

The elements in thought picture 4.5 are not, like beads on a string or links in a chain, confined to strict temporal sequence; they are constituents of simultaneously retrospective and prospective groups whose elements are both separated in sequential time and synchronously conjoined. Linguistics has traditionally understood such disjacent constituency as the province of syntax. The argument here, however, is that all such groupings are only superficially grammatical; they are instead mnemno-semantic schemata (cf. Thompson 1980, Halliday 1967, Chafe 1980). They are similar to the phrasal groupings that constitute commonsense knowledge and function as basic information units in discourse.

Phrasal schemata are also rhythmic. They tend to be broken into breath groups or prosodic groups marked by rising and falling tones, and accentual groups not unlike those of the ABC example. Consider the following selection from the Susan/Karen tape.

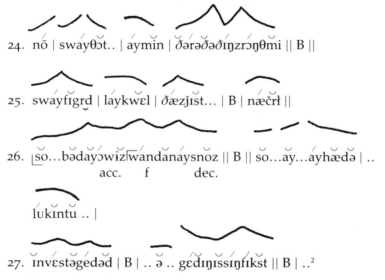

24. nõ | swayθɔt.. | aymín | ðərəðəðɪŋzrɔŋθmi || B ||

25. swayfígrd | láykwɛl | ðæzjíst... | B | næčrɫ ||

26. ⌊só...bədayɔwíz⌐wandánaysnóz || B || só...ay...ayhædə | ..
        acc.   f   dec.

lúkɪntu .. |

27. ínvɛstəgedəd | B | .. ə .. gédɪŋɪssɪŋfíkst || B | ..[2]

The rhythm of lines 24–26 is something like:

24. DAAH DAHda DAHda daDAHda daDAHda REST
25. DAHda DAHda DAHda REST DAHda REST
26. da REST dada DAHdaDAHdaDAHda REST

Even this brief sample chosen at random illustrates the way prosodic features mark schemata. In line 24 each phrase (terminally marked by | or ||) is a piece of rhythmic format: "so I thought," "I mean," "there are other things wrong with me." So, too, in line 24: "so I figured," "like, well," "that's just." And in lines 26 and 27 there are: "so, but (I)," "I always wanted a nice," "so I had a" "look into" or "I had a look into," "getting this thing fixed." Their unitary wordlike character is clearer in the phonetic transcription than in ordinary print. Their prosodic patterns mark them off from one another, though that is obviously not the whole function of prosody in communication. The point is that schemata are often rhythmically and tonally defined units of information similar to those of the ABC example. They are not, of course, fixed musical patterns, for that would prevent us from using stress and intonation to focus attention on different points of a schema when needed as in:

That is, "I'm going to HIT you!" vs. "I'm going to hit YOU!" vs. "I'M going to hit you."

Moreover, I do not suggest that rhythm is important only in the word. As meaningful in conversation and other forms of oral discourse is the synchronization of movement and utterance that gives a conversation, for example, its pace and rhythm. Speakers' turns are synchronized with the perception of beats, accents, and rests as are movements displaying the hearers' attention and involvement. How we as speakers and hearers attend to or fail to attend to these features of synchrony is a sign of how we feel about ourselves, the speaker/hearer, what is being said, or all three. They are, then, part of our construction—our memory—of what was said. They may be used to dismiss utterly the cognitive content of what was said, as when we attend more carefully to how someone speaks than to what she says as a surer guide to her meaning.

Returning to the memory picture of thought picture 4.4, we can illustrate how Karen and Susan use different schematic forms in accomplishing their interview/conversation. As speaker, Karen uses the macrostructure "The story of having my nosed fixed" as the whole toward which her utterances work. Implicated substories are generated as parts of this larger whole, such as "how noses are" (9–36, 81–110), "how my nose got to be the way it is" (147–68), "what the doctor will do" (39–79), "how things will be afterwards" (112–44, 179–98, 319–79). Each of these is part of a larger story. They correspond to setting, complication, resolution and evaluation, and unfold in the manner of a Proppian folktale.

As the page numbers above indicate, however, Karen's story does not develop as a straightforward sequence of related substories or episodes in the manner of a written narrative or well-known folktale. It is, instead, cumulative and cyclical. Substories appear in disconnected parts, separated by other substories or parts of substories, and they are recycled as topics or themes in other stories. She uses the mode of *sorites*, the "heaping up" of bits of information in a manner reminiscent of Ezra Pound's ideogramic method of heaping together the components of thought. Part of this drift from a straight narrative line arises from Karen's following out incidents and observations peripheral to the main story of the moment. She drifts into new stories tangential to her main narrative instead of repressing them in favor of tighter narration. Part of this drift is due to Susan's questions which pick out themes for emphasis or identify implications that lead to new divergences. The "interruptions" of interviews and conversations work against ordered exposition and fixed narration of a single story, particularly when the interviewer or conversational partner has a different story in mind. Part of the drift is also verbal play, especially in the latter parts of the conversation where "absurd" associations or implications became the focus in place of exposition and narration. Here it is no longer story and narration or even dramatic narrative, but a cooperative exchange of witty and exaggerated comic situations. The two cooperate not so much in creating a story as in making the story a metaphoric source of amusing possibilities.

These different "drifts"—from interview to topic-oriented conversation to verbal play—are marked by different incidences and types of "interruption." From lines 1–100, there are only two speaker overlaps. All other speaker turns occur at phrase boundaries or at appropriate speaker silences in the form of turns at the end of an idea sequence or as cooperative fill-ins or repetitions when the speaker is stuck. Susan, in effect, helps the story along by interrupting only in the interests of clarification, emphasis, flow, and as a sign of empathetic listening. In the next 100 lines there are, by contrast, 10 overlaps, not all of which are strictly cooperative from the standpoint of narrative flow and clarity. In the next 100 lines there are 15 overlaps, and most of them are "playful" metaphoric "take-offs."

From the hearer's point of view, the outline of memory in thought picture 4.4 illustrates how each speaker is able to interrupt the other, complete the first speaker's sentence in a word or phrase and go on to a new and implicated topic. The hearer knows where the speaker is going before she gets there. The hearer anticipates the other's destination—"gets her drift" as we say—arrives there first, interrupts, and sets off on a new journey. This reflects "hearing for meaning" or "getting the gist" of an utterance which is not dependent on having the whole utterance in all its parts in mind as such. It is a meaning "for now" which is sufficient to present purposes.

Thought picture 4.4 also makes clear the organization and role of schemata themselves. The whole utterance or story may be a schema, or their parts may be schemata. The implication here is that the units of utterances and stories are themselves schemata operating at different constructional levels, all the way from the relatively fixed format of idioms, common expressions, and metaphors to such larger units as routines, episodes, plots, stories, genres, narration, and exposition. Very little in discourse can be accounted for metonymically as the mechanical conjunction of parts. There is no smooth, step-by-step, inductive transition from sensory signal to concept. The sensory signal itself is a sign only in a schematic context. The past (= schema) always precedes the present (= iconic sign) and makes its future context. The movement then is not just from sense to concept *via* percept but from concept to sense via percept or from percept to concept or percept to sense. This, of course, parallels, in part, the distinction between thoughts, perceptions, and memories that are "data driven" or processed from the "bottom-up" (inductively) vs. those that are "concept driven" or processed from the "top-down" (deductively). Both are mediated by schemata, and the consequence is that concepts are neither built-up analytically as generalizations abstracted from data nor understood by reductive analysis to concrete particulars.

Concluding Objection

This "picture of memory" is consistent with the kind of physicalist understandings of memory that have predominated in memory research, and that is the surest sign that it is wrong. It portrays memory as an instance of the conservation of objects. Our memories are like objects subject to the ravages of entropy. They "decay," they "fade," they "disappear" from mind, they leave "traces," they can be "stored," they can be "retrieved," sometimes even after they have been "lost" or "repressed." We like to think of memory not only as a collection of *loci,* of places where memories are stored, but as a place itself, having a *locus* in the brain. This whole vast and persistent metaphor of objects and places is a peculiar metaphor for memory, which, after all, is more intimately implicated by time than by space and its congeners of objects in places. It is part of a tradition of speculation that ties memory to writing and visualization, to the idea of representation, whether of the cruder sort known as images or of the subtler variety called symbols. The idea of representation makes sense only in a context of writing and visualization, of the spatialization of sound. It confirms us in that false analogy between the behavior of bodies and the behavior of minds which encourages us to think of memory on the model of a physical transaction (Reid 1895:536). When we think of memory for sound rather than the memory of visual pictures of sound the idea of representation is less persuasive. What could be re-presented in the case of sound? An echo? A vibration? (cf. ibid.). Unlike images, the idea of sound does not implicate spatial representation, it implies instead, time, which is not a thing, has no dimensions, and cannot be perceived. It is reasonable, then, that memory for speech is neither representation nor the conservation of an object. We would do better to think of memory as the conservation of time rather than the conservation of an object. We would no longer think of memory as if it were the recurrence of a thing known before, an object identical in two different times—past and nonpast. Rather than differences in time confirming identity of objects, differences in objects would only confirm differences in subjects, but no difference in time. We would no longer think of time as a locus or container and we would no longer speak of "being on time" or "being in time," but of "being time," and we would find it stranger to say "I am an object" than to say "I am time." Who knows, we might even be able to hear the voice of God.

Appendix: Text of Conversation

1 Susan: (snort ha-S) What I would like to find out more about[1]
2 is your operation . . . that you are having.
3 Karen: My nose operation.
4 S: Yes, your nose operation(giggle-S)
5 You see, I have a similar problem and I've been postponing
6 doing something about it for a very long time, so tell me what
7 you're having done an' . . . what condition you're gonna be in when
8 you're having it done.
9 K: Well, maybe I should preface this thing, why I want it done.
10 First of all, I want it for cosmetic reasons. I'm sort of tired
11 of everyone going like this to my nose, so I thought, well, . . . I
12 would get it cosmetically changed, and then someone told me that
13 I had a problem, you see. That was great! My friend who is a
14 nurse said, "listen, you've got a deviated septum."
15 S: (sympathetic laugh)
16 K: I said, ah, does that mean I can get my nose(giggle-S) operated on?
17 Will someone else pay for it? She said, "sure, it's a medical
18 problem an' they'll . . . "
19 S: Didn't you notice, you had a deviated septum?
20 K: No, I mean, everything else
21   ⎡   is crooked an' stuff, you can't even (?) . . ⎤
22 S: ⎣ . . . that you couldn't breathe through the   ⎦
23 side, one side of your nose?
24 K: No, so I thought, I mean there are other things wrong with me,
25 so I figured, like, well, that was just . . . natural, so . . . but I
26 always wanted a nice nose, so . . I . . I had, uh, looked into,
27 investigated, uh, getting this thing fixed. But it was a long
28 time ago, so I couldn't do it. And it was just time and money
29 and all that other stuff. So then I thought, well, . . . its about
30 time I changed it. I got new insurance, you see, so I thought,
31 well, . . and someone also this summer told me that, uh mm that he had the
32 operation done, and that you really should get it done,
33 because you can breathe better and all sorts of things, so . . so,
34 when I went to the hospital this time, I just inquired, and
35 they said, "sure, you've got a real problem. (small sympathetic
36 laugh-S) Let's just fix that nose right up!" But I wanted, . . .
37 you see, then I had to figure out how to get plastic surgery
38 done . . also. So I said, well, I can trade art work(small laugh-

This conversation has been transcribed from a videotape made in the Department of
Linguistics, Rice University. It was originally intended for use in a symposium on discourse at Rice in 1984.
  1. Brackets indicate simultaneous conversation. Laugh indications immediately following a word begin on that word.

39 S) . . uh . . (small laugh-K) extra, or I give em money . . . anything, that
40 once they were going to break my nose, let's do everything . . .
41 why do it twice? So, uh mm, he said he couldn't do plastic surgery.
42 So . . . in the conversation with him, I just said, "well . . I
43 mean, I don't want to go pay someone else . . . a second time to
44 break my nose again, . . to do this," and so he said, "well . ."
45 S: Do they have to break your nose to correct your deviated
46 septum?
47 K: They may have to . . they may not. But they do have to completely
48 alter . . inside . . . at least . . . they still have to change the whole
49 shape, so I'm sure that they're going to do something sort of drastic,
50 so . . uh, . . so I got around it by saying, "well, listen . . . is it going
51 to be straightened?" you see and he said, "yes." I said, "well, what
52 about this part, you said that you could file that down a little
53 bit." He said, "well, . . ok(ha-K)!" I said, "well, then, if that's
54 all straight, this is gonna look really funny, can you . . like
55 straighten that up?" And so he said "well, ok." . . and that's all I
56 wanted done anyway, as far as plastic surgery's concerned, so he
57 did consent to it then, so . . I'm gonna get this new nose.
58 S: And what are . . . are they going to put you to sleep when you
59 have it done? . . . or do you have to be awake, while it's being
60 done?
61 K: Well, normally you're awake, and . . if I understood it
62 correctly, they're gonna do it under general anesthetic, so
63 that's ok, . . so I'll be asleep . . . But, uh, my friend, Emma,
64 said that all the doctors, when they get their noses fixed, or,
65 corrected, then they want to be put asleep, you see(long ha-K),
66 but they tell these patients, "this is nothing" (sympathetic laugh-
67 S), . . except that you see this hammer(long ha-K) whacking your
68 face, and that's sort of traumatic. So . . Emma told me not to get it
69 done under . . uh . . local, cause it will hurt, and uh, . . so?
70 S: And how long afterwards are you going . . . to be black and blue,
71 or . . ?
72 K: I don't know. I asked him if I could teach on the following
73 Monday, since the operation is on Thursday, . . would I be ok? . .
74 and he said, "yes", but he said, "you won't be able to
75 breathe out of your nose" . . so . . but he said uh, "you haven't
76 been able to breathe anyway(giggle-K), so why not?"
77 S: How long have you not been able to breathe out of . . is it is it the . .
78 which side of the nose can't you breathe out of?
79 K: This side . .
80 S: Out of your right side?
81 K: Uh hum it's just collapsed . . . I mean, I just . . . always thought that
82 that's . . . the way . . people breathed, . . you know, sort of less(low
83 ha-K), . . just use your mouth a lot . . . to breathe . .
84 S: Uh huh, yeah(giggle-K) . . . right(sympathetic giggle-S)! . .

85 K: Right, so . . . I think it's . . . the problem, they say, is that you
86 get a lot of colds, . . stuff like that, and, . . . and, uh, I'm tired of
87 colds. In fact I said if this doesn't work, I want my tonsils
88 out . . . if that doesn't work, maybe a big pipe(giggle-K), . . .
89 S: Just . . .
90 K: ⌈That's right! . .
91 S: ⌊Irrigation system . . . ⌋
92 K: In fact I was so desperate to sort of get rid of colds and
93 coughing and all that other stuff, that I even went in for . . . new
94 allergy tests, . . so on the same day that I scheduled my operation
95 I had sixty-two shots up my arm, . . . to see what I was allergic
96 to . . and . . . you know, I just really want to breathe . .
97 S: Did they tell you what you were allergic to?
98 K: All sorts of stuff . .
99 S: Have you gotten . . .
100 K: Yes, I'm . . . but I'm a good allergy patient.
101 S: They can treat every one of the allergies, . . huh? . .
102 K: Yes, after having all these diseases, you see,
103 tuberculosis, all that other stuff, they said, that, . . .
104 "you're lucky"(low contained giggle-K), you see, . . "because you can be
105 treated" and that's nice. I mean the fact that I can get shots and
106 that I don't have a problem . . . is sort of nice . . And my allergists
107 gave up on me back in Pittsburgh, because they can't do anything
108 anymore . . . all these molds and mildews and stuff . . . so if I get my
109 allergies taken care of, my nose fixed, . . keep my tonsils, I think . . .
110 I think life can be ok!(short giggle-K) . . ⌈and then, maybe . . .   ⌉
111 S: ⌊This is gonna be a big year . . . ⌋
112 K: . . . also get a good nose . . . yeah . . . I'm gonna look black and
113 blue, though . . . when I come out of this operation.
114 . . . .
115 S: Probably pretty swollen? . . . ⌈all through   ⌉
116 K: ⌊that's right . . ⌋
117 that's right so I have my sunglasses ready . .
118 S: Yes, big ones that come . . .
119 K: Yes, but I am sort of, . . I think I'm, I'm ready for this
120 operation, cause I need like three days in the hospital for
121 rest . . read cheap novels . . stuff like that . . so I'm up
122 for . . convalescing . . I won't give up my phone ⌈number out . . .   ⌉
123 S: ⌊What kind of cheap ⌋
124 novels are you going to read? . . Harlequin
125 romances or something like that . . to . . . .
126 K: Who knows? . . I think *The Nurses* . .
127 S: *The Nurses*(small laugh-S—giggle-K)
128 K: Yeah, ⌈something definitely general . .   ⌉
129 S: ⌊ In between soap operas on television? . .   ⌋
130 K: ⌊   Well,   ⌋

131 I don't like those soap operas, but I sort of . . . I like
132 reading better than watching TV, I think, . . so, I, I would rather
133 read something like *General Hospital*, but in . . besides they can
134 ⌈ be more graphic . . .   ⌉
135 ⌊ S: Big print . . and . . . ⌋
136 K: . . in those books . .
137 S: . . yes . .
138 K: . . and they don't really do all that stuff, so . . besides you have
139 to wait too long . . . this way I can jump over paragraphs, you see,
140 K: ⌈ and get . .
141 S: ⌊ . . find out what happens to . .
142 K: . . the real good stuff . .
143 S: . . yeah . .
144 K: Instead of having to wait 'til tomorrow . . to get the
145 information
146 S: So how long have you had this? . . has it been since you were
147 a kid?
148 K: . . I don't know. I, . . I swear it was when my brother, Jeff,
149 pushed me out of the bunkbeds when we were about . . two and three . .
150 y'see, . . . I think I broke my nose then, but my mother . . . maybe its
151 child abuse!
152 S: Child abuse(giggle-S then K), yes.
153 K: I don't know . .
154 S: Let's make this statement on(giggle-S then K) TV right
155 now(giggle S).
156 K:That's right! so, uh . . .
157 S: Broker is the victim of child abruse(ha-S)abuse . . .
158 K: That's right, I mean, I wish I could just go in and get a
159 total body overhaul, I mean, I wish you could go in for sort of things
160 like that, but you have to be . . have aesthetic reasons, they have
161 to . . instead of saying, "I don't like it, . . it seems to me
162 that's enough . . . I don't like my ankles, let's cut off . . .
163 S: ⌈ . . put in some new ones . . ⌉
164 K: ⌊ . . a few inches . . . ⌋
165 that's right! . . But now you have to have
166 really good reasons, so luckily with my nose, I've got a great
167 reason . . . it happens to be, uh, physical, but luckily it fits in there,
168 you see . .
169 S: Yeah, I was always disappointed, I was in an automobile accident
170 about eight years ago and smashed . . . my mouth, and . . . when I was taken
171 to the hospital I didn't really realize what state I was in and
172 the plastic surgeon came in and completely reconstructed . . . my
173 bottom lip, but had I known, what he was doing, I would have
174 asked to see a book of mouths(giggle-S, then K) first, and pick out
175 a new one . . . I was tired of my old one . . .
176 K: I hadn't thought of it like that. . . .

177 Well, I, . . . it's a good thing I don't like my nose, you see . .
178 S: I think your nose is perfectly fine . .
179 K: . . because you don't own it(sympathetic giggle-S) . . You
180 don't(giggle-K)have to look at it all the time. No, but it's like,
181 all crooked and stuff like that . . and it goes up, and I mean, I'm
182 thinking ahead . . . when I'm forty . . .
183 S: You mean it's not gonna go up anymore?
184 K: That's right! . . it's gonna come down . . . . a little bit. You see,
185 then I don't have to be a 'cute' forty-year-old, in a few years,
186 you see, it's gonna be like . . .
187 S: This is gonna alter your appearance altogether . .
188 K: . . gonna alter my-whole-outlook-⌈ on-life (giggle-K) . . . ⌉
189 S: ⌊ . . your demeanor   ⌋
190 S: and presence and . . . everything.
191 K: That's right, that's right, you never know . . . dates . . .
192   ⌈ and things like that . . .   ⌉
193 S: ⌊ personality(giggle-K), too, ⌋ who knows . . .
194 K: Right! yes. . . . Maybe more, . . higher enrollment(giggle-K) . . .
195 S: . . (giggle-S)higher enrollment in your classes . .
196 K: . . they're gonna come in and say, "look at that
197 nose!" . . . anyway, I'm sort of excited about this, cause I waited a
198 long time . . .
199 S: There's some guy, . . we heard a story a couple of weeks ago,
200 Uh mm, . . of this this family . . . and there was a young child in the
201 family, a young boy . . and he was . . he was having tremendous
202 problems in school, he was a a very difficult child . . . he was too
203 active and he was always getting in trouble, and . . and, uh mm, a long
204 lost relative came into this family, and who had been to India
205 and studied with some of the Eastern mystics . . an' so he suggested to
206 this child that he stuff cotton up the right side of his nose . .
207 and so they stuffed cotton up the right side of his
208 nose(giggle/laugh-S) and his personality completely changed, he
209 became this very passive, nice docile child(giggle-S) . . .
210 K: (giggle-K)yeah, he had to sort of writhe on the floor for a while . . . he
211 couldn't breathe . . . poor guy! . . . . Well, uh, I, as a kid I used to
212 tape my nose down though . . every night I would get this masking
213 tape and I would put this tape on, you see . . .
214 S: Was that to change the shape of it? . . to ⌈ flatten out your . . . ?⌉
215 K: ⌊ That's right,   ⌋
216 I thought it would hold it down, 'cause
217 everybody would go like this, you know, and say, "oh, look at
218 that cute Broker nose," . . . well they (long contained ha-K), you know,
219 like . . . they . . I wanted words like . . . beeyoudiful (sympathetic
220 giggle-S) . . . gorges . . great . . not cute (laugh-K). . . .
221 S: . . . nstead of cute . .
222 K: So I learnt right off, that I've got to get a new nose . . . but I

223 would last in bed for about . . . ten minutes . . . with this tape, you
224 see, and then I'd . . .
225 S: . . then breathing became more important(sympathetic giggle-S) . .
226 K: . . whip it off . . . I'm surprised I just didn't have little
227 welts going up my nose, but I just couldn't stand it, so . . you
228 can see, I . . . I've thought about this for a while . . I mean . . even
229 though my mother complains, and says that it's, because I had to
230 blow my nose as a child . . . my first reaction is . . . why? . . you see,
231 and . . and their their response to me blowing my nose was . . uh . . stop
232 blowing it! just stop! . . it's all in your head. Course,
233 then I'd(laugh/giggle-K)try and I'd sort of be(giggle-K) this kid with . . .
234 S: . . (sympathetic giggle-S) runny nose . .
235 K: That's right(ha-K)! . . . that's right! . . and I would have to apologize
236 for blowing my(sympathetic giggle-S) nose . . . I kept thinking, like, I'm
237 mentally deficient, because I'm blowing my nose . . . and I know it sounds like
238 such a stupid subject, but those sort of things really sort of
239 last, you see, . . . long enough . . .
240 S: They really stay with you, . . that's . . yeah . .
241 K: That's right! . . . long enough for me just to out of the blue . . . to
242 have someone say, "well, I had my nose operated on" . . . Why? . . you
243 know, "because I had a deviated septum," and then, I just . . it
244 sort of fired, it rekindled all that enthusiasm, and . . . here I am!
245 S: Do you know what they have to do with a deviated septum? Do
246 they have to reconnect? Do they . . move . . . it's cartilage, isn't
247 it, that they have to move over, so that it . . . Do they have to
248 reconnect that to something . . that it has torn away from . . or s-?
249 Do you know what they are doing?
250 K: Well, it seems to me, . . . and I must be totally, I'm hoping
251 I'm wrong, but I think they just take these poles and they just
252 sort of(giggle/laugh-K) . . . make . . .
253 S: . . (sympathetic giggle-S)they violently knock your . . .
254 K: . . that's right! I think they're . . basically it's like breaking
255 inside, I think . . . now . . . ⌐And the reason I don't kn- . . .⌐
256 S: ⌊ . . but how do they set it again? ⌋
257 K: Well . . they pack it!
258 S: . . oh, pack it . . .
259 K: . . you see, they pack it . . and it resets . . . and so it's like . . .
260 S: . . so that's why you can't breathe until they take out the
261 packing.
262 K: . . that's right! . . . you see, so that's the only problem I
263 foresee, is that I . . .
264 S: You can't breathe for . . you have to breathe through your mouth . .
265 K: Right! . . . an the thing is that if you choke on food, I mean
266 you could die(sympathetic giggle-S) . . . all these years . . .
267 S: Yes . . there's danger involved in this operation . .

268 K: . . that's right! . .

269 S: . . high risk(ha-S)! . .

270 K: . . well, imagine this, I mean, all those years you've been

271 keeping yourself away from muggers, rapists, things like

272 that . . and then all at once you die, because you've got

273 ⌈ a nose . . .

274 S: | . . . choked on a piece of food(giggle-S . . ⎱

275 K: ⌊ . . operation . . ⌋

276 I mean that's a real sort of ⌈ a disgusting way to go . . .

277 S: ⌊ You have to be very careful ⌋

278 for a period of time . . . this is . .

279 K: I mean it's Murphy's Law! I know that(small giggle-S)this could

280 possibly happen . . .

281 S: . . . on chocolate mousse or(sympathetic giggle-S)something like that . . .

282 K: . . that's right! . . and . . . besides, I can't taste anything, so at

283 least if I . . I can go to cheap restaurants now, because I can't

284 taste anything . . I could be eating dogmeat and it wouldn't

285 matter, because I can't taste it.

286 S: . . mmm be an economical week!

287 K: . . Right! I . . and, it might pay for my

288 operation(giggle/laugh-K&S), . . so . . I hope this . . . this better be a good

289 nose that's all I can say! . . .

290 S: . . yeah, maybe you should look at a book of noses or something,

291 before you go in . . . ⌈ he doesn't

292 K: | No, he doesn't want me to do that, . .

293 S: ⌊ want you to . . . ⌋

294 K: because then he's gonna feel like he's doing plastic surgery, you

295 see, I mean, ... I HAD a nose . . I could DRAW him a nose . . that I would

296 want; but then I may have to get other things done, too. I mean,

297 I do think . . . that the curve and things of your nose sort of goes with the

298 rest of it . . . like I . . if I had a real pointy nose, I'd have to

299 have half my chin taken off, you see, or something like

300 that(laugh/giggle-S), so(giggle-K) I can't be real radical about

301 this. I don't want someone looking at me, and saying,

302 "oh, what's wrong with you," you see, . . . I just don't want them

303 to say, "what a cute nose". . . . . fact, I'd like them to drop the

304 subject(laugh/giggle-K, then sympathetic giggle-S) . . .

305 S: . . just not even notice your nose anymore . .

306 K: That's right . . just forget it . . . so . . I don't know. That's about

307 the only operation I've had. I mean other than . . sort of foot

308 reconstruction, and . . but . . but that was a real physical

309 problem . . so this is the first time, and, and, and at . . at least

310 this time when people say, "Why are you getting your nose

311 fixed?" . . as a female, they already think that it's because you

312 want a nice nose, you see. Well, they're right!(laugh-S), but but

313 but(giggle-K) I'm not gonna admit to that . . . yeah . . so I
314 immediately say, ⎡ "Ah, I can't
315 S: ⎣ I have a deviated septum ⎦
316 K: breathe(ha-S), I haven't been able to breathe for years" . . . They say,
317 "Ah, that's a shame." See, so it's nice . . . maybe it's catholic
318 guilt . . . something like that . .
319 S: It's gonna be a new experience. Probably for the first time in
320 your memory, you'll be able to breathe out of both nostrils? . .
321 K: Yeah . . I was hoping that my voice was gonna change, like, I'd
322 go really low or something . . . that it would . . that I would sound
323 more like the way I hear it . . . but . . uh . . after talking to, uh, Jim
324 and, . . he just said, "Forget it!" It's not where voice comes from, or
325 whatever. Although he may be wrong! . . see . . . I mean maybe he's
326 wrong . . .
327 S: Hey, . . if you . . . if these Eastern mystics are right, you see,
328 what they figure is it's right and left brain kind of stuff, so
329 that . . the air that goes into your right nostril controls your
330 left . . . brain thinking . . . which is your more analytical,
331 intellectual kind of stuff. And the air that goes in the left
332 side controls your right brain thinking . . .
333 K: . . so the more the artistic side . . uh-oh!
334 S: Yeah, ⎤
335 K: ⎡ Uh oh! ⎦
336 S: ⎣ so this ⎦way your more intellectual side is going to
337 surface more . . . right?
338 K: Oh God . . . I'll(giggle-K) ⎡ be a Renaissance professor . . . ⎤
339 S: ⎣ You're going to be a ⎦
340 (giggle-S)Renaissance professor of art.
341 K: That's right! . . and, you see, now that I only have a right
342 brain(giggle K&S), basically cause I'm not using the left one, right?
343 and . .
344 S: ⎡ . . . a new dimension . . . ⎤
345 K: . . . and, have you ever read that ⎣ book, *Drawing on the Right Side* ⎦
346 *of the Brain?*
347 S: . . Uh-uh . .
348 K: . . well, it's an ok book . . I mean, I wouldn't use it, uh . . it's
349 nice for evening reading, sometimes . . . but, . . so I use my right
350 hand, see, and they do feel that you could use the right side of
351 your brain better . . . and uh . . . , so this way . . maybe I'll learn how to
352 use computer now . . maybe it will . . .
353 S: ⎡ Right! . . it will open up ⎤
354 K: ⎣ . . . all make sense(low giggle-K) ⎦
355 S: a whole new(giggle-S)G world to you . .
356 K: Instead of saying—bashing in there—, "Hey, you in there,
357 send up(low giggle-K) that information!" or, "Stop saying things like,

358 'doesn't compute', or whatever" (low giggle-K) . . . you know . . .
359 S: You'll invent the perfect one.
360 K: . . . or when the paragraph goes off the page, when you're just
361 trying to type in that little bit of information, and I'm
362 screaming to Jim, "it just left, I didn't do it(sympathetic
363 giggle-S)! I only wanted to put an 'a' in there instead of an
364 'e,'" and he keeps saying, "you have . . . you know you are the
365 person in charge of this computer, an' it only listens to
366 whatever you punch in" . . . but . . . I know(low giggle-K) . . . that . . .
367 S: . . . it has a mind of its own . .
368 K: . . . that's right! . . . so maybe if I get the left side working, I
370 S: (sympathetic giggle-S)You won't have to be so. . . . yes!
371 K: . . . violent with it . .
372 S: violent with it, yes . .
373 K: . . . or in lithography it's . . . I won't say, "Well, it's magic,"
374 while I'm teaching it, you see, . . not that it's chemistry, that
375 it's magic, so . . but if it doesn't work, I'll stuff the right side
376 (giggle K and S)of my, my nose with stuff, ok? . . so . . .
377 S: You would just take it out at night to sleep . .
378 K: That's right!
379 S: (loud mock whisper)I think we've finished . . .
380 K: OK.
381 S: Let's call it "The End."

PART TWO

INVENTIO, TOPICA, ET

DISPOSITIO

5

THE VISION QUEST IN

THE WEST, OR WHAT

THE MIND'S EYE SEES

Verily truth is sight, for verily truth is sight. Therefore if two
come disputing, saying "I have seen!" "I have heard!"
we should trust the one who says "I have seen."
Brhādaraṇyaka Upaniṣad 5.14.4

Say it! No ideas but in things.[1]
William Carlos Williams, *Patterson*

My thesis is simple, consisting of these four truths of
common sense:[2]

(1) *Things*, both as fact and concept, are hegemonic in Standard
Average European language and thought.[3]

---

1. It is amusing that both of these quotations extoll the visible, but do it in a context of "saying." I am indebted to Paul Friedrich for the quotation from the Brhādaraṇyaka Upaniṣad.

2. Versions of this chapter were previously given as talks at anthropology colloquia at the University of Chicago and at Rice University in 1982. It has profited from discussions in those contexts, but it has benefited more from comments and suggestions made by Paul Friedrich. Since this paper appeared in the *Journal of Anthropological Research* 40, 1 (1984):23–40, several papers on this topic have been brought to my attention (Dundes 1972, Latour 1985, and Stoller 1984). The general theme of "ocularity" is also discussed in books by Derrida (esp. 1974), Fabian (1983), and Rorty (1979).

3. "Standard Average European" or "SAE," is, of course, Whorf's term. As this borrowing of the term SAE suggests, this whole paper is a sort of footnote to Whorf's "The Relation of Habitual Thought and Behavior to Language" (1956), and is partially intended as a rejoinder to Black's charge that Whorf merely built from the wreckage of Aristotelian philosophy (Black 1959:432–37, and 1968:94). The rejoinder takes the form of asking, "Who has not thus recapitulated Aristotle?" and of showing, *à la* Whorf, why that recapitulation is unavoidable. I will argue in another place that much of the so-called refutation of Whorf's theses are based on systematic and ideologically motivated misreadings of his text. In particular, note that the "tests" of the "hypothesis" are devoted to vision as if that were the critical reading of "perception." That color perception became the index of Whorf's arguments about the verbal world demonstrates the power of the visualist metaphor, but says nothing about Whorf's arguments. In fact, one could

The Vision Quest in the West

(2) The hegemony of things entails the hegemony of the visual as a means of knowing/thinking. *Seeing* is a privileged sensorial mode and a key metaphor in SAE.[4]

(3) The hegemony of the visual, among other things: (a) necessitates a reductive ontological correlation between the visual and the verbal; (b) creates a predisposition to think of thinking/knowing as seeing; (c) promotes the notions that structure and process are fundamentally different and that the latter, which is only sequentiality, can always be reduced to the former, which is simultaneity, and thus being dominates becoming, actuality dominates possibility.

(4) The hegemony of the visual, of this way of seeing things, is not universal, for it: (a) has a history as a commonsense concept in Indo-European influenced particularly by literacy; (b) is not "substantiated" in the conceptual "structures" of other languages; and (c) is based on a profound misunderstanding of the evolution and functioning of the human sensorium.

The first thesis merely asserts what every SAE speaker knows— "thing" is the dominant concept in the semantic hierarchy of "what there is."[5] Things come in two packages: one, the dominant package, is "Platonic," the other, the subordinate package, is "Heraclitean"; or, "real things" vs. "occult things." The former are "substances" or "objects." The latter are "attributes," "qualities," "actions," "events," "relations," or, in general, things that change either autonomously in themselves or transitively change other things by their connection with them. They are only "derivatively real" by this connection with things that are "really real." To put it differently, occult things are what

say that nothing proves Whorf's thesis so well as its refutations. Friedrich has suggested, and I concur, that it would be better to make claims for Germanic or Romance or Slavic rather than SAE, particularly with respect to conversational practices. In that wider sense of discourse, though, which refers to lettered traditions of thought and encoded forms of folk knowledge, I think we can speak of SAE, and even of Indo-European as a single, more-or-less coherent discourse, and what I seek here are some of the key tropes that organize and direct that discourse.

4. The most influential work on the cultural significance of sensorial metaphors is, of course, Ong (1977), whose influence is obvious throughout. Other relevant sources here are: Goody (1968 [with Watt], 1977), Havelock (1963), Auerbach (1957) and Kelber (1983), particularly in the latter, the chapter entitled "Orality and Textuality in Paul" (pp. 149–83).

5. For an excellent account of the child's acquisition of this "thing," see Keil (1980). On this point, Wittgenstein's Tractarian distinction between "What can be said" (= the real) and "What can be pointed to" (= the mystical) merely takes apart the two possibilities inherent in predication.

can be predicated[6] of the real, what can be said of the seen. Their reality is a condition of saying rather than a fact of seeing. Or, to put it grammatically, nouns (substantives) are more real than verbs.[7] So too in logic, functions are queerer than arguments because functions are names of odd apparitional appearances of continuous becomings and possibilities rather than of discrete beings and actualities. And in rhetoric, the *expositio,* the simultaneous structure of arguments, dominates and relativizes the *narratio,* which is sequential and processual.

"Real things" as substances are of two sorts: "elemental" and "composite," or in Peircian "visualist" semiotics, icons ("firstness"), and indices ("secondness"). In the Port Royal Logic,[8] these correspond respectively to reasoning from part-to-part (metonymy) and from part-to-whole (synecdoche), and in Peirce's system to inference by abduction and by induction. Both grammatically and logically this is the source of the distinction between "names" and "compound names." Elemental things are "the really real," composite things are part of the "derivatively real," and taken together they comprise "the seen," "what there is," or in Port Royal "the real as cause and caused."

"Occult things" are always "complex." The Peircian analogue is "thirdness" or symbol, which, as its derivation suggests, arbitrarily "throws together" a name and a thing. In inference, it corresponds to Peircian deduction and to Port Royal "whole-to-part." In rhetoric, function or predication is the source of metaphor as the "substitution of names," and in grammar more generally it is the means of name

6. The etymology of predicate (>IE *deik-,* "point to," L *dicere,* "to say," *praedīcāre,* "to proclaim") reveals its kinetic and oral basis, and thus its appropriateness for "showing the occult." These points are made by Whorf (see esp. 1939:147,152). Here he also notes the distinction, largely neglected by his detractors, between common sense and its special sublanguages. It is amusing to note how Whorf anticipated current "dual brain" theses in his distinction between "spatial" and "nonspatial" consciousness. He links the former with the visual and the latter with hearing and notes the tendency to use visual perception as a metaphor of auditory perception (1939:155–56). The term "occult" is itself connected with saying by way of its derivation from "hiding" and "breathing" (IE *kel-,* "to hide," L *hālāre,* "to breathe"). The connection between speaking and the mystical breathing of the cosmos turns up again and again in all branches of Indo-European. On rhetoric, ecstasy, and mysticism, see Yates (1966), with thanks to Werner Kelber, who brought this work to my attention.

7. "Nouns" (>IE* nem-,* "name") and "substantives" are what "stand under" appearance. See note "d" to thought picture 1.

8. I refer to the Port Royal Logic (Arnauld 1865) here for two reasons: to draw attention to the source underlying the Port Royal Grammar which Chomsky mistakenly uses as the paragon of rationalism; and because it is a pivotal work in the transformation of rhetorical categories into logical operations.

relations or syntax. All occult things are synthetic and are only derivatively real by analysis. They comprise "the said," "what can be said of the seen," "the true."

Taken together, the two divisions of things comprise "the real," "what can be thought clearly." The real is thus constituted by a dominant visual mode of referential naming (names for real things) and a subordinate verbal mode of abstract and arbitrary name substitutions (names for occult things or for other names). All merely verbal aspects are by reductive ontological correlation identified with the visual as substitutions of appearances, that is, names for things. The manner of substitution is iconic, indexical, and symbolic, or in older terminology iconic and indexical are "natural," and symbolic is arbitrary and conventional. The architectonic of these concepts is illustrated in Thought Picture 5.1.

This thought picture represents both our commonsense notion of "the way things are" and the background, as well as some of the content and structure, of our scientific presuppositions about the "nature of things." It is a diagram of our contemporary inexplicability as represented by science and common sense,[9] of how science and common sense interpenetrate, common sense providing the background structure which constitutes a conditioned *a priori* that enables and structures scientific speculation, sets its boundaries, provides its problems, and relativizes its findings. I return to this topic in the conclusion, noting here only that science and our common sense are both metaphysics of substance, our science is but a sophisticated version of our naive physicalism, and both are derived from and are sustained by the metaphysical hegemony of the visual.

The Thing Is . . .

To begin with "things": The word itself has a history, originally denoting in Anglo-Saxon and Germanic an "assembly," specifically a "legislative assembly," a meaning that still survives in Norwegian *storting* ("great assembly"), the legislative body of Norway, and in the English term "husting," where politicians are always going when they want to be reelected. Derived from "hus" ("house") "ting"

9. Here I rephrase Barthes (1972, as quoted in Frake 1980:61) who says: "someday we must diagram our contemporary inexplicability, as it is represented to us not by science but by common sense." I am arguing that the relation between science and common sense is synecdochic, science being only a part of common sense.

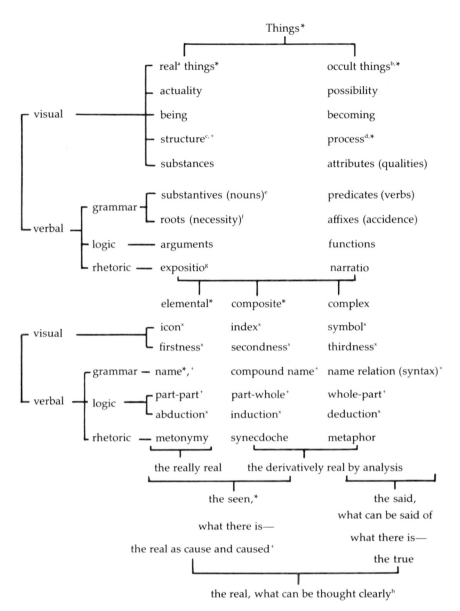

Thought picture 5.1. The real "inSight." Asterisks (*) denote commonsense categories; plusses (+) indicate categories as represented in the Port Royal Logic (Arnauld 1865); and (x) indicates categories from Peirce. This thought picture derives from the original "synOptic" method of Petrus Ramus (cf. Ong 1958).

a. A reprehensible redundancy here. Since "real" is derived from L *rēs*, IE **rē*- ("goods, riches, property thing"), a "real thing" is tantamount to a "real real" or a "thing thing." All etymologies are from Partridge (1958).

b. consisting of actions, events, relations, qualities

c. structure = simultaneity = stasis = space

d. process = sequentiality = change, movement, = time

c and d are the source of the Newtonian distinction of "things at rest" and "things in ("assembly"), it meant an assembly of representative heads of houses for legislative purposes. Beyond this, "thing" is perhaps etymologically connected with the *tem-per* group of IE words. Significantly, all the words in this etymological group have to do in one way or another with the mixing together of elements ("temper") or with cutting up space and time as in "temple," "template," and "temporal."

Whatever may be its more remote history, "thing" as word and concept in modern English and German is unavoidable. Try, for example, to spend a whole day in normal talk without once using the term in one or another of its simple or compound forms, "the thing is that" "things," "somethings," "everythings" and "nothings" overpopulate our everyday patterns of speech and confirm that "thing" is an indispensable tool of communication, which fact leads us too soon to the correct conclusion that "things" are only a manner of speaking.

It is not just that the word occurs with unbecoming frequency in discourse, but that it demands its avatars in its absence, so that our

---

motion." The relative importance of structure or stasis can be assessed in the reflexes of IE *sta-, "stand," as in "substance" and "understand," both implicating that which "exists or persists" (and both of these from L sist-, "to cause to stand") beneath appearances, in contrast to "process" (L pro-cēdere) as "that which goes, gives way," and compare Skt utsad-, "step aside," "disappear." The conjunction of structure and process or space and time in the hypotactic category "Things" reveals that the physicists' seemingly modern and revolutionary notion of space-time is no more than another way of saying, "Things!" They have thus succeeded in recapitulating the structure of IE thought.

e. "noun" is, of course, only another name for "name" (cf. L nōmen, etc.) which is also the source of the grammatical categories "nominative" and "pronoun." "Verb" reveals the verbal nature of the occult. It derives from IE *wer-, "to speak" and thus L uerbum, "word," E "word," and "verb," G rhetor, "speaker," and compare Skt vratam, "vow." "Predicate" is from IE *deik-, "to point to, to show" and reemphasizes the kinetic aspect of the occult, so that one could say that the real distinction between nouns and verbs is that of mimesis vs. kinesis. The verbal aspect of "predicate" is revealed in L praedīcāre, "to cry out, preach," and praedīcāmentum, "something predicated, a quality or condition." In general the category of "occult things" implicates "an action of speaking," or "saying." It is what is said.

f. The grammatical distinction between roots and affixes notes the difference between that part of a word which is changeless and therefore necessary (>L ne cess-, "not yield") because it does not yield to analysis, and what happens to a word by chance, hence "accidence" as the earlier grammatical term for affixation. An affix is only probable and changeable. This treatment identifies logical functions with affixes and verbs, or to put it differently, verbs and functions are "affixes" in their role of changing the condition of their nouns or arguments, a feature early grammarians noted in their characterization of "agglutinative" language. In logic, functions have always been stranger than arguments, as for example in Frege's concern about the "incompleteness" of argumentless functions, in Wittgenstein's torturous phrasings of "relations" as being neither thinking must be of *something*, about *something*, with *something*, even when nothing much is there and we say "I wasn't thinking of anything," as if we could. Because of a common locution, or grammatical function, which makes these words objects of "think," we are tempted to equate their "objecthood" with that of such "things" as apple pie and Fords. Grammar, by means of collocation, confirms us in our lexical addiction to things and makes us unresistant conspirators to the continuing hegemony of things as objects of thought and topics of discourse. This is how things "pile up" and "get the better of us."

Though they sometimes "get us down," "things" are good to think about in any form, but they are best when visual, as our manner of speaking about thinking confirms. When we talk of the "things that go on in our minds" we call them "images" or "visions" and speak of "examining ideas" as if they were suspicious coins, or of "seeing concepts" from our "point of view" much as if we were surveying from a prominence the vista of some peculiar interior landscape, for this is

---

"between" nor "had" by arguments, and also in the Batesonian slogan "not the things, but relations." These are all part of a propagandistic effort to change the commonsense notion about nouns and reality and to promote a Heraclitean and kinetic notion. They reveal by their concerns just the pattern indicated in thought picture 5.1, and they confirm its constraints by their inability to "speak" consistent and sensible "Heraclitean." In this respect, the modernist poets Pound, Williams, Olson, Creely, Duncan, and Snyder have actually been more successful in "speaking" consistent "Heraclitean," but the consequence has been that they speak sensibly only to a restricted audience of leisured Mandarins who have the time and inclination to translate their work back into "Platonic." Like the logicians they do not write originally in "Heraclitean," but first compose within the constraints of "Platonic" and then translate into "Heraclitean." For both, the commonsense world is the ground of speech and communication which makes the transition to "Heraclitean" possible, and like it or not, "Platonic" is still their mode of exposition (which see below).

g. *expositio*, from IE *po-, L *ponere*, "to put (away, aside), place, set" implicates not so much the act of placing, but the idea of "location," of being in a position. It is a placing or location of arguments relative to one another outside of the *narratio* on which they comment. Like "stand," which implicates it as the "place" where something stands, "place" has been a fertile trope for grammatical, logical and rhetorical concepts, for example, "composition," "deponent," "preposition," "post position," "suppositio," "presuppositio," "dispositio," "proposition," "opposition," "transposition," and "juxtaposition." All of which reveal a "predisposition" for structure, for location in space. By contrast, *narratio* is verbal; it is the act of telling or what is told. The connection between these visual and verbal categories as well as the distinction between kinds of things in the upper part of thought picture 5.1 are discussed by Henle (1958:426).

h. In this thought picture the ontological reduction is from "verbal" to "visual" or "the said" to "the seen." It is not without significance that Wittgenstein refers to this relationship as "picturing" in the *Tractatus*.

how we "get the picture." This common function as objects of visual inspection also betrays the visual bias of the terms "ideas" and "concepts." "Idea," after all, is derived from the Greek *idein* "to see" and concept (>IE *kap-*, "to take in hand") expresses the notion (>L *nōtus*, "make a mark") of an image formed by abstraction (>L *tractāre*, "to make a visible mark such as a furrow") from particulars. So when we fancy (>G *phantasia*, "appearance") that we are thinking of or with abstractions we are at best only trafficking in representations (>L *esse*, "that which truly exists") of the visualizable. Now, it may be that when we, in unaffected speech, use "idea," "concept," "notion," "image," and so on, we do not really have in mind a picture, and may be entirely persuaded that nothing beyond a vague sense of discomfort is manifest therein, but it is at least odd that the overwhelming majority of our words for the inhabitants of our minds are derived from words whose earlier meanings are connected with the seeable, and it is equally queer that our grammatical usages should be so persistently derelict in informing us, even unwittingly, of differences in the visual status of "things" that may be "objects" of predicates.

Even without these historical connections with the visual, our common expressions betray our fascination with appearances (>L *parere*, "to be visible"), for we say: "I see" when we understand, or "I see what you mean" as if we could, or "I can see where you're coming from" as if arriving all hot and dusty from a distant place, or "I see where you're going" as if a hidden path through a thicket had opened up, or "I can see through your argument" as if looking through a smudged window. We even say:

$$\text{"I just wanted to see what it} \begin{matrix} \text{felt} \\ \text{tasted} \\ \text{smelled} \\ \text{sounded} \end{matrix} \text{ like"}$$

as if we could see feels, tastes, smells, and sounds. The latter expression is not just a colloquialism, but a semantically marked preference for seeing. Try reversing the positions of "see" and the bracketed words and you get such unreasonable statements as: "I just wanted to taste what it looked like." We thus affirm the privileged position of the visual in the sensorium. I return to this question of the sensorium below, my point here being to remind you of what you already know and profess in daily discourse: "a picture is worth a thousand words."

It is not just our homely, commonsense way of talking that elevates the visual; learned discourse too indulges in it even more flagrantly. The whole history of psychology documents the search for—and failure to find—such substantial and seeable things as "memory traces," "engrams," and "stimulii," and what can we conclude about an anthropology that "looks at culture" as if watching a bug, or a philosophy that "seeks the source of ideas in conditions of life" as if on a journey to discover the Nile. Science at least affirms its predilection outright. As Bronowski says: "The world of science is dominated by the sense of sight" (1978:11), even though modern physics now finds it difficult to differentiate between itself and mysticism since its elementary particles are not strictly seeable as such, but are, like God or Bigfoot, knowable only by the tracks they leave behind. As mystical physics asserts, science without sight is unthinkable.

This same emphasis on sight accounts for the fact that most of the critical instances used to illustrate the primacy of perception in psychology and philosophy texts are visual, the auditory and tactile senses being added only as afterthoughts if they are mentioned at all. Bishop Berkeley's lonely God in the quad is a case in point, and his soundless tree one of the few exceptions.

Talk Is Cheap!

It would be one thing if vision were simply valued as the dominant sense, but we go further than that, for we actually denigrate the veracity of the other senses, especially the verbal/auditory. Not only do we declare that a picture is worth a thousand words, we also claim that "seeing is believing," all else is merely (delightful word) "hearsay," or just "what I heard," or "so I was told." Even kinesthesia takes precedence over the verbal, for everyone knows that "actions speak louder than words" and who has not been exhorted to "put your money where your mouth is," or (in my favorite) "I see your lips movin' but I don' hear you sayin' nothin." Moreover, we "play with ideas," "turn things over in our minds," or "mull" over them, or they "revolve," presumably until they become twisted and we need "to get things straight in our minds," and no one finds it odd if we "weigh our impressions," have "weighty" thoughts and declare "that idea shits!" or say of someone: "His mind jumps all over the place." Our ideas "flow," "run," and "surge" through our minds where our thoughts have a "course" or may even be "planted," "grow," "ripen," "bear fruit," and, here is food for thought, we think so little of the relation between saying and thinking that we have more terms for thought based on gustatory tropes than on verbal ones. Thus we "ruminate," "digest thoughts," "chew the cud," and even find some thoughts "hard to swallow." It is no accident that one of the major verbs for "know" in the Romance languages derives from the Latin *saper* "to savour, taste," for it confirms the well-known Latin and Gallic preference for gustatory sensation. Given this overwhelming preference for other sensory modalities, it is no wonder that we think of the hearing of inner voices as an index of pathology far more serious than "having visions," and that the hallmark of hallucination is not just having queer and silent visions, but engaging them in discourse.

These everyday notions imply a classification of the senses with respect to their capacity for providing true and accurate information about the external world. The visual sense is dominant because of its superior mimetic ability; the verbal/auditory is degraded because its mimetic capability is flawed; and the kinesthetic is somewhere between the visual and the verbal/auditory. This classification is revealed in thought picture 5.2.

Sophisticated Western discourse is no less certain of the superiority of the visual. Thus Schopenhauer:

> Outer sense is . . . divided into five senses and these accommodate themselves to the four elements, i.e., the four stages of aggregation. . . . Thus the sense for what is firm (earth) is touch; for what is fluid (water), taste; for what is in the form of vapor, i.e., volatile (vapor, exhalation), smell; for what is permanently elastic (air), hearing; for what is imponderable (fire, light), sight. . . . From this classification there also follows the relative dignity of the senses. *Sight has the highest rank*, because its sphere is the widest and its susceptibility the finest. . . . Hearing has second place. . . . However touch is a more thorough and well-informed sense (1962: 192, italics mine).

Primacy of the visual is not altogether a recent phenomenon, for the evidence of Indo-European etymology suggests that it is an ancient pattern, reflected most clearly in the equation "seeing = knowing," especially in the reflexes of IE *weid- (to see, to know truly"; G. *idein*, L. *vide* "to see, idea") from which we have among others, in English "idea," "vision," "view," "evidence," "wit," "wisdom," "witness," "wise," and "visible." Perhaps the best instance of the equation of vision and knowledge is in Hittite, which we might say preserves the primeval vision in all its concrete glory in the reflexes of IE *sekw- (from which English "see"), thus *sekw* "to see," *sak* "to know," and *sakw* "eyes." This Hittite equation (though not its form) expresses that overpowering redundancy of the visual which our legal system enshrines in its preference for the "evidence of eye witnesses."

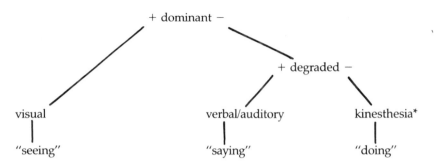

Thought picture 5.2. Commonsense classification of sensory modalities. *Kinesthesia here includes gustatory tropes of action like "eating," "swallowing," "digesting," but does not include those of taste and smell as such. The latter are usually expressions of attitudes toward thought, not direct judgements of mimetic quality nor tropes of thought processes, as in: "his ideas stink," "he savoured the thought," "that is a delicious thought," "that's a shitty idea." So, too, for the tactile modality: "that is a painful thought" and more globally: "he's sharp," "he's dull," "he's soft in the head," "he's a Californian mush-head." The latter are transitional to intermodal tropes of defective process like: "he has shit for brains," "he's a vegetable," "he's a meat head," "he's gappy."

In contrast to this pattern, a brief survey of Indo-European terms turns up only one clear cut case of a standard term for "thinking" that derives from a word meaning "to say," and that, significantly, in Irish *im rādim* ("think," from *im* "about *rādim* "speak"), which is related to a dubious verbal set in English, namely "reason," "ratiocinate," "rational," all from IE *ra- or *re- (*rē-*) and meaning "to count." In that counting was from earliest times probably verbal, I count "counting" verbal, and the exception that proves the rule.

This is not to say that Indo-European languages or the Western tradition of thought have totally neglected the possibility that thinking might be just "saying to oneself." Plato endorsed such a view—endorsing a view is, I suppose, the mental equivalent of signing a picture. In the *Theaetatus* he says: "When the mind is thinking, it is simply talking to itself," and this despite the fact that the idea is the dominant idea in his thought. Aristotle hastened to refute this heresy, declaring that "spoken words are the symbols of mental experience . . . which is the same for all . . . as are the things of which our experiences are images (1952: p. 25). More recently, Plato's notion of thinking as saying reemerged explicitly as part of a program to relieve us of the burden of the mental. Watson, as is well-known, identified thinking and saying and even argued that thinking was accompanied by motoric movements of the speech organs; it was merely "speech minus sound." The materialist basis of this idea has an obvious and enduring appeal to Russian psycholinguists for whom the concept "inner speech" has a direct physicalist interpretation in the form of electromyographs which provide *visible* evidence of motoric movements accompanying silent reading and problem solving (Shokolov 1972). It is ironic that the evidence for kinesis must be in the form of visible marks, but it is wholly consistent with the reductive ontology of the visible.

Analytic philosophy, too, rediscovered language, and Ryle and Wittgenstein, in different ways to be sure, reduced thinking to saying. In analytic philosophy, though, it is not a question of sensorial representation or of representation of any kind. Analytic philosophers and extreme behaviorists like Skinner avoided the whole issue of representation and the sensorium through an exclusive focus on the outward manifestation of speech, on the external form of orality. They did so for a good visualist reason: to defeat the reality of mentality as an invisible inner process. They affirmed the ambiguity of these lines from Stefan George's *Words*: "So I renounced and sadly see / Where word breaks off no thing maybe" (quoted in Heidegger 1971:140).

Actions Speak Louder Than Words

In a sense, neither Watson, the Soviet neurolinguists, nor the analytic philosophers have anything to say about the purely auditory aspect of representation except, perhaps, to reduce it to a motoric and kinetic feature. For them, the hearing of voices in thought is at best only the thinker's own voice speaking or preparing to speak. Hearing is first a form of saying; as we listen to another we, as it were, speak along with him, silently saying the words he utters (Shokolov 1972:49). The ideological aim here, as in all motor theories of speech perception, is to derive auditory imagery from originally overt motoric acts which have become internal motoric acts. Speech perception derives from speech production.

The truthfulness of this "motion picture" does not interest me here, though indeed many things, such as the child's ability to understand speech before he can begin to produce it, point to its inadequacy. What interests me is the shape of the underlying metaphor, the clue to which is the term "speech production"—not just speech or speaking, but speech *production.* Speaking and thinking are forms of *work*. The idea is clearly stated by Blonski: ". . . both speech and thought have developed from work. Primitive speech was really action. Primitive mental operations were actions, and it was only gradually that true action became replaced by mental action" (quoted in ibid., 48).

Here the inner form of saying and thinking is derived not from seeing, but from doing. Words and thoughts are internalized deeds. This kinetic theory of thinking not only reduces thought to external action, it locates its origin in social life, in acts of verbal communication which are the dialogical models of internal thought. Its program is thus an attack on both the imagists and rationalists, on the imagists because it deemphasizes visual representation in favor of kinetic representation, and on the rationalists because it negates the idea of "pure thought"—thought arising universally and independently of the signs that express it and of the conditions of life that support it.

The most famous formulation of these wordless and imageless pure thoughts is in the polysemous Greek term *"logos."* For Plato the *logos* was not the product of the senses but the archetypal idea behind the flawed representations of the senses; for Aristotle it tended to be an emergent synthesis of the *sensorium communis;* for Heraclitus it was a form of knowledge, the origin of action and speech, a word, reasoning, and the cosmic law of the clash and harmony of opposites; and for Parmenides, the means of freeing oneself from the appearances which impose on sense. Though the *logos* has an increasingly mystical and extrasensorial interpretation in later Greek philosophy, its connections with the sensorium are straightforward. In the first place, its more remote history connects it directly with the semantic territory of "thing" as "that which is assembled," for it derives from IE *leg- meaning "to gather, collect." Second, it is related to vision and orality, and to thought generally, by way of its connection with reading and writing and calculating, as: in G *legein,* ("to reckon, say"), *logos,* ("counting, reason, narrative"), and L *legere* (from which *lēctiō,* "a reading"), in compounds G *analekta* ("collection of sayings"), *analogia* ("proportionate"), *apalogos* ("story"), *dialogos* ("conversation"), L *intellegere* ("choose among"), *colligere* ("collect"; and in a host of English words primarily pertaining to thought and literary expression— "logic," "intelligence," "lecture," "analogy," "epilogue," "prologue," "lexicon," "dialogue," "syllogism," "select," "trilogy," "monologue," and many others. On the whole *logos* indicates a peculiar class of "things"—assemblages assembled with the eyes by means of the intermediary alphabet, the visible substitutes for the things themselves which are the words we have for them and the word we have of them.

Pure thought, then, is either something derived from the senses, albeit indirectly, or something beyond the senses and not representable by them at least in this life. The former is the product of the Aristotelian *sensorium communis,* the Kantian "concept," that Hegelian joining together of diversity into the unity of the "imageless sign," knowledge emergent by synthesis and abstraction, and the latter is the Platonic *logos* and the Kantian "pure reason," the *ding an sich* of thought which Schopenhauer says "lives the true, full life only so long as it does not transgress the boundary where words begin" (quoted in ibid., 20).It is that which the Wurzburg school sought to substantiate by means of introspective verbal accounts of nonverbal thinking.

Cognitive psychologists to this day are still divided into "verbalists," who, under the influence of modern linguistics, understand thinking as propositional, and "visualists," who have recently revived the mental image as the vehicle of thought. Even linguists, who might be thought on *a priori* grounds to be obvious verbalists, are generally not, for they mostly revile Whorf and few even know of Max Müller. They tend to be either Platonist believers in wordless ideas underlying expression as in "The basic idea is what remains when complete abstraction is made from any way of representing the idea—from any wording of it." (Grace 1981:59), or "closet visualists" who settle for one or another version of the Kantian concept which is, to put it paradoxically, equivocally verbal and nonverbal. As in psychology, the hegemony of the visual has recently reasserted itself in the contemporary work on "prototypes," "basic reference," and "schemata" (cf. Lakoff 1982). If these trends in psychology and linguistics are harbingers, then it is likely that the preponderance of the Heraclitean heresy in psychology and philosophy by way of language and linguistics is to be short-lived.

In neurolinguistics two similar lines of contradictory visualist and verbalist interpretation are current; one stresses communication, the other representation. Thus, the evolution of language has been traced to brain mechanisms directly linked with vocalization and communication in lower animals, or it has been sought in the hyperdevelopment of visual representations as if language was only a more sophisticated mode of combining visual representations (Jerison 1976). Aphasiology, too, has been a contest between whole-brain theorists like Goldstein (1948), for whom language and thought are inseparable because all brain activity is integrative, and locationists like Geschwind (1968) who favor an internal version of Gall's phrenology in which different brain functions are physically separated and act in concert only by means of specific connections. The latter, in its emphasis on centers and connections, is little more than a repetition of the Indo-European distinction between place and process. It hinges on the separation of language from the sensorimotor aspects of speech and hearing, and is an attempt to locate the *logos* in some part of the brain (the *planum temporal*) that is not simply a speech or auditory center. It is a "physicalization" of Lichtheim's fictional "idea center." The argu-

Left Hemisphere	Right Hemisphere
temporal	spatial
sequential	simultaneous
auditory	visual
verbal ideation*	nonverbal ideation**
analytic	holistic

Thought picture 5.3. Hemispheric distribution of functions of thought. *Verbal ideation includes speech, writing, and calculation. **Nonverbal ideation includes spatial orientation and pictorial representation. These correspond, respectively, with Hughling Jackson's distinction between "propositional" and "nonpropositional" thought, and with Whorf's "nonspatial" and "spatial" consciousness (cf. footnote 5). This thought picture is contructed from: Sperry 1968, Bogen 1969, and Luria and Simmernitskaya 1977.

ment between holists and locationists has been recently relativized in a Manichaean interpretation of brain function which assigns holism to the right hemisphere and analysis to the dominant left hemisphere. It is not surprising that the opposed features of this dualism recapitulate the distinction between the visual and the verbal. Compare the distribution of features in thought picture 5.1 with those in thought picture 5.3.

Though the two thought pictures agree in the distribution of features, they seem to imply different evaluations, thought picture 5.1 favoring the visual, thought picture 5.3 the verbal, but that is only because thought picture 5.3 makes no overt ontological claim. It obscures the issue of representation by means of the representationally opaque terms "verbal ideation," and "nonverbal ideation," which are either silent about representation or have, so to speak, secretly accomplished it beforehand. At this point I must emphasize that I am not interested here in the correctness of the ideas to which I have been alluding; I am fascinated only by the trope that makes them possible and enlivens the clash of oppositions. This brief history is now complete enough to reveal the essential features of that trope. There are two ways of thinking about thinking in Indo-European languages: thinking is either a metaphor of the visual, for which the picture or image is the organizing basis; or it is a metaphor of the verbal, for which speech is the basis. At another level these symbolize mimesis, *thinking as representation* (visual) versus kinesis, *thinking as communication* (verbal). Both are ancient patterns in Indo-European, but whereas the visual metaphor has suffered little change through history, the verbal metaphor has been under constant threat of reduction to the visual metaphor. The principal source of the threat has been from two related conditions of Indo-European life and thought: the visually reductive technology of writing and the mystical concept of "language" that writing created, for writing is that figure of speech that makes speech visible, divisible, and immortal, and transforms it from an activity or happening into a superorganic object of thought, a "thing" capable of division into parts and assembly into wholes of discourse—that now familiar object of linguistics whose only real connection with speech is its etymology. This facilitative relationship between writing and "language" is revealed by the etymology of "grammar" which derives from IE *gerbh-* ("to carve"), G. *gramma* ("a letter of the alphabet") and *grammatikos* ("the art of reading"), and L. *grammar* "the Latin language." Without writing there could be no "language" nor any of the other *logoi* which descend from the gramarye of writing.

In part, it is this ambivalent character of language-as-logos that makes us think of words as a kind of activity (speech) or as a kind of structure deriving from visible marks, and tempts us to reduce one mode to the other, but this ambivalence, reflected in the history of thought about thought, and made critical by the new technology of thought called writing, is actually a problem set for us by the ancient Indo-European two-fold division of "knowing" into kinetic knowing, as in "knowing how" (IE *gana-*, "be able," from which E "can" and "know"), and mimetic knowing, as in "knowing that" (IE *weid-*, "see"). This dual character of knowing is reflected in the classification of things, for what is known about is also either kinetic or mimetic. Thus both knowing and the known are divided into kinetic and mimetic. Writing mystically harmonizes these two opposites, for reading and writing are at once skilled action ("knowing how") and mimesis of the *logos* ("knowing that"), but it also separates them because it freezes thought in visible form that is forever disconnected from the activity that fixed it. Skillful or inspired speech is also a conjunction of kinesis and mimesis, but its transitoriness ensures that the harmony it creates cannot be broken.

The point of this historical excursion is that the verbal/auditory aspect of the sensorium has always been problematic in Indo-European thought, for as "saying" it is a kind of doing or kinesis, but as writing it becomes a thing seen and a representation of the unseen *logos*. We can now understand why English has so many mimetic and kinetic images of thought and so few verbal ones—the verbal has always been subordinated to these two dominant tropes. The tension between kinesis and mimesis draws the verbal as speech/hearing into the orbit of action, even if only of the cheaper mental sort, but as writing/reading the verbal becomes a substance of sorts, an imitation of substance and thus forever suspect as substance, for its substantiality is accomplished as a magical trick, an illusion; it is not the thing, only its shadow. All mimesis is dual. On one hand it is the surest sign of the real, but by virtue of being a sign it is only a substitute for the real and we suspect it of hiding more than it reveals, for a copy of something, no matter how artfully constructed, is still only a copy, not "the real thing." This dark, other side of mimesis is obvious in its etymology. Derived from IE *mei-, its root meaning is "to deceive," as in the Skt reflex *māyā* ("illusion," "the magical power of illusion") or in G *mimos* ("a play," "a grotesque imitation"), all of which comes down to us in English as "mime" and "mimic." What Plato recorded in his theory of ideas was this ancient suspicion of representation and the inconsolable sense of separation from the real that it creates even as it seems to draw us closest to it. It accounts for our longing for a reality made inaccessible by the very means of its accessibility, and it is in that moment of deepest alienation and loss that we remember the occult and flee from the *logos* to seek in kinesis what we were denied in mimesis.

The whole history of Indo-European thought is little more than the repetition of this dual theme. The contrary traditions of India are variations on what the West takes to be the minor key, so too its own Heraclitean and hermetic traditions. The disputes between verbalists and visualists, too, are part of this clash of opposition. All, however, are played out within a cocoon of common sense that provides the background reality, engenders oppositions and makes their harmony in the way things are. Things being what they are, deviations from the commonsense predominance of the visual merely confirm in their opposition that the dominant view in Western thought, commonsense or otherwise, is that the sensory takes precedence over the nonsensory, for sense is better than nonsense, and the visual sense is best of all.

Another Point of View

It is tempting to think that the way things are is the way things are everywhere, but this way of seeing things is not dominant in Dravidian languages. Among the 20 or so words used in the various Dravidian languages to express thinking or knowing, approximately one-fourth makes no reference to sensory representation—are not sensory tropes—being translatable by such notions as "desire," "intention," "hope," "wish." About three-fourths are translatable cross-modally by a variety of sensory terms. The remainder are nearly evenly divided among visual, verbal, and kinesthetic tropes. This simple count of instances reveals no consistent tropological pattern associated with the sensorium. There are sensory tropes but they are not preferentially clustered around one of the senses. In particular, verbs of vision do not predominate as metaphorical bases of thinking/knowing.

Language use does, however, reveal that a verbal trope is one of the commonest ways of talking about thinking. It involves the use of "saying/telling" verbs in reports of thinking. This grammatical feature is common in most Dravidian languages and in others as well, but I illustrate it here with examples from Koya. When a Koya wants to talk about thinking he may sometimes use the verb *tos-* (a visual trope), or *odis-* (tropologically neutral), or *innuko-* (a verbal trope, literally "to say to oneself"), or *alocintsu-* (a tropologically neutral borrowing from Skt via Telugu), but the commonest mode is to use *in-* ("to say"), as in: "'I will go to Nallabali,' he thought," where the "he thought" is represented by *ittōṇḍu* ("he said"). Similarly, in the sentence "thinking it was his, he brought it," the "thinking" would be represented by *inji*, the past-passive participle of *in-*. In Koya: *nādinji tattōṇḍu* (literally, "my it, having said, he brought"). "He had a thought" would be: *tanaki ittōṇḍu* (literally, "to himself he said"). These usages parallel the English form of figuratively reporting thought, as in: "I said to myself . . ." (= "I thought"), as if reporting the speech of another, but in Koya they are the standard not the figure. The general principle is clear: in reporting thought, report it as speech in a direct quote. Koyas are rustic Platonists. Apart from this usage Koyas seldom speak of thoughts as such; it is far commoner to mention their happening without mentioning them, as in: *ōni matki paḍte* (literally, "to his mind it befell," or "it happened in his mind" = "he had a thought"). This signifies that the "thing" that "befalls" is not a proper thing. Neither a picture nor even a colorless idea, it is more of an emotion like "desiring," "hoping," "expecting," "wishing," what we prefer to think of as nonrepresentational "feelings" rather than thoughts. To put it grammatically, thoughts are generally not nouns. There are, to be sure, nouns that mean "thought," such as *alōcanu, inta(na), talapu, uddeṣam, abhiprāyamu,* but all except *talapu* are loan words from Sanskrit and are seldom heard in ordinary discourse. *Talapu,* though indeed a noun grammatically, is not the name of a representation, being derived from *talacu* ("to think"), and both ultimately are borrowings from Telugu. In fact, none of these is the name of a representation. The first three are sensorially neutral, *talapu* may also mean "desire," and the last two are better translated as "opinion."

All of this may lead us to conclude that when a Koya thinks, he has nothing in mind, which may well be correct from our point of view, but it is also the case that he hasn't much to say about it either, for thought and thinking are not major topics of discourse. The first Koya "Symposium" is yet to be held and what someone says, does, and desires is far more important than what he thinks about thought. In the commonsense world inhabited by Koyas, saying and doing—words and deeds—are far more important than thinking, and this is reflected in their linguistic habits.

Koya, and by implication, Dravidian languages generally, are the converse of Indo-European languages, but there is more here than the reversal of pattern, for the structure of Indo-European sensory concepts implicates representation as a central issue in a way that Dravidian does not. Even though Dravidian languages have sensory tropes for knowing/thinking they do not involve directly the idea of ideas as representations.

Apart from previous examples, two lines of evidence are relevant to this conclusion. The first is the absence in Dravidian of a metaphysical category corresponding to "thing," which is, after all, the enabling concept for representation. In order to represent, some *thing* must represent and some *thing* must be represented. Terminological equivalents for "thing" in Dravidian, such as Tamil *porul* include in their range of meaning inappropriate "things" like "the meaning of a word" and "power," which point to the fact that Indian and Western ideas of "substance" do not correspond. In the great religious and philosophical traditions of India, substance is not a permanent, unchanging essence, it is the stuff of *māyā,* the illusory, endlessly changing flux. Second, the Dravidian terms for "knowing/thinking" do not so fastidiously separate "knowing" and "feeling" in the way SAE terms do. In Dravidian, "rationality" is not just a way of knowing/thinking but a way of feeling/knowing.

Both of these patterns are consistent with the Indian philosophical tradition which, in most of its versions, derives both the material world and the means of knowing it from intentionality and desire. These "feelings" are not irrational sources of subjective error that rationalism must contest and defeat in the quest for objective truth, but are instead the very source and enabling condition for any rationality whatever. What for SAE is only a disturbing philosophical afterthought, in the form of phenomenology is, in Indian tradition, the starting point and foundation of philosophy.

Whereof We Cannot Speak

"Thing," "sensorium," "representation," and "rationality" are mutually implicated in SAE, for it is the role of the senses to represent the things thinking thinks. The sensorium "makes sense," and the only quarrel in the philosophical traditions of SAE is over the functions and priorities of the different sensory modes, for questions about the sensorium are meaningful only in the context of representation and those who would find in the differences between idealism and realism a refutation of Whorf's determinism have failed to see that these two ways of seeing, like all other Western philosophies, are merely predictable implications within the more encompassing structure of possibilities permitted by "thing," "sensorium," "representation," and "rationality."[10] True challenges to all of these key limiters are practically nonexistent in the philosophical tradition of SAE, for such a challenge could only be classified as nonthought, irrational, beyond the limit of language. Our thinking about thinking presupposes the commonsense meaningfulness of these tropes and rejects whatever falls outside them. That is the reason "reason" is not universal; it is relative not to an *a priori* form of thought, but to a discourse that forms a cultural *a priori* sedimented from common sense.

Common sense, the reasonable, that language of culture, conditions the *a priori* and relativizes it to a framework of facts that reason can at best express, but never deny, for to deny them would be to deny reason. Reason cannot change the reasonable, for that is the role of history, of the irrational, and thus common sense—the reason-

---

10. This refers to Feuer's rather silly argument to the effect that though European philosophies are fundamentally different, they are expressed in the same language and this proves that language does not determine philosophy. He neglects the fact that all European philosophies are predictable permutations of possibilities set by the features indicated in thought picture 1. See Feuer (1953, in Manners and Kaplan 1968:412).

able—is the product of unreason, of the will, of passion, of ideology and power. Reason is born of unreason and not, as Kant thought, of itself, or so we must think if we are reasonable. Reason is conditioned by life and culture and its expression is the subject of history not its maker, for it was ideology, not necessity of thought, that prompted Plato to emasculate rhetoric and evict poetry from the house of reason, and urged Aristotle to drive apart dialectic and logic.[11] The birth of reason in that reduction of *oratio* and *ratio* to mere *ratio* is an accident of history, and though it is tempting to believe with Kant that nothing new has or even could be discovered in logic since Aristotle's invention of it, that temptation dwindles when we recall that his "invention" consisted only in elevating into the transcendental realm of the *logos* the semantic and grammatical categories of the Greek language.[12]

Descartes, too, discredited ancient authority and sought to supplant its agonistic mode of deductive disputation with dispassionate inductive inquiry. Invention, the rhetorical means for locating topics in the stock of commonplace ideas, he radically reinterpreted as induction, and he located the source of ideas not in the already known—in the store of knowledge inherited from Greece and Rome—but in inquiry itself, and knowledge, thus suborned by method, became not what everyone knew, but what they might know if they employed the critical method that would lead reason from observation of things to inductive generalization.

Reason, thus shrunken to observation of particulars and inductive generalization, and become an engine of objective inquiry, no longer functioned in its former communicational context, for its *communis*, its *consensus omnium* was no more the commonsense world, but a party of adepts in critical method whose sole purpose was the discovery of new and distinct knowledge of *things* that would replace the flawed knowledge of *words* received from the unreason of tradition. Questions might be of words or things, but those addressed to things took precedence.

Such, in brief, is a narrative of that connection between words and things which issues in the hegemony of things. In this triumph of things over words was accomplished the triumph of logic over rheto-

11. On the implications generally of the transition from orality to writing, see Ong (1967, 1977, 1982), Goody (1968 [with Watt], 1977), Havelock (1963), Kelber (1983), Maxwell (1983), Carothers (1959).

12. On this point, see Jaeger (1944), especially vol. 3, which is devoted almost entirely to this topic.

ric, of representation over communication, of science over common sense, of the visual over the verbal. This is the history of our logophobia, of our common belief that things are better than words. Although these visual arts seem to us to form the hard framework of all thought deserving of the name, they are instead historical emergents within a structure of common sense, and being thus relative to a cultural tradition cannot function as universals capable of constituting a fusion of all cultural horizons into a single integrated whole. Except as ideology (that instrument of power), logic and science, those arts of the visual, have no more claim to universality than the traditions they pretend to dominate, for these traditions speak of other things and even remind us, in the words of a Bemba saying, that:

"The eye is the source of the lie" (Maxwell 1983).

6 POSTMODERN ANTHROPOLOGY

Postmodern anthropology is the study of man— "talking."[1] Discourse is its object and its means. Discourse is both a theoretical object and a practice, and it is this reflexivity between object and means that enables discourse and that discourse creates. Discourse is the maker of the world, not its mirror, for it represents the world only inasmuch as it is the world. The world is what we say it is, and what we speak of is the world. It is the ". . . saying in which it comes to pass that world is made to appear" (Heidegger 1971:101). Postmodern anthropology replaces the visual metaphor of the world as what we *see* with a verbal metaphor in which world and word are mutually implicated, neither having priority of origin nor ontic dominance (see Chapter 4). Berkeley's *esse est percipi* becomes "to be is being spoken of." Postmodern anthropology rejects the priority of perception, and with it the idea that concepts are derived from "represented" sensory intuitions that make the intelligible the sensible "re-signed." There is no movement from originary substance to derived "spirit," from thing to concept, nor from mind to material, nor from the real to the less real, for the mutuality of word, world, and mind, or of language, things, and selves is beyond time and space, located nowhere, but found everywhere, as in the harmonic reverberations of a chord never struck but always heard.

Seeing is always mediated by saying, and postmodern anthropology is thus the end of an illusion, of that separation of word and world created by writing and sustained by language-as-logos, that "univocal picture" projected in words from the standpoint of the all-seeing tran-

1. That is, speaking and writing. This chapter is based on a talk given to the Washington Anthropological Society in November 1983, and in revised form to the Rice Circle in January 1984. It also incorporates some remarks given in a talk at the Conference on Language and Culture at Canberra in July 1982. My thanks to Phyllis Chock at Catholic University for inviting me to speak to the Washington Anthropological Society and to the organizers at the Canberra Conference, especially Judith Irvine, for inviting me to attend. This chapter is a mediation of two strong and partly contradictory authorial voices, both speaking to me at once. I refer to Jaques Derrida and Walter Ong, whose works are cited throughout, and whose voices sing contrapuntally in my inner ears with those of Reid, Wittgenstein, Heidegger, Whorf, Laksmayya, and Kapila of the "three-fold misery."

scendental ego whose real message is that the world is a fable (cf. Nietzsche 1911:24, Derrida 1976:14).

In its positive aspect, postmodern anthropology seeks to atone for the original sin of LANGUAGE,[2] that separation of speech and world we know as the disjunction of words and things, and to make that atonement by means of a return to the commonsense, plurivocal world of the speaking subject. In its negative aspect, it seeks to encarnate the transcendental object called LANGUAGE, and to cast out the doxology of "signs" and "signification" that is the means of transcendence and false objectification.[3]

By this return to the immanence of language, postmodern anthropology aims to complete the revolution of consciousness begun in ancient Greece and so far accomplished in the deconstruction of "things"—the object of perception—in the physical sciences, and in the deconstruction of "selves"—the subject who perceives—in the social sciences. The impudent moderns have stood Bacon on his head and left Descartes's *cogito* for dead. Their "thing" is only a trace of being in its moment of death, and their ego is a Leibnitzian infinity of perspectives on the becoming of the "thing" that never is, even in death. Their "thing" is impotent and cannot rise up as the single image of a dispersed mind.

Postmodern anthropology is both the fulfillment of that revolution and its nemesis, for it is that third, and final, stage of a revolution that destroys the means of revolution. This decomposition of things and selves was an accomplishment of textuality, of the fetishization of language by writing that constituted things and selves as CONCEPTS whose reality was totally contingent on the ontology of LANGUAGE as a transcendental object (cf. Nietzsche 1911:21). Both subject (self) and object (thing), knower and known, are mediated by LANGUAGE, which transcends, encompasses, and constitutes them. Thus the amaurosis of LANGUAGE, the means of that mediation, must be the final act in the decomposition of the commonsense world of words and things. It will also be the recreation of a commonsense world, for postmodern anthropology refuses the transit to absolute knowledge that establishes an identity between the subject and the object by means of LANGUAGE. It denies that "I speak of the world by means of language," is identical to "LANGUAGE speaks of itself by means of itself," and declares that "The world is what we say it is." It does not mean "The world is all we

2. The use of even small capital letters here and throughout signifies concepts in the *logos* or as the *logos*.

3. Thus Derrida, "This . . . amounts to destroying the concept of "sign" and its entire logic" (1976:7).

say it is," and asks "What sense can we make of a silent universe with no voice to speak the name of its silence?" (cf. Foucault 1965:xi).

This program denies the absolute difference between signs and things, and the arbitrariness of the relation between signs and things that depends upon their absolute difference. The consequence is the denial of LANGUAGE and what its transcendence implies,[4] specifically, the five Platonic emanations:

(1) the transcendence of METHOD and the WILL to TRUTH;
(2) the transcendence of the SIGN in the substitution of appearances that enables REPRESENTATION and SIGNIFICATION;
(3) the transcendence of the TEXT as a transcendental OBJECT;
(4) the transcendence of the INTERPRETER as transcendental SUBJECT—the critic as oracle;
(5) the transcendence of FORM enabled by the separation of FORM and CONTENT;

and the four Plutonic mysteries:

(1) the myth of the text as cypher;
(2) the myth of appearance vs. reality;
(3) the metaphor of surface vs. depth, in which our deciphering "penetrates" the hymenic surface of the text, fathoming its underlying, real meaning, reveling in the revelation of orgasmic mystery;
(4) the myth of the unconscious.

The aim is to demystify both Thoth and our chthonic connections.

Only 1, 2, and 5 of the Platonic emanations are addressed here,[5] but hear first a brief account of this two-fold world of transcendence and suppression (cf. Derrida 1972:75) in the form of a history written after the end of the history which is not a history, but an essay on metalepsis, on how the *logos* was always a mythos of

A Certain Picture of the World[6]

The story of this picture begins and ends in a commonsense duality that is the vehicle of metaphoric implicatures,[7] a

4. Much of this was already worked out in Tyler (1978).

5. The remainder are reserved for later treatment or have appeared piecemeal in other papers.

6. The allusion here is to Lyotard (1974).

7. Metaphoric implicature is the sort of implication that moves thought not by identities, but by equivalences that are unities of identity and difference. It is thus different

mimesis	kinesis
representation	*ergon,* will
sameness, identity	difference
permanence	change
stasis	movement, activity
substance*	accidence**
real	derivatively real
noun	verb
space	time and telos
nonliving	living, *anima****
seeing	saying
writing	speech

Thought picture 6.1. The duality of mimesis and kinesis and their metaphoric implicates. **ens per se,* the first Aristotelian category. ***ens per accidence,* the remaining nine
Aristotelian categories. ***consisting of: vegetable, animal (beings having sense, memory, and imagination), and rational (beings having reason and judgement). From Aristotle, *Categoria* and *De Anima.* The Aristotelian schema here is as given in thought picture 6.2.

family of founding symbols whose interconnections, maintained
through time, have been the perduring problems of philosophy. Its
source, if such it may be called, is the intersection of mimesis and
kinesis and their metaphoric implicates. Thought pictures 6.1 and 6.2
illustrate the implicates of this duality.

Some sense of the persistence of these metaphors can be intuited
from the metonymic substitutions that constituted different (but
equivalent) understandings of mind and brain in Western speculation. Consider thought picture 6.3.

As the inclusion of Peirce suggests, these same anima distinctions
translate directly into the language of semiosis, becoming the means
of representation: iconic signs; indexical signs; and symbols, and

from logical implication which uses only identities and is thus paralyzed, goes nowhere, and cannot be the source of movement within a discourse. Metaphoric implicature moves ceaselessly through a genealogy of concepts and over a field of concepts, sometimes even coming back to what might seem to be a point of origin.

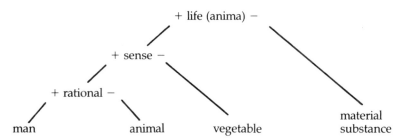

Thought picture 6.2. Aristotelian schema. This schema has the interesting consequence of making life "unreal," just an accident of substance (see thought picture 6.1),
but substance, too, is unreal as a consequence of being implicated by mimesis which
creates only appearances of reality. *Anima* also refers to different states of man's soul,
expressing distinctions still in use today as when we speak of someone in an irrevers-
ible coma as being a "vegetable" or in a "vegetative" state. Man is not only a "rational
animal," he is also a "sensitive vegetable," and a "living substance," but his reality is
nonetheless compromised, achieved only as an illusory substance after death. This is
the original "death wish" of Western thought and the analogue of "life negation" in
Indian thought. It suggests the Heraclitean conclusion that the "real" should be classed
under kinesis rather than mimesis.

symbolizing the dominance of mimesis over kinesis, for the categories
of the latter become the means of mimesis. In addition to these means,
mimesis is achieved through sensorimotor modalities in a movement
from the sensible to the intelligible, from concrete to abstract. These
modes are "saying" (thought), "seeing" (representation), and "doing"
(will, work), or "words," "things," and "deeds," whose permutable
combinations constitute the realm of semantics in the relations "words
and things" (reference), "words and words" (sense), "words and
deeds" (pragmatics).[8] These are also the means of prudence (judgments based on past, present, and future) and are equivalent to the
Augustinian faculties: *intellectus* (saying), *memoria* (seeing), and *voluntas* (doing). Moreover, they are the metaphoric equivalents of modern
divisions of the cerebral cortex into associative, sensory, and motor
areas. They are metaphors of present, past, and future respectively,
and of time, space, and movement as categories of intuition, and of
subject, object, and verb as grammatical categories of the understanding, and of *ethos, eidos,* and *pathos* as rhetorical categories. As the latter
suggests, they also correspond to the basic divisions of *logoi*—aesthetics, science, and politics—as these are realized synecdochically in
poetry, philosophy, and rhetoric, whose respective forms of discourse

---

8. Here, too, belong Austin's "locutionary," "illocutionary," and "perlocutionary,"
though he might say "with different force" (1962) since they are "acts."

	Aristotle	Reid	Peirce	McLean
conscious, abstract	rational (reason, judgement)	rational (reason, conceptions)	cognition = triad = synechism (continuity) = symbol	neomammalian brain
↕	animal (imagination, memory, sense)	animal (perceptions, will)	volition = dyad = agapism (evolution, growth) = index	old mammalian brain
unconscious, concrete	vegetable	mechanical (sensations, instinct)	feeling = monad = tychism (chance) = icon	reptilian brain

Thought picture 6.3. Metaphoric equivalents of Aristotle's categories of *anima* (kinesis, action). With few exceptions, this triad has been the standard interpretation of man's essential character and, as in Peirce, the character of the macrocosm as well. Based on Reid 1895:543–52; Peirce 1932:1:148–80, 2:56–60, 134–73; McLean 1973. These designations are largely self-explanatory. To these we could add, reading up, the Kantian categories "phenomenon," "schematismos," "noumenon," or "person," "society" and "culture," or physical = mechanical, neural = organic, conceptual = mental. They are, in effect, the major tropic orders: metonymy, synecdoche, and metaphor (see thought picture 6.7), which chronicle the emergence of mind or spirit. They are metaphors of past, present, and future, of doing, seeing, and saying, and as such are also faculties of the emergent mind (see thought picture 6.4).

are tropical, logical, and dialectical and whose functions are evocation, description, and provocation, and which have as their object value, fact (truth), and opinion. Such are the metaphoric equivalents of the sensory modes. These metaphoric connections are illustrated in thought picture 6.4.

The intersection of these two families of metaphors (kinesis as manner of signification and mimesis as mode of representation) constitute an interlocking episteme, a paradigm of semiosis, as illustrated in thought picture 6.5.

Note that none of these metaphors is actually "foundational," even in Western discourse, not even mimesis and kinesis. They appear "inside" and "outside" of paradigms, signifying that they are sometimes means of other metaphors and sometimes metaphoric creations; they are sometimes "defining," sometimes "defined," what is understood, and what the understanding makes. It is not the case that there are no foundational concepts, but rather that there are many of them, and they are constantly shifting about from steeple to foundation and back again, forming new and different figural possibilities which have not so much an origin, something suggested by beginning my tale with Aristotle, as they have a more-or-less predictable cycle of permutations, in which, one after the other, each, or each pair, seems to be the center of orientation for all the rest, like the principal character on a stage. Aristotle is only the central figure in the play that ends with Descartes, and we see him, through the Renaissance, receding from center stage until he fetches up in the wings, quietly waiting for his turn to come round again. All welcome the Stagirite!

Places on the stage suggest what is next in this history, namely, the theatre of *topoi*, those locations in memory of the words and things we want to speak and think about. *Topoi* are metaphorically connected with work, duty, and fundamental character, for things are stored in memory analogically, according to their character, as in a rebus, or relatively, according to the work they signify, according, in other words, to what will best evoke them when needed for speech and thought.[9] *Topoi*, and memory itself, are vast, interlocking, figurative orderings in which things are remembered not by what they are in themselves nor by their direct resemblance to other things, but by what they are for and by arbitrary analogical circumstance. *Topoi* make the mother matrix, the web that makes the figure of the cosmos and encloses the cosmic man.

9. Yates (1966: 378–88) makes the point of the relation between character and *characteristica* in her discussion of Leibnitz.

Thought picture 6.4. Means of mimesis.

Means of Mimesis		Sensory Modes		
		Verbal/Auditory	Visual	Kinesthetic
Faculty (*anima*)		saying thought *intellectus* associative (Present)	seeing representation *memoria* sensory (Past)	doing = work (*ergon*) will *voluntas* motor (Future)
Kategoria	semantic	words-words (sense)	words-things (reference)	words-deeds (pragmatics)
	grammatical	subject	object	verb
	metaphysical	time *ethos*	space *eidos*	movement *pathos*
Logoi		aesthetics	science	politics
Discourse	genre	poetry	philosophy	rhetoric
	colligational mode	tropical	logical	dialectical
	rhetorical function	evocation value	description (demonstrate) fact (truth)	provocation (persuade) opinion

These are the metaphoric implicates of the three sensory modes. Note that "seeing" has no "voice" (evocation and provocation derive from *voce*, "voice"). Its rhetorical mode is given by writing, de-scription (L *scribere*, "to write") which "shows" (*de-monstrāre*, "show," "loom"). *Ethos* is the essential character of a people or work of art; *eidos*, a picture, image, phantasm, representation; *pathos*, what moves to action.

178

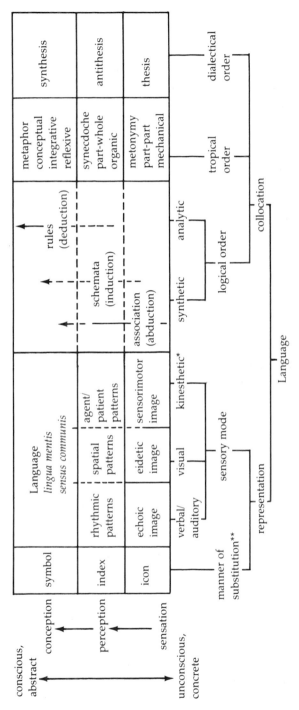

Thought picture 6.5. The intersection of mimesis and kinesis. This paradigm is the Cartesian product of thought pictures 6.3 and 6.4. It illustrates the modes of representation and collocation that define signs and sign functions. Thus, for example, perception is indexical, sensory specific, schematic, and part-whole. Schemata are analytic "logical" means of collocation. This parallels the function of the antithesis in dialectical reason. The whole is a metaphor of the movement from sensation to perception. Language, or the *lingua mentis* is as much outside the paradigm as in it, for it creates (recreates?) the whole paradigm. The whole is thus a feature of language that produces language and that language produces. *includes kinesthesia and tactile. **that is, how the sign substitutes its appearance for what it signifies.

179

Work (doing, *ergon*) is linked with character and duty because one is what one does, and one does what one must; so spoke the ancients. Work is first a symbolic value before it is a material value, and only by being the former can it be the latter, and it is not so just as a signified, but as a signifier pointing to the mode of signification that characterizes each kind of work.

Consider the world of antiquity and most of that world we choose to call underdeveloped. They have, like us, two kinds of work: "real" work and "phony" work, but for them, unlike us, phony work is the privilege of the few, real work the condition of the many. What do I mean by real and phony work? A simple distinction marks their difference: real workers "move" things, phony workers "move" no-thing except symbols. In between these two extremes is a third kind of work, that done by those who "move" others as if they were things, the work of politicians, soldiers, and bureaucrats. In other words, workers are classified by the signs that characterize their work. Thus, real work:iconic :: phony work:symbolic :: political work:indexical. We may think of the contrast between these other worlds and ours by means of population pyramids, as in thought picture 6.6.

Beyond this realistic Aristotelian world of work are other worlds, pyramidal also. They are "the other of unity," the Platonic world of oneness, and "the other of difference," the Plutonic world of separation. The pyramids are arranged hierarchically, the Aristotelian in the middle, joined at its tip by the inverted tip of the Platonic, and at its base by the inverted base of the Plutonic, and below the latter, joined to its inverted tip is a fourth pyramid, the world of animals and dumb material. These are homologous with the four *Yugas* (periods) of the Hindu cosmic cycle, the "four ages of man" in Platonism, the "four emanations" of spirit in Zoroastrianism and the Kabbalah, and the gyres or windings of the cosmos in Yeats, and the "four-fold" of Heidegger. They are the material, formative, creative, and archetypal worlds that provide the stasis of myth and the movement of history generally as well as of that history called evolution particularly. They are the *anima mundi*, the "world memory," and they make the figure of cosmic man that we know as person, society, and culture.

As part of the "great memory" they intersect with other *topoi*: cosmic, social, corporal, and communicational. Thus, the cosmic *topoi* (celestial, atmospheric, and terrestrial) of the Ṛg Veda, for example, correspond with the three kinds of work and are *loci* of gods, kings, and men, respectively (cf. Dumézil 1958; Benveniste 1969:227–60). Corresponding to the "other of unity" is the supercelestial realm, the locus of abstract supernaturals, and corresponding to the "other of difference" is the subterranean world, locus of the demons. The corre-

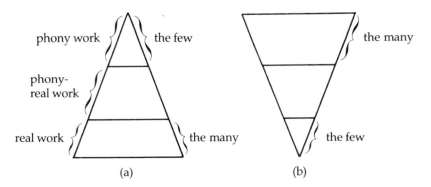

Thought picture 6.6. (a) The population pyramid of the ancient world and of the "underdeveloped" world. (b) The population pyramid of the "developed" world. In our world, most people do phony work, the manipulation of symbols as opposed to the manipulation of things. The underdeveloped world is the converse. The major work of phony workers is to justify the necessity of phony work and to reconcile phony-real workers and real workers with one another and to their relatively less fortunate forms of life. Each of these pyramids has a "dark twin" which is its opposite. For the underdeveloped world it is the dream of a future paradise—of which pyramid "b" is an approximation—and for the developed world it is a romanticized memory of the past—of which "a" is an approximation. We see, then, how the dreams and memories of these two worlds complement one another, forming a single unity of inverses, a universe of interlocking fantasy as in the star of Lakśmi.

sponding social categories are priests (*literati*), warriors (nobles), folk (*rustici, vulgari*), and barbarians and slaves. This set of *topoi* is homologized with the human body as spirit, mind, and body, a movement from inner to outer; or in other versions as heart, mind, and body; or, with the outer body as locus, head, shoulders and chest, and lower extremities. The inner man of St. Bernard is *voces* (speech), *res* (text), *ratio* (reason), and *veritas* (the voice of God within), while the now better known inner *loci* of Freud are id, ego, and superego, corresponding more or less to the *loci* of St. Bernard. The *loci* of communication give the powers and privileges of communication appropriate to each division of work. Thus, the Hegelian categories in-itself, for-itself, and in-itself–for-itself refer ultimately to forms of language appropriate to each form of work. Different possibilities of the subject-object relationship are similarly located as in: pure objectivity : animal :: pure subjectivity (desire, greed, vice, and illusion) : demonic (Plu-

	Corporal				Social[1]	Cosmic
	Inner		**Inner-Outer**	**Outer**		
	Freud	St. Bernard				
	super-ego	*veritas* see God in person				super-celestial abstract deities
	ego	*ratio* voice of God within	spirit (heart)	head	saints sages priests literati ☿	celestial astral deities
		res (text)	mind (head)	upper body, arms	kings warriors nobles professionals tradesmen bureaucrats ♂	atmosphere atmospheric deities
		voce (voice)	body (hands)	lower body, legs	folk craftsmen laborers ♀	terrestrial earth deities
	id				barbarians slaves savages primitives	demons subterranean

Platonic other of identity (unity) logos ☉

phony work

phony-real work

real work

Plutonic other of difference (separation) ani-

mal

material

eros as spirit ⊕

ergon[2] ♂

eros as substance ♀

Powers and Privileges of Communication

Form of Language	Subject/Object	Form of Communication[3]	Medium of Communication	Mode of Interpretation	Mode of Evidence
	Ⓢ unity of subject and object	music Pythagorean astronomy		anagogy	*monstrāre* (know things as they are)
in-itself-for-itself (discourse its own object)	S O person ↔ God	logic number dialectic grammar	written	tropology	*metaphorica* figurative
for-itself (pragmatic-instrumental)	person ↔ PERSON[4]	rhetoric	oral text[5] secondary orality	synecdoche	*significāre*[6] (know things as they appear)
in-itself (unselfconscious speech in the world)	person ↔ person	poetry	oral	metonymy	*propria* literal
	S pure subjectivity as vice, desire, greed, avarice, lust, illusion	techne		irony	
	O pure objectivity				

the limit of language[8]

Mode of Signification		Metaphoric Value			
Representational	Constitutive	Light	Time	Direction	Substance
	$S^?$ "mark" *davar*	*lux* pure light	future	high inner	spirit, perfect, mind, rational, form, conscious, abstract, civilized, living
symbol whole-part "thirdness"	S ⟷ s	*sol*	present		
index part-whole "secondness"	S → s	*calor* shadow			
icon part-part "firstness"	S ← s	*energeia*	past		
	s	pure darkness		low outer	matter, imperfect, body, irrational, content, unconscious, concrete, primitive, nonliving

Thought picture 6.7. The matrix of *topoi*. The categories of *ergon* are metaphoric implicates of iconic, indexical, and symbolic (reading up).

1. On these "social-cosmic-corporal" categories, see, for example, the Rg Veda, and
    for Indo-European generally, Dumezil (1958).
2. Work (*ergon*) and love (*eros*), the two themes of Freud, but here the union of Marx
    and Freud. The world (*ergon*) is bereft of love, for it is only a place of work, war,
    and worship. The three levels of *ergon*, are antagonistic and dialectical. The world
    of real work is creative, that of phony-real work destructive, that of phony work
    aims for atonement and reconciliation through the manipulation of the symbols
    that constitute ideology. Phony work is the neutralization of the opposition be-
    tween real work and phony-real work, thus:

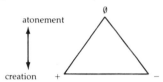

    The world of *ergon* repeats in microcosm the dialectic of the macrocosm, for *eros* as
    substance is creative (*energeia*), in opposition to the world of *ergon* which is de-
    structive, while the world of *eros* as spirit is the neutralization and reconciliation
    of these opposing forces. This is the reversal of the Indra myth in the Rg Veda
    where gods and men symbolize creation, generation, and evolution, and the de-
    mons stand for antigrowth and permanence. Gods and men are in endless battle,
    an unreconcilable dualism. The world picture in thought picture 6.7, not only re-
    verses the character of these antagonists, it gives them a dialectical resolution in
    the world of *eros* as spirit. Only the world of *ergon* is strictly entropic because only
    it is an-tropic. Note that these pyramids in Kabbalistic tradition are collapsed and
    interlocked with each point of base and apex as the locus of a planet and a period
    of life. In Hinduism, the triangles interlock in the form of a *yantra* meant for use as
    a meditative vehicle to lead the mind in toward the infinite.
3. Thus, the seven liberal arts make a hierarchy, with poetry or grammar at the bot-
    tom. Below that, of course, is mere *techne*, skilled practice. Grammar tends to get
    above its proper station.
4. This notation with "person" capitalized signifies communication between real per-
    sons and things or institutions as fetishized persons, or conversely between per-
    sons as if one of the persons was a thing, so, persons as things, things as persons,
    which characterizes the whole of politics and economy. In the realm of phony
    work, person ↔ God signifies communication between real persons and concepts
    or abstractions as persons. In real work, communication is between real persons
    in face-to-face, concrete situations. Each of these represents a different sense of
    "dialogue," and each may be dialogue between real persons, but in the levels
    above real work, one of the persons is a category, stereotype, institution, concept,
    or fantasy. Each kind of work, then, is characterized by its own objectifying mode.
    Rhetoric, in the adjoining box, is predictably "agonistic" as the means of the world
    of war. Thus Lakoff and Johnson (1980) are able to show that "argument is war."
5. Oral texts are texts based on oral models of organization, as in the case of much
    early written poetry and the dialogues of Plato. Secondary orality is oral discourse
    based on texts as in classical rhetoric and the dialogues of Plato (cf. Ong 1982:
    93–116, 168–69). The distinction is: text based on speech and speech based
    on text.

tonic) :: communication among equals:real work :: communication between superiors or things fetishized as persons and persons fetishized as things:the middle class :: the communication of persons to God:the priestly class :: the union of subject and object:the supercelestial realm. Forms of communication are similarly hierarchically topologized from poetry upward through rhetoric, dialectic, grammar, logic, and number, to music in the supercelestial. Media of communication are included, too, as written for priest and literati, oral text or secondary orality (rhetoric) for kings, and orality for the workers. Modes of textual interpretation, the great problem of the Chris-

---

6. This is the dualism between "showing" reality and showing only its appearance. Mathematics and logic arrogate to themselves the supercelestial function of *demonstrāre*. This is equivalent to St. Bernard's idea that in heaven we shall see God as he is, but elsewhere we must be content with signs of his presence (*significāre*). The world is only a place of signification, as is made clear by St. Augustine (*On Christian Doctrine*, book II, ch. 6, and in book III, the discussion of "literal and figurative" meaning). So too in Aristotle, the sign is an inference to the nonapparent (*Rhetoric* 1.1357a, b36.). In St. Augustine (*Confessions* 11:7), the word becomes flesh because man cannot otherwise understand it. Human knowing is only synecdochic and occurs in time; God's word is timeless, not a linear sequence of sound but a whole and eternal. Wittgenstein as well, in the concluding parts of the *Tractatus*, tells us that what cannot be said (i.e., the mystical, which is beyond the limit of language) can be "shown" (1961). By contrast, Heidegger unites "saying" and "showing" as the "showing of saying," which he reconstructs as the original meaning of Greek *semeia* in the famous passage on signification at the beginning of Aristotle's *De Interpretatione*. This unity of "showing saying" was later broken apart in the development of the idea of signs and signification. *Monstrāre* and *significāre* were separated (1971:114–15).

7. This is the medieval idea of the "mark," the sign that shows a thing's real character, as in the expression, "the mark of the beast (the devil)." In Leibnitz it becomes the search for a universal character (*characteristica universalis*) as a system of marks for all things on which all men agree. *Davar* is the Hebrew concept of the unity of signifier/signified. The lowercase "s" at the bottom here is the Kantian thing-in-itself. The terms "firstness," "secondness," and "thirdness" are Peirce's. Note Derrida (1976:11), "The written signifier . . . has no constitutive meaning."

8. The "limit of language" is also the limit of the world of *ergon*. Compare Wittgenstein (1961) and Humboldt's famous distinction between *ergon* and *energeia*, which identifies language as the former, not the latter (1970:27). Language is ". . . a true world which the intellect must set between itself and objects" (ibid., 135). On the fourfold division here, compare with Heidegger: "The movement at the core of the world's four regions, which makes them reach one another and holds them in the nearness of their distance is nearness itself" (1971:105).

Note that the threefold distinction of "lust" (eros as substance), "work," and "love" (eros as spirit and the "play" of the gods) is an "externalized" metaphor of the threefold of "work," or conversely, the threefold of "work" is an "internalized" metaphor of

tian tradition, were hierarchized in order of ascending subtlety as: irony (saying other than you mean is a form of illusion appropriate to the demonic and academic), metonymy, synecdoche, tropology, and anagogy. So, too, modes of evidence correspond to this hierarchy, the most general being the distinction between *significāre* and *monstrāre*. Men know only by signification, and that is either literal (*propria*) or figurative (*metaphorica*), but in the supercelestical realm they know things as they really are; things *show* themselves, and as St. Bernard says, we shall then *see* God as he is; but for now we can only hear his voice within us as a *sign* of his presence. Modes of signification fit this

---

"lust," "work," and "love." These correlative threefolds correspond to the trinitarian systems of Popper, Parsons, and Habermas in addition to those noted elsewhere (cf. thought picture 6.3). Popper distinguishes among the "first world" as the physical world, the "second world" as the world of consciousness, and the "third world" of Platonic spirit consisting of texts. These worlds emerge sequentially in the order given. Later emergents cannot be reduced to earlier ones (cf. Lakatos 1978:108). Habermas' three "domains of reality," which have corresponding "modes of communication," "validity claims," and "general functions of speech," are: "my world of internal nature," "our world of society," and "the world of external nature" (1979:65–68). In Parsons' well-known system these are the separate subsystems of personality, society, and culture (1949). These are all different ways of speaking of the three Kantian categories: phenomenon, schematismos, and noumenon, or, in a slightly different dialect, of the Augustinian categories *sensus, imaginatio,* and *intellectus.* Thus the internal order from particular to universal in cognition mirrors the exterior world. Each follows the same sequence in the upward movement from material to spiritual. The order of thought : the order of society :: the order of society : the order of the cosmos. This is the fundamental theme of Western thought in all its variants throughout history. The three levels are also the solution to the Platonic problem of the relation between form and content. The middle term (schematismos, *imaginatio,* representation) was called into being as the mediation between form and content. It is the familiar notion of the sign that mediates between signifier and signified in Saussure's system as in: signifier ← sign → signified.

Note, too, that the three Kantian critiques of pure reason, practical reason, and judgement are allegories of the sensory modalities "seeing," "doing," and "saying," respectively. *Eidos/logos, pathos,* and *ethos* are their respective subject matter.

Finally, this whole thought picture is really only a reminder of the Dantean rhetoric, or perhaps it's a queer sort of revisualization of Pound's phanopoetic *Cantos.* As in the Schiffanoia frescoes that so captivated Pound by their pagan combination of narrative and myth in their depiction of the casual, the recurrent, and the permanent, it has its Triumphs (Hermes) and Thrones (Taurus) and is both narrative and myth, movement in time and juxtaposition in space.

The ultimate paradox is that this whole edifice, built in order to surpass itself, can do nothing more than reproduce—endlessly—allegories of itself. So the imperious urge to symbol and metaphysics makes no metamorphosis after all, and succumbs finally to its own allegory. And that is why Hermes is the tutelary deity of the postmodern age rather than Prometheus.

same pattern, the system of Peirce has already been noted, but there is also the system of St. Augustine, differing in its hierarchic arrangement of modes.[10] Metaphoric values also follow this hierarchic system. Thus we have the metaphors of high (= good) and low (= bad); up is better than down (Lakoff and Johnson 1980), light vs. dark; a light-heat series downward from *lux* (pure light), through *sol* (the sun, heat and light), *calor* (heat), to energy (the "dark," hidden power of light); union vs. separation; abstract vs. concrete; conscious vs. unconscious; primitive vs. civilized; past (dark, obscured, ghostly, and demonic), present, and future; living vs. nonliving; and on and on. These correspondences are illustrated in thought picture 6.7.

Such then, are the *topoi* that have in the past formed the structure and content of our imagination. We do not yet know what new *topoi* will emerge from the revolution created by inverting the old pyramid of work that informed and animated this vast system of metaphors, this Brunoesque kaleidoscope in which each rank is a memory wheel inscribed with the signs of its loci and each is aligned to each to yield a total episteme. But standing now amid the rubble of this wondrous machine, the shattered bits and pieces of colorful metaphors glinting in the feeble, postmodern light, we know, at last, that only the [ay] peering through the other end of the shadowy tube was real, that its vision was deceived by movements caused by a hand it could think and feel, but not see, and only when the wheel was turned by the hand of the other did it suspect the reality of what it saw. And we know, too, at the end of this history that is not a history of a history that was not a history, that the *logos* was always a *mythos* obscured by

The Transcendence of Method and the Will to Truth

> *The distinguishing feature of our . . . century is not the triumph of science, but the triumph of the scientific method over science*
>
> Nietzsche 1913:3

One of the constant themes of western thought has been the search for apodictic and universal method. We can trace it in the reforms of rhetoric, in the emancipation of logic from dialectic,

---

10. See the discussion "The Transcendence of Signs."

in the allegorical textual hermeneutics of the scholastics, and in the Cartesian and Baconian revolt against tradition that produced scientific method. In our own times we see it in the triumph of formalism in all branches of thought, its analogical model being, of course, mathematics. The transcendence of method derives from one simple assumption: *rules of interpretation and analysis are separate from what they interpret and analyze.* Rules are separate from what rules are for; they transcend their objects and conditions of use; they have universal and unequivocal application; they are neither contingent on, nor contained in, the content they order. This is the fetishization of logic, of reason enthroned by right (cf. Derrida 1967:59).

Apart from rather pointless debates about rationality centering around such notions as "primitive mentality," "concrete operations" and *bricolage*, which imply a different kind of reason that can only be unreasonable by the standards of reason, no one has ever demonstrated the independence of reason, of logic and mathematics, from the discourses that constitute them. They are, after all, historical emergents, and are thus not self-constituting, for their emergence depends upon two conditions: (1) a founding written discourse, and (2) a background of presuppositions that makes the historical quest for method reasonable. Only if reason had no history could it, by means of itself, justify its claim to universality and demonstrate that it is anything more than the means by which we justify the lies we tell.

Method, then, is immanent in a larger, founding discourse, and every application of it to a given discourse is conditioned by that immanence. Its transcendence is a condition of its immanence, and its immanence is given by the need for its transcendence. The source of this need is the "will to truth," and its means is the written text. Texts provide the ground for the emergence of method and are its original objects. From the need to interpret texts arises the will to truth, and from the will to truth arises method.

The will to truth is contingent upon writing in the "vulgar" sense and is not principled by "arche-writing" (cf. Derrida 1976:27), for the truth of orality is momentary in its expression and depends for its duration on the durable character of the speaker as one who speaks truly whether or not she speaks the truth.[11] In a word, truth before writing is honesty, a feature of the speaker and only derivatively connected

11. The etymology is revealing here. "Durable" and "duration" derive from Indo-European *drū* ("strong, resistant, hard") which is adjectival of *dreu- ("tree, the oak"), from which come "trust," "fidelity," and "truth." Other reflexes include "troop" (of soldiers), "to rule," "Queen," "chief," and "Lord" (Benveniste 1969:84–90). The association of truth and reason with nobility and power is clear, calling to mind Lyotard's "Reason and power are one and the same" (1974:13).

with her words, for the speaker's honesty rests in some harmony between her words and deeds and not in her words alone, nor in any correspondence between words and things, as these are only the means of lying. Truth is always part of a fable, of something told, a thing of words alone, but honesty is both word and deed and that is why English gives truth no agentive force outside the context of telling. One may be a liar but not a "truther." Truth is born with the *logos* and dies with it (Derrida 1976:10).

Textuality is not only an historical emergent (Ong 1982:78–116); texts are always incomplete. They cannot speak at once of what they speak and tell us of their means of interpretation; if they speak of one, they can only point to the other by silence (Heidegger 1971:115). Texts, as Derrida says, always are in need of a supplement (1976:141–65). They entail a method of interpretation because they are occult; they reveal only inasmuch as they conceal, and this is the mystery that generates the will to truth, the urge to discover what the text has hidden beneath the surface of its content, but neither text nor method is absolute, their sufficiency is relative to the mutuality of their lack.

What, then, of oral discourse? Is it too so constrained by the will to truth that it must extrude methods to ensure its interpretation? In general, the answer is no, for it is writing that facilitates the mystery that engenders the will to truth; it alone creates the illusion of a higher truth that lives beyond the momentary, particular act of speaking and indexes more than the speaker's character and intent. The image of truth universal and incorruptible thrives only in the dry labyrinths of text or in the moist mouths of immortals whose language we no longer understand. Paradoxically, it is its failure to keep its promise of truth writ large that feeds and encourages the will to truth. The less truth it delivers, the more we long for it. In the end it provides not truth immortal, but only its means, and hopes to satisfy our lack with this changeling called method.

Oral discourse, even among literates, has no exterior method of interpretation, no consistent set of abstract rules whose function is to provide universal truth. Its method is in it, or in its conditions, and such method as there is, is entrained not universally in order to lay hold of truth, timeless and immortal, but in problematic circumstances and in order to solve problems arising from unclear meaning and uncertain honesty. It does not treat all discourse as if it were universally problematic and therefore in need of universal method. Oral discourse has its hermeneutics, but it is a hermeneutics of language-in-the-world, of reflexivity and immanence, of contingent and *ad hoc* transcendence. Holy and mystical speech apart, it has no will to truth except in a secondary and derivative imitation of writing (Ong 1982: 31–77, 139–54).

And what of logic? Is oral discourse illogical, its *dispositio* guided only by the speaker's random associations, which miraculously harmonize with those of the hearer, or does it too submit to the authority of logic without which it would be incoherent? Oral discourse has order, but it is not an order imposed by a fixed logic either from within or without. Its order is instead emergent, shifting, changeable, impermanent, created in the negotiation of speakers and hearers seeking to understand and be understood. No textlike object intervenes between speaker and hearer, and there is no fixed method, for that too is emergent and contingent. Order, then, is not *in* the discourse or *in* its method of interpretation, but in the juxtaposition and reflexivity of emergent discourse and emergent "method." The order of discourse is in the method of interpretation which is in the order of discourse. Method is immanent in the discourse that is immanent in the method, and each may be temporarily transcendent under proper circumstances as when we say: "But you said . . ." invoking the discourse, or: "If you say x, then y," invoking method.

Logic, then, is not separate from oral discourse, the discourse itself is logical in a wider sense. That is to say, it is "reasonable," but not necessarily rational in any strictly logical sense. Reasonable oral discourse may include features that we would be tempted to equate with logical operations, but it uses many other "nonlogical" devices that contribute far more to its reasonableness. Moreover, logical operations are themselves objects of interest only in unusual circumstances. *Ratio* is embedded in the reasonable (cf. Cole and Scribner 1973, Luria 1976). *Ratio* out of context is unreasonable. As its derivation from *logos* suggests, logic emerges as a fully separate means and object of discourse only as a product of writing after discourse has become a visible "thing" and has taken itself as its object, as in Aristotle's *Prior Analytics*. Texts are the "kingdom of desire" out of which logic emerges and are the means by which ". . . the world seems logical to us, because we have made it logical" (Nietzsche 1913:27,37).

In the West, traditional rhetoric, which we might think is not only oral but oral method, is actually secondary orality—orality based on written discourse which, as the *Phaedrus* makes clear, is the analogical source of its method. Secondary orality (Ong 1982:168) is generally characterized as the organization of oral discourse on the model of written discourse. The method of primary orality, inasmuch as we may speak of method, is not primarily oriented to the *dispositio*—the structure of argument—but to *inventio* and *memoria*, the sources of ideas in which the organization of ideas is already given in the world in the form of schemata, formulae, semantically rich key terms, fixed metaphors, and other holistic means. *Memoria* and *inventio* are not, in other words, analytic (cf. Ong 1958:114).

The absolutism of the text is founded in that *ratio* which texts themselves created. It emerges from focusing on the *dispositio* as order and arrangement, and from the backgrounding of *inventio, memoria, ethos* ("speaker"), and *pathos* ("hearer"). It marks the supremacy of *eidos*, and is the condition for the separation of form and content in which *dispositio* = form (*eidos*) and *inventio/memoria* = content. It enables signification, of which it is itself the paragon (cf. Ong 1958:112–16). It is the sign of

The Separation of Form and Content and the Transcendence of Form

The transcendence of method indexes the separation of form and content, for method is the expression of that separation and is also an expression of form, of the rules that order content. Form is the operation of ordering that is independent of what it orders so that it constrains and structures content. Content itself has no order; it is to be ordered by means that are external to and independent of it. In order for there to be a method there must be something other than the method to which the method applies, and when method makes itself its object that is the beginning of logic and the end of socio-logy. Method applies to content and is the means by which "data" are created and acquire order. It imparts form to the formless content from which it is itself utterly separate and independent. Form, in the sense of "formula," is the method by which substance achieves form in the sense of "shape." Form, in other words, produces form; it is both process and structure.

The separation of form and content motivates the separation and regionalization of the sensorium. In the faculty psychology of St. Augustine, for example, the mind has separate faculties: *intellectus, memoria,* and *voluntas.* In modern neurology these are similarly understood as differentially localized brain activities. Memory provides the representations, the phantasms, the substitutions of appearances that are the data of thought, what thought thinks.

What then is the source for the separation of form and content if all our instantiations of the separation merely reflect back on one another in self-confirmation and provide no grounds for its necessity? Inasmuch as the condition for it is writing, then writing is its source. Writing is the means for a systematic separation of form and content more pervasive than that conditioned by pictorial representation and more accessible than anything provided by hearing or touch. Writing expresses the separation of form and content, produces it visually, and promotes our consciousness of it.

Consciousness of form arises when action produces a substitution of appearances, that vision of the one-in-the-many (= shape), or in the succession of acts themselves (= formula). Writing accomplishes this dual constitution of form in a way that speech and hearing cannot, for it visualizes the succession of acts (= formula), and it is the lineal succession of the act of visualization (= shape). The succession of elements in the sentence is the order of things or the visual order of action, and the succession of sentences is the order of events in narration or the order of things. Thus Albertus Magnus could rightly say that the memory image of a wolf contained the intention to flee (Cf. Yates 1966:64).

The economy and means of written discourse—its order, arrangement, and visualization, its mode of substituting appearances— become the object, the source, and the model of any theoretical discourse on order, arrangement, and signification. Theoretical discourse is discourse on discourse and arises when the form of language takes itself as its content. Writing provides the means by which discourse takes itself as its object, and in so doing extrudes forms of discourse which emerge in ordered sequence, each as the underlying form of its predecessor—as ghosts arising from corpses. Thus rhetoric comes from the objectification of speaking, dialectic from the objectification of rhetoric, and logic from the objectification of dialectic, but as Wittgenstein saw, the objectification of logic produces only antilogic, not metalogic. This, perhaps more than anything else, marks the end of writing, for writing has finally closed entirely upon itself and produces nothing new. No new form of writing can grow in this nautilus; its builder is dead and its finished chambers are let out to a new tenant. We can hear the creature's claws scrabbling on the inner walls as it crawls toward the light, and do we hear it singing?

The Transcendence of Signs

Writing, which is the paragon of the separation of signs and signifieds creates only the shadow of reality and establishes the prior condition for treating the world given by normal perception and common sense as an illusion. It shifts the locus of reality from this world to a world of form indirectly available to the knower—not through senses but through signs. Writing displaces the subject from the world and alienates it from him. It produces as equal possibilities: (a) the transcendence of signs à la Derrida, or (b) the transcendence of signifieds as an unknowable Kantian "thing-in-itself." In either case, it sets up the universal problematic of reconnecting signs and signifieds, words and things. In contrast, postmodern anthropology asks "how did signs and signifieds get pulled apart?" and, identifying writing as the culprit, argues that sign and signified are mutually constituted in "saying," where the sign is immanent in the signified and the signified is immanent in the sign (cf. Heidegger 1971:115–35; Tyler 1978:459–65). The effect of this argument is to make symbols concrete rather than abstract and arbitrary, for it asks not "how do signs represent?" in the fashion of contemporary semiotics derived from Saussure and Peirce, as if one could know the origin of it all, or as if some kinds of signs constituted themselves independently of conventionality—"naturally" in the older terminology of signs. It asks instead, "how is the signifier/signified *constituted*?" There are three possibilities: (a) the signifier is conventionally constituted by the signified (s → S), as if in iconic representation; (b) the signified is intentionally constituted by the signifier (S → s), as if in indexical representation; (c) the signified and signifier are mutually constituted (S ↔ s), as if in symbolic representation. In thought picture 6.8 we show the dialectical relation of these possibilities.

In thought picture 6.8, "a" and "b" are inverses and "c" is their synthesis. Both "a" and "b" are "picturing" modes, but neither is necessarily representational, for "a" might be ideographic writing and "b" syllabic or phonetic writing. Of course, "c" is not "picturing" or visual in any way, for it is the *presence* of the word in the world and world in the word, but not as "being," or as we *say*, "Speech," which amends thought picture 6.8 as in thought picture 6.9.

Apart from their "sensory" differences, the chief difference between "c" and "a/b" is that the latter "point to" the difference between themselves and what they "picture," whereas "c" neutralizes that difference. In effect, this is the difference between Saussure's "signification" and St. Augustine's "significatio." The latter is a restatement of the idea of the trinity in the series: "incarnate" (present), "excarnate" (future), "noncarnate" (past), and reflects the earlier opposition between "significāre" and "monstrāre," and also points to the tension between the "senses" of "word" in Christian hermeneutics—the word as im-

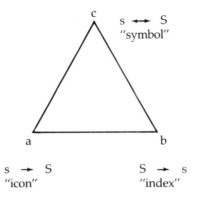

Thought picture 6.8. Dialectical relation of constitutive signs. s = signified, S = signifier. "a" is the inverse of "b," and "c" is the sublation of "a" and "b." The dialectic thus "rationalizes" the order of signs and encompasses logic (cf. thought picture 6.5) by means of will (intention-convention, à la St. Augustine) and person (speaker-hearer, or "interpretant," à la Peirce).

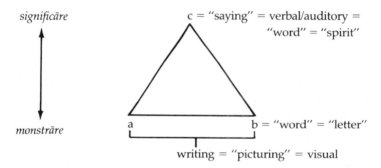

Thought picture 6.9. "Saying and showing." "a," "b," and "c" have the same values as in thought picture 6.8, except that "a" also signifies hieroglyphic or ideographic writing, and "b" signifies alphabetic writing. Note that this diagram inverts the relation of *significāre* and *monstrāre* given in thought picture 6.7. Writing is thus a "showing-saying" and speech a "saying-showing." The reversal of *significāre* and *monstrāre* is the consequence of inverting the ancient pyramid of *ergon,* which thus "demystifies" the oriental and exotic role of the hieroglyph in Western thought.

manent speech, "the word was in God, and God was the word" and the word as transcendental logos.

The chief advantage to eliminating the idea of representation is that representation emphasizes the difference between sign and signified at all levels. There is always a constant world of things and a separate world of signs, and this defines the essential problematic as one of words and things and leads us to overemphasize mimesis, description, and correspondence theories of truth, and tricks us into thinking of language as if it were a form of calculus where we can abstract signs away from their representational functions and treat them as "pure forms," focusing exclusively on their modes of collocation. The "constitutive" mode emphasizes not the separateness of signs and signifieds, but their interpenetrability and mutuality. There is no problematic relationship between word and world, for both are mutually present. It is only where there is the possibility of the ABSENCE of one or the other that problems arise, and it is, of course, just this possibility that writing enables. Writing either focuses on itself, absenting itself from the world, or in focusing on the world and absenting itself, tricks us into thinking that we can compare and describe as we will without being constrained by the means of composition and description. Do I "refute" Derrida here? No, I merely supplement his text, for he "says," "There is neither symbol nor sign but a becoming-sign of the symbol" (1976:47), which is precisely what thought picture 6.8 "says." Derrida argues against the idea of signs as "substitutions of appearances" in which things become phantasms or images in the mind, are represented as speech, and then re-represented as a written sign (Aristotle, *De Interpretatione*). One appearance precedes the other as its origin and original, and is thus prior in both time and reality. The order of representation is from the earlier to the later, from the real to the unreal, from nature ("natural" signs) to culture ("conventional, arbitrary" signs). In this world-picture the real "for-us" is only a "hand-me-down" reality or a "dime-store" imitation of "the real thing."

The implication is not, as the concept "arche-writing" might seem to suggest, that we simply reverse the order of emergence to writing → speech → mental image → thing, but to see these as copresent possibilities within a single participatory whole where signs are used by speakers and hearers not only to represent things, thoughts, and speech, but to communicate about communicating, which is the intentional means by which signs represent conventionally and is also the convention of that intention. The participatory whole is just the possibility of the intersubstitutability and integration of the triad will, representation, and person in the pairs intention/convention, signifier/signified, speaker/hearer, respectively. This is the fulfillment of the Peircean-Augustinian semiotic as opposed to that of Saussure (cf. Tyler 1978:462–64).

What then of writing? Is it forever excluded from the participatory reality of speech, or can it somehow capture the interdependence, the mutual involvement of sign, signified, and interpretant? Two methods have been tried in the past—mystification and imitation. In mystification, the sign is taken to be both a sign and realia, as in the use of Sanskrit letters in mantras and on the lotus leaves of the Yogic *chakras,* or in Hebrew tradition where the letters of the alphabet are mystical "sign-things," or in medieval theories of the "mark" in which things bear the mark of their creation. This idea is attractive, but tends to make the notion of writing redundant. Writing imitating speech, of course, is what we have in the written dialogue of Socrates, and the idea of dialogue is a perennial favorite of those who wish to capture in writing some sense of the mutuality of speakers and hearers, as witness the rebirth of this and other conversational forms in recent ethnographic writing. Other strategems suggesting techniques of oral discourse have been deployed from time to time throughout history. Parabolic discourse is one such; so too are the sermon, the method of sorites, repetitious figures, polyphony, ellipsis, the use of enigmas and paradox, and the "fragment" or "negative" dialectics of Benjamin and Adorno. Just as rhetoric is speech imitating writing, this kind of writing is writing imitating speech. Postmodern experiments in ethnographic writing are the inverse of the modernist experiment. Where modernists sought by means of ideographic method to reveal the inner flow of thought hieroglyphically—as in Joyce or Pound, for example—postmodern writing focuses on the outer flow of speech, seeking not the thought that "underlies" speech, but the thought that is speech. Where modernists sought an identity between thought and language, postmodernists seek the "inner voice" that is the equivalent of thinking and speaking. Modernists sought a form of writing more in keeping with "things," emphasizing, in imitation of modern science, the descriptive function of writing—writing as a "picture of reality," which is not "realism" but "surrealism" or better, "orientalism." Postmodern writing rejects this modernist mimesis in favor of a writing that "evokes" or "calls to mind," not by completion and similarity, but by suggestion and difference. The text is not to be seen as a depiction or revelation within itself in what it says, but is to be "seen through" by what it cannot say, to show what it cannot say and say what it cannot show. When postmodern writing tries to achieve what speech does by imitating speech, it fails, as it must, for in imitating speech it merely displaces the focus of representation without changing it. The great problem for postmodern anthropology is either to give up on writing altogether or to achieve by written means what speech creates, and to do it without simply imitating speech. It may well be that some kind of naive realism is what common sense will demand. At any rate, one may be certain that postmodern writing will not achieve its goal merely through experimentation with form, for that favorite preoccupation of the modernist depends upon the presupposition of the independence of form and content—a presupposition postmodern anthropology denies. Nor will it come about through some technological advance in sound and video recording, for every technological means merely imposes new forms of representational constraints without really addressing the problem of representation itself. Nothing yet, as mere *techne*, is "saying-showing." These technologies are instead archaisms, hold-overs from an outmoded era of writing whose whole *ergon* was based on the separation of saying and showing, on their differences rather than on their union, which is not an identity, but an identity within difference and a difference within identity.[12]

This is the end of the first chapter of the "Lust for the Logograph." "Oh Egyptians, give us your pyramids and hieroglyphs."[13]

12. Here beginneth an essay entitled "Postmodern Ethnography: From Text of the Occult to Occult Text."

13. Thought pictures are the satisfaction of hieroglyphic desire. They are logographic writing, the complete spatialization and visualization of thought that the western tradition has always envied and sought to emulate (cf. Derrida 1967:24–26). They are signs of the end of alphabetic writing and of the narrative that was never a narrative.

POSTMODERN ETHNOGRAPHY

FROM DOCUMENT OF THE OCCULT

TO OCCULT DOCUMENT

First Voice: Context

Neither part of the search for universal knowledge nor an instrument for the suppression/emancipation of peoples, nor just another mode of discourse on a par with those of science and politics, ethnography is instead a superordinate discourse to which all other discourses are relativized and in which they find their meaning and justification.[1] Ethnography's superordination is the consequence of its "imperfection." Neither self-perfecting in the manner of scientific discourse nor totalizing in the manner of political discourse, it is defined neither by a reflexive attention to its own rules nor by the performative instrumentality of those rules. Defined neither by form nor by relation to an external object, it produces no idealizations of form and performance, no fictionalized realities or realities fictionalized. Its transcendence is not that of a metalanguage—of a language superior by means of its greater perfection of form—nor that of a unity created by synthesis and sublation, nor of praxis and practical application. Transcendent, then, neither by theory nor by practice, nor by their synthesis, it *describes* no knowledge and *produces* no action. It transcends instead by *evoking* what cannot be known discursively or performed perfectly, though all know it as if discursively and perform it as if perfectly.

Evocation is neither presentation nor representation. It presents no objects and represents none, yet it makes available through absence what can be conceived but not presented. It is thus beyond truth and immune to the judgment of performance. It overcomes the separation

---

1. This paper was given at the Conference on the Writing of Ethnographic Texts at the School of American Research in Santa Fe, New Mexico, 1984. It has been revised and "sandwiched" between the "Context" and "Supplement" appearing here. Both "Context" and "Supplement" were written after the conference and are as much dialogical responses to conference papers and discussion as they are the working out of themes and conflicts in other parerga to *The Said and the Unsaid* (Tyler 1978).

of the sensible and the conceivable, of form and content, of self and other, of language and the world.

Evocation—that is to say, "ethnography"—is the discourse of the postmodern world, for the world that made science, and that science made, has disappeared, and scientific thought is now an archaic mode of consciousness surviving for awhile yet in degraded form without the ethnographic context that created and sustained it. Scientific thought succumbed because it violated the first law of culture which says that "the more man controls anything, the more uncontrollable both become." In the totalizing rhetoric of its mythology, science purported to be its own justification and sought to control and autonomize its discourse. Yet, its only justification was proof, for which there could be no justification within its own discourse, and the more it controlled its discourse by subjecting it to the criterion of proof, the more uncontrollable its discourse became. Its own activity constantly fragmented the unity of knowledge it sought to project. The more it knew, the more there was to know.

All its textual strategies—its method—depended on a prior and critical disjunction of language and the world. It made visual perception unmediated by concepts the origin of knowledge about the world, and it made language the means by which that knowledge appeared in descriptions. Science depended, in other words, on the descriptive adequacy of language as a representation of the world, but in order to move from individual percept to agreed-upon perception, it also needed a language of communicative adequacy that could enable consensus in the community of scientists. In the end, science failed because it could not reconcile the competing demands of representation and communication. Every move to enhance representation threatened communication and every agreement in communication was the sign of a new failure in representation.

Science adopted a model of language as a self-perfecting form of closed communication that achieved closure by making language itself the object of description. But closure was bought at the cost of descriptive adequacy. The more language became its own object, the less it had to say about anything else. So, the language of science became the object of science, and what had begun as perception unmediated by concepts became conception unmediated by percepts. The unity of communication brought about by language displaced the unity of perception that language had formerly wrought. Language as communication displaced language as representation, and as science communicated better and better about itself, it had less and less to say about the world. In an excess of democracy, agreement among scientists became more important than the nature of nature.

Still, this would not have been fatal had it not been for the stubborn refusal of language to perfect itself. As science increasingly defined itself as the mode of discourse that had its own discourse as its object, every move to perfect that discourse and fill every gap of proof revealed ever-new imperfections. Every self-perfecting, self-corrective move created local orders that spawned new imperfections requiring new corrections. Instead of a coherent system of knowledge, science created a welter of local orders unrelated to one another and beyond the control of anyone. Scientific knowledge was systematized only by the unity of a rational method that produced greater and greater irrationality. The utopian unity of science disappeared from sight along with all the other unreal objects of scientific fantasy.

Caught up in the fascination of this glass bead game with its everchanging rules of play and promise of the always new and different, scientists fulfilled in their discourse that dream of capitalist production in which new self-destructing products automatically remove themselves from competition with still newer self-destructing products created to fill an insatiable demand for the consumption of the latest scientific break through, the latest change in the rules of the game. In this world of ever-changing fashions, the mark of the provincial was the player who continued to play a game that had already been abandoned by those in the "forefront" or on the "cutting edge" of research.

As science came to be thought of more and more as a game, it became distanced from praxis and disrupted the taken-for-granted relation between theory and practice. What consistent practice could flow from an inconstant theory that understood its significance as a play in a game? The less theory was guided and stimulated by a reflexive relation to practical application, the less it could justify itself as the source of practice. And since the infinite game led only to provisional knowledge ever subject to revision as a consequence of changes in the rules, it produced no universal knowledge and could not justify itself by holding out the promise that it would. Its involution closed off both the return to the concrete world of practice and the transit to the wholly transcendental world of universal knowledge. Consequently, it had to look outside its own discourse for justification, to seek legitimation in a discourse that was other than its own and not subject to its rules. It needed a discourse that could not be part of the self-perfecting discourse of science nor foundational in any scientifically acceptable way. Science chose an uneasy compromise, subjugating itself both to the discourse of work (politics and industry) and the discourse of value (ethics and aesthetics), but since politics and industry controlled the means of play and could always threaten to withhold the funds on which the game depended, science succumbed more and more to limitations on play imposed in the interests of its masters.

Enlisted first as the propaganda arm of science, asserting the lie of theory and basic research as the source of practice and technological innovation, the discourse of value eventually became the ideological means for the justification of work, and all talk of value was linked inseparably to objects and to performance relative to objects—the reality fictions of work. What had originally presented itself as the context of practical reality within which the aesthetics of the play of science would find its meaning and justification became the condition of a bureaucratic unreality establishing the limits of reality through the exercise of power disguised as reason. All discourse was reduced to the rhetoric of work. But, at this moment of its triumph of total control, do we sense the first tremors of the eruption of the uncontrollable?

This is the tale of the origin of the postmodern world as told by Habermas (1975, 1984) and Lyotard (1984)—allowing for certain intentional interpretive liberties. It is the framing story for the

Free Voice: Postmodern Ethnography

A postmodern ethnography is a cooperatively evolved text consisting of fragments of discourse intended to evoke in the minds of both reader and writer an emergent fantasy of a possible world of commonsense reality, and thus to provoke an aesthetic integration that will have a therapeutic effect. It is in a word, poetry—not in its textual form, but in its return to the original context and function of poetry which, by means of its performative break with everyday speech, evoked memories of the *ethos* of the community and thereby provoked hearers to act ethically (cf. Jaeger 1945:3–76). Postmodern ethnography attempts to recreate textually this spiral of poetic and ritual performance. Like them, it defamiliarizes commonsense reality in a bracketed context of performance, evokes a fantasy whole abducted from fragments, and then returns participants to the world of common sense—transformed, renewed, and sacralized. It has the allegorical import, though not the narrative form, of a vision quest or religious parable. The break with everyday reality is a journey apart into strange lands with occult practices—into the heart of darkness—where fragments of the fantastic whirl about in the vortex of the quester's disoriented consciousness, until, arrived at the maelstrom's center, he loses consciousness at the very moment of the miraculous, restorative vision, and then, unconscious, is cast up onto the familiar but forever transformed shores of the commonplace world. Postmodern ethnography is not a new departure, not another rupture in the form of discourse of the sort we have come to expect as the norm of modernist aesthetics' scientistic emphasis on experimental novelty, but a self-conscious return to an earlier and more powerful notion of the ethical character of all discourse, as captured in the ancient significance of the family of terms "ethos," "ethnos," "ethics."

Because postmodern ethnography privileges "discourse" over "text," it foregrounds dialogue as opposed to monologue, and emphasizes the cooperative and collaborative nature of the ethnographic situation in contrast to the ideology of the transcendental observer. In fact, it rejects the ideology of "observer-observed," there being nothing observed and no one who is observer. There is instead the mutual, dialogical production of a discourse, of a story of sorts. We better understand the ethnographic context as one of cooperative story making which, in one of its ideal forms, would result in a polyphonic text, none of whose participants would have the final word in the form of a framing story or encompassing synthesis—a discourse on the discourse. It might be just the dialogue itself, or possibly a series of juxtaposed paratactic tellings of a shared circumstance, as in the Synoptic Gospels, or perhaps only a sequence of separate tellings in search of a common theme, or even a contrapuntal interweaving of tellings, or of a theme and variations (cf. Marcus and Cushman 1982, Clifford 1983). Unlike the traditional teller of tales or his folklorist counterpart, the ethnographer would not focus on monophonic performance and narrativity, though neither would he necessarily exclude them if they were appropriate in context.

I do not wish to suggest that such a text would resemble an edited collection of authored papers or one of those authorless books produced by committee, or an accidental collage like an issue of the *American Anthropologist*. These three used together, though, do characterize a ubiquitous ethnographic form called the "newspaper." In fact, had there been a modernist movement in ethnography it would have taken the newspaper as its literary model. The collection and the collage preserve differences of perspective, but differ on the dimension of accident vs. purpose, though we can all think of edited collections that are in fact collages, so little do their selections relate to common themes or topics that their presence in the same volume seems accidental, and we are all familiar with thematized collages like the newspaper, whose items are minimally linked by the common theme, "here are today's relevances for nobody in particular as put together by nobody in particular."

Polyphony is a means of perspectival relativity and is not just an evasion of authorial responsibility nor a guilty excess of democracy, though, as Vico might say, it articulates best with that social form, and it does correspond with the realities of field work in places sensitive to the issue of power as symbolized in the subject-object relationship between he who represents and she who is represented. And, it is not that ethnographers have never before used the idea of authorless texts, for myths and folktales, even when related by someone, are pure examples of the form, though we must think in that case of a committee extended in time whose participants never convene to compose the work.

The point is that questions of form are not prior; the form itself should emerge out of the joint work of the ethnographer and his native partners. The emphasis is on the emergent character of textualization, textualization being just the initial interpretive move that provides a negotiated text for the reader to interpret. The hermeneutic process is not restricted to the reader's relationship to the text, but includes as well the interpretive practices of the parties to the originating dialogue. In this respect, the model of postmodern ethnography is not the newspaper but that original ethnography—the Bible (cf. Kelber 1983).

The emergent and cooperative nature of textualization also indexes a different ideological attitude toward the ethnographic other and the uses of ethnography. The history of ethnographic writing chronicles a cumulative sequence of different attitudes toward the other that implicate different uses of ethnography. In the eighteenth century, the dominant mode was "ethnography as allegory," centering around the key concept of utopianism in which the "noble savage" played his ennobling role as a therapeutic image. In the nineteenth century, the "savage" was no longer noble; she was either "fallen," in the continuing Biblical allegory, or a figure of therapeutic irony—a minatory Satanic finger, or an instance of the primordial "primitive," a "living fossil" signifying past imperfection healed by time in the emerging evolutionary allegory. In the twentieth century, the "savage" was no longer even "primitive." She was only "data" and "evidence," the critical disproving instance in the positivist rhetoric of political liberalism. Later, in the twentieth century's structuralist and semioticist revival of the seventeenth century, he became again pure "difference," a formal pattern of collocated signs totally robbed of therapeutic significance. Now, in addition to these, each or some combination of which still feeds the imagination of some ethnographer somewhere, she has become the instrument of the ethnographer's "experience," the ethnographer having become the focus of "difference" in a perverse version of the romanticism that has always been in ethnography, no matter how desperately repressed and marginalized by the objective impulses of seekers for pure data. As in the utopianism of the eighteenth century, the other is the means of the author's alienation from his own sick culture, but the savage of the twentieth century is sick too; neutered, like the rest of us by the dark forces of the "world system," IT has lost the healing art.

Having perceived the limiting meaning of the second member of the compound term "ethnography" ("-graphy" <G *graphein*, "to write"), some ethnographers have tamed the savage, not with the pen, but with the tape recorder, reducing him to a "straight man," as in the script of some obscure comic routine, for even as they think to have returned to "oral performance" or "dialogue," in order that the native have a place in the text, they exercise total control over her discourse and steal the only thing she has left—her voice. Others, in full and guiltless knowledge of their crime, celebrate it in "ethnopoetry," while the rest, like Sartre, their faces half-turned from the offending pen, write on in atonement—little finger of the left hand on the "erase" button, index finger on the "play" button—in the sign of the cuckold-counterfeiting voice in text.

Like Derrida, they have missed the true import of "discourse," which is "the other as us," for the point of discourse is not how to make a better representation, but how to avoid representation. In their textualization of pseudodiscourse they have accomplished a terrorist alienation more complete than that of the positivists. It may be that all textualization is alienation, but it is certainly true that nonparticipatory textualization is alienation—"not us"—and there is no therapy in alienation.

As the utopians knew, ethnography can perform a therapeutic purpose in evoking a participatory reality, but they were wrong in thinking that reality could be explicitly projected in text. It is this echo, then, of participatory reality that the postmodern ethnography seeks to evoke by means of a participatory text in which no one has the exclusive right of synoptic transcendence. Because it is participatory and emergent, postmodern ethnography cannot have predetermined form, for it could happen that participants would decide that textualization itself is inappropriate—as have many informants in the past, though their objections were seldom taken to be significant in themselves, being treated instead as impediments to the ethnographer's monophonic text. Whatever form the text takes—if any—it will stress sonorant relativity, not only between the text and the community of discourse of which it is a part—the usual sense of "cultural relativity"—but within the text itself as a constitutive feature of the text.

Though postmodern ethnography privileges discourse, it does not locate itself exclusively within the problematics of a single tradition of discourse, and seeks, in particular, to avoid grounding itself in the theoretical and commonsense categories of the hegemonic western tradition. It thus relativizes discourse not just to form—that familiar perversion of the modernist, nor to authorial intention—that conceit of the romantics; nor to a foundational world beyond discourse—that desperate grasping for a separate reality of the mystic and scientist alike; nor even to history and ideology—that refuge of the hermeneuticist; nor even less to language—that hypostasized abstraction of the linguist; nor ultimately even to discourse—that Nietzschean playground of world-lost signifiers of the structuralist and grammatologist; but to all or none of these, for it is anarchic, though not for the sake of anarchy but because it refuses to become a fetishized object among objects—to be dismantled, compared, classified, and neutered in that parody of scientific scrutiny known as criticism. The ethnographic text is not only not *an* object, it is not *the* object; it is instead a means, a meditative vehicle for that transcendence of time and place that is not just transcendental but a transcendental return to time and place.

Because its meaning is not in it but in an understanding, of which it is only a consumed fragment, it is no longer cursed with the task of representation. The key word in understanding this difference is "evoke," for if a discourse can be said to "evoke," then it need not represent what it evokes, though it may be a means to a representation. Since evocation is nonrepresentational, it is not to be understood as a sign function, for it is not a "symbol of," nor does it "symbolize" what it evokes. The postmodern text has moved beyond the representational function of signs and has cast off the encumbrances of the substitution of appearances, those "absences" and "differences" of the grammatologist. It is not a presence which calls into being something that was absent; it is a coming to be of what was neither there present nor absent, for we are not to understand "evocation" as linking two differences in time and place, as something that evokes and something else evoked. Evocation is a unity, a single event or process, and we must resist the temptation of grammar which would make us think that the propositional form "x evokes y" must mean that "x" and "y" are different entities linked by a third rather peculiar "process-entity" called "evoke," and that, moreover, "x" must precede "y" in time, and consequently "x" must be a condition of "y" or "y" a result of "x."

These are all illusions of grammar which make us dismember unities into discrete entities and punctuate events. We might think to correct this situation by writing English nonlineally, as if it were Chinese, in imitation of Fenellosa and Pound: evo$\overset{x}{k}$es, but since we could still read lineally "x evokes y," and the elemen$\overset{y}{t}$s "x," "evokes," and "y" are as discrete as ever, this is no solution. Perhaps the best we can do, short of inventing some new logograph, is a Heideggerian "evoking," or better yet, be wary of the snares of grammar.

The whole point of "evoking" rather than "representing" is that it frees ethnography from mimesis and that inappropriate mode of scientific rhetoric which entails "objects," "facts," "descriptions," "inductions," "generalizations," "verification," "experiment," "truth," and like concepts which, except as empty invocations, have no parallels either in the experience of ethnographic field work or in the writing of ethnographies. The urge to conform to the canons of scientific rhetoric has made the easy realism of natural history the dominant mode of ethnographic prose, but it has been an illusory realism, promoting, on one hand, the absurdity of "describing" nonentities like "culture" or "society" as if they were fully observable, though somewhat ungainly, bugs, and on the other, the equally ridiculous behaviorist pretense of "describing" repetitive patterns of action in isolation from the discourse that actors use in constituting and situating their action, and all in simple-minded surety that the observers' grounding discourse was itself an objective form sufficient to the task of describing acts. The problem with the realism of natural history is not, as is often claimed, the complexity of the so-called object of observation, nor failure to apply sufficiently rigorous and replicable methods, nor even less the seeming intractability of the language of description. It is instead a failure of the whole visualist ideology of referential discourse with its rhetoric of "describing," "comparing," "classifying," and "generalizing," and its presumption of representational signification. In ethnography there are no "things" there to be the objects of a description, the original appearances which the language of description "re-presents" as indexical objects for comparison, classification, and generalization; there is rather a discourse, and that, too, no thing, despite the misguided claims of such translational models of ethnography as structuralism, ethno-science, and dialogue, which attempt either to represent native discourse or its unconscious patterns, and thus recommit the crime of natural history in the mind.

Ethnographic discourse is itself neither an object to be represented nor a representation of an object. Consequently, the visualist rhetoric of representation, depending from the concreteness of the written word—of *de-scribere*—subverts the ethical purport of ethnography and can only give us as replacement a sense of incompleteness and failure, since its goals and means are always out of reach.

Ethnographic discourse is not part of a project whose aim is the creation of universal knowledge. It disowns the Mephistophelian urge to power through knowledge, for that, too, is a consequence of representation. To represent means to have a kind of magical power over appearances, to be able to bring into presence what is absent, and that is why writing, the most powerful means of representation, was called "grammarye," a magical act. The true historical significance of writing is that it has increased our capacity to create totalistic illusions with which to have power over things or over others as if they were things. The whole ideology of representational signification is an ideology of power. To break its spell we would have to attack writing, totalistic representational signification, and authorial authority, but all this has already been accomplished for us. Ong (1977) has made us aware of the effects of writing by reminding us of the world of oral expression that contrasts with it. Benjamin (1978) and Adorno (1977) have counterposed the ideology of the "fragment" to that of the whole, and Derrida (1967) has made the author the creature of writing rather than its creator. Postmodern ethnography builds its program not so much from their principles as from the rubble of their deconstruction.

A postmodern ethnography is fragmentary because it cannot be otherwise. Life in the field is itself fragmentary, not at all organized around familiar ethnological categories like kinship, economy, and religion, and except for unusual informants like Ogotemmêli, the natives seem to lack communicable visions of a shared, integrated whole; nor do particular experiences present themselves, even to the most hardened sociologist, as conveniently labeled synecdoches, microcosms, or allegories of wholes, whether cultural or theoretical. At best, we make do with a collection of indexical anecdotes or telling particulars with which to portend that larger unity beyond explicit textualization. It is not just that we cannot see the forest for the trees, but that we have come to feel that there are no forests where the trees are too far apart, just as patches make quilts only if the spaces between them are small enough.

We confirm in our ethnographies our consciousness of the fragmentary nature of the postmodern world, for nothing so well defines our world as the absence of a synthesizing allegory, or perhaps it is only a paralysis of choice brought on by our knowledge of the inexhaustible supply of such allegories that makes us refuse the moment of aesthetic totalization, the story of stories, the hypostatized whole.

But there are other reasons, too. We know that these textual transcendentals, these invocations of holism, of functionally integrated systems are literary tropes, the vehicles that carry imagination from the part to the whole, the concrete to the abstract, and knowing them for what they are, whether mechanismic or organismic, makes us suspect the rational order they promise.

More important than these, though, is the idea that the transcendental transit, the holistic moment is neither textually determined nor the exclusive right of the author, being instead the functional interaction of text-author-reader. It is not some secret hidden in the text, or between texts, nor in the mind of the author and only poorly expressed/repressed by him; nor in the reader's interpretation, no matter what his critical persuasion—if any. It is not the negative dialectics of Adorno, for its paratactic oppositions are participatory functions rather than textual forms; they derive from dialogue rather than the monophonic internal dialectic of the author with his text. Even though Adorno argues that the essay, by means of negative dialectics, aims at the liquidation of all viewpoints, it cannot achieve this goal so long as it is monophonic, projected from the viewpoint of a single author. It expresses only the cognitive utopia of the author (Kauffmann 1981: 343–53). Unlike negative dialectics, the oppositions of dialogue need not be held in unresolved suspension without the possibility of transcendence, but like negative dialectics, postmodern ethnography does not practice synthesis within the text. The synoptic transit is a nonsynthetic transcendence that is not immanent in the text, but is evoked by the text. The text has the paradoxical capacity to evoke transcendence without synthesis, without creating within itself formal devices and conceptual strategies of transcendental order. In common with Adorno's program, it avoids any supposition of a harmony between the language-conceptual order of the text and the order of things, and it attempts to eliminate the subject-object nexus by refusing the possibility of their separation or of the dominance of one over the other in the form of the text-as-mirror-of thought. It accomplishes a cognitive utopia not of the author's subjectivity nor of the reader's, but of the author-text-reader, an emergent mind which has no individual locus, being instead an infinity of possible loci.

Here then is a new kind of holism, one that is emergent rather than given, and one that emerges through the reflexivity of text-author-reader and which privileges no member of this trinity as the exclusive locus or means of the whole. Moreover, this emergent whole is neither a theoretical object nor an object of theoretical knowledge, and is consequently neither evoked by explicit methods nor the derivational source of practices. It does not motivate or enable practice in the expected manner of the usual theory-practice correlation. It is not, in other words, a dialectical synthesis of the manifold of impressions which neutralizes their differences in a higher order pattern of their same type. It is neither an abstract "thing" nor an abstraction from "things," and is thus not the product of an inference whose line of development could be traced step-by-step from the concrete particulars of its origins, through transformations, to its abstract and universal terminus.

It goes against the grain of induction, deduction, synthesis, and the whole movement to "symbol," for its mode of inference is abductive, and the elements it conjoins, though used up in the fantasy, do not deliver up their separateness in the resolution of some organic totality. In Sir William Hamilton's way of speaking, they are similar to correlatives like part-whole, cause-effect, the one unthinkable without the other, a conjunction of terms that mutually explicate but do not determine one another nor induce a synthetic reduction. They express the "Law of the Conditioned": All positive thought lies between two extremes, neither of which we can conceive as possible, and yet as mutual contradictories, the one or the other we must recognize as necessary (1875:911).

Just as the metaphor of the upward spiral into the Platonic "other of unity," the "light of reason," the "higher, rational" realm of conscious thought and faceless abstraction—into the future, mind excarnate—is inappropriate, so too is the opposite metaphor of descent "beneath the surface" into the Plutonic "other of separation," the "lower" gyre of the unconscious, where dwell in mutual antagonism the dark forces of the irrational animal and the demonic rational powers of "underlying structures"—into the past, in memory, the mind carnal and incarnate.

That ancient metaphor of thought as movement, a species of motion, bequeathed to us by Aristotle is in question here, for it is the simultaneous juxtaposition of these contrary motions and their mutually neutralizing conflict that enable the whole I seek to evoke, that stillness at the center where there is neither higher nor lower, forward nor back, past nor future, when space and time cancel one another out in that familiar fantasy we all know as the everyday, commonplace world, that breach in time, that ever-present, never-present simultaneity of reality and fantasy which is the return to the commonsense world, floating, like the Lord Brahmā, motionless in the surfaceless void, all potentiality suspended within us in perfect realization, a return which is not a climax, terminus, stable image, or homeostatic equilibrium, but a reduction of tension as the moment of transcendence simultaneously approaches, draws near, and departs without having arrived. And that is why the postmodern ethnography is an occult document; it is an enigmatic, paradoxical and esoteric conjunction of reality and fantasy that evokes the constructed simultaneity we know as naive realism. It conjoins reality and fantasy, for it speaks of the occult in the language of naive realism and of the everyday in occult language, and makes the reason of the one the reasonableness of the other. It is a fantasy reality of a reality fantasy whose aim is to evoke in reader and writer alike some intimation of a possible world already given to us in fantasy and common sense, those foundations of our knowledge which cannot themselves be the objects of our knowledge, . . . for as by them we know all else, by nought else can they be known. We know them indeed, but only in the fact that with them and through them we know. (Hamilton 1875:755)

Postmodern ethnography is a return to the idea of aesthetic integration as therapy once captured in the sense of Proto-Indo-European *ar- ("way of being," "orderly and harmonious arrangement of the parts of a whole"), from which have come English "art," "rite," and "ritual," that family of concepts so closely connected with the idea of restorative harmony, of "therapy" in its original sense of "ritual substitute" (cf. Hittite *tarpan-alli*), and with the poet as *therápōn*, "attendant of the Muse." A postmodern ethnography is an object of meditation which provokes a rupture with the commonsense world and evokes an aesthetic integration whose therapeutic effect is worked out in the restoration of the commonsense world. Unlike science, it is not an instrument of immortality, for it does not hold out the false hope of a permanent, utopian transcendence which can only be achieved by devaluing and falsifying the commonsense world and thereby creating in us a sense of permanent alienation from everyday life as we live in constant expectation of the messianic deliverance from it that can never come, or comes only with death, and science thus encourages us to die too soon. Instead, it departs from the commonsense world only in order to reconfirm it and to return us to it renewed and mindful of our renewal.

Because the postmodern world is a postscientific world without the illusion of a transcendental, neither transcendental science nor transcendental religion can be at home in it, for that which is inhospitable to the transcendence by abstraction of the one must also be unfriendly to the similar character of the other. Neither the scientific illusion of reality nor the religious reality of illusion is congruent with the reality of fantasy in the fantasy reality of the postmodern world. Postmodern ethnography captures this mood of the postmodern world, for it too does not move toward abstraction, away from life, but back to experience. It aims not to foster the growth of knowledge but to restructure experience, not to understand objective reality, for that is already established by common sense, nor to explain how we understand, for that is impossible, but to reassimilate, to reintegrate the self in society and to restructure the conduct of everyday life.

Save in the commonsense world, discourse cannot autonomously determine its rhetorical effects. Neither its form nor its authorial intention determines how it will be understood, for it is impossible in text or speech to eliminate ambiguity and to structure totally for all time the auditor's purposes and interests. Her reading and listening are as much expressions of her intentions and will as is the author's writing and speaking. Not even the conjunction and consequence of their joint interests and purposes in a shared interpretation denies ambiguity and affirms determinative meaning; it only expresses a temporary sufficiency for present purposes and conditions that will be insufficient for other purposes and different conditions. Even less can the text, by means of its form, dictate its interpretation, for it cannot control the powers of its readers. They respond to a text out of various states of ignorance, irreceptivity, disbelief, and hypersensitivity to form. They are immune in the first extreme to any nuance of form, reading through it, not by means of it, unconscious of it except perhaps in confusion or annoyance. In the second extreme a paranoid conviction of authorial deceit feeds a search for hidden meanings— and the finding of them; or in one with heightened sensibility to the necessary structures of thought and language it is less a search for things hidden by the author than of things hidden from the author by the structure of language and thought. Of these latter two, the one thinks the author a charlatan, the other a dupe, but to both the text is a coded secret hiding a necessary inner meaning irresponsive to those obscuring or concealing appearances of outer contingencies that implicate a community of belief. Because the text can eliminate neither ambiguity nor the subjectivity of its authors and readers, it is bound to be misread, so much so that we might conclude, in a parody of Bloom, that the meaning of the text is the sum of its misreadings.

Such may indeed be the fate of the text, but the meaning of this inherent failure to control ambiguity and subjectivity is that it provides good reason for rejecting the model of scientific rhetoric, that Cartesian pretense that ideas are effable in clear, unambiguous, objective, and logical expression, for the inner form of text is not logical, except in parody, but paradoxical and enigmatic, not so much ineffable, as overeffable, illimitably effable, possessing a surplus of effability that must always exceed the means of its effability, so that the infinite possibility of its effability becomes the condition of its ineffability, and the interpretation of text must struggle against this surplus of meaning, not with its obscurity or poverty.

For postmodern ethnography the implication is, if not clear, at least apparent that its text will be projected neither in the form of this inner paradox nor in the form of a deceptive outer logic, but as the tension between them, neither denying ambiguity nor endorsing it, neither subverting subjectivity nor denying objectivity, expressing instead their interaction in the subjective creation of ambiguous objectivities that enable unambiguous subjectivity. The ethnographic text will thus achieve its purposes not by revealing them, but by making purposes possible. It will be a text of the physical, the spoken, and the performed, an evocation of quotidian experience, a palpable reality that uses everyday speech to suggest what is ineffable, not through abstraction, but by means of the concrete. It will be a text to read not with the eyes alone, but with the ears in order to hear "the voices of the pages" (St. Bernard, quoted in Stock 1983:408).

Other Voices: Supplement

Yes, but what you really mean is don't you think that how is it possible that what you're trying to say is . . .

1. Consensus in form and content belong to the other kind of discourse, and whose ethics is not the question. If one is deaf to the tune, one need not to dance to it, and besides there is no presentation of an ethic, only the possibility of its influence.

2. No, there is no instance of a postmodern ethnography, even though all ethnography is postmodern in effect, nor is one likely, though some recent writing has the right spirit, for example Crapanzano (1980), Tedlock (1983), and Majnep and Bulmer (1977). The point anyway is not how to create a postmodern ethnography or what form it ought to take. The point is that it might take any form but never be completely realized. Every attempt will always be incomplete, insufficient, lacking in some way, but this is not a defect since it is the means that enables transcendence. Transcendence comes from imperfection not from perfection.

3. No, it is not a question of form, of a manner of writing as such, and even though I speak of polyphony and perspectival relativity,

fragmentation, and so on, these are not necessary components of form. There is here no aesthetic of form. Lyotard (1984:80) notes two possibilities. Let us call one "writing at the limit," where we seek to push against limits imposed by conventions of syntax, meaning, and genre, and let us call the other "writing within the limit," writing so clear and commonsensical that its very reasonableness evokes what is beyond reason. In both cases the writing is antigenre, antiform.

4. Perspective is the wrong metaphor. It conjures images appropriate to descriptive writing, writing in thought pictures or hieroglyphs. It is not a business of "seeing" at all, for that is the metaphor of science; nor is it a "doing," for that is the metaphor of politics. There is no attempt to go beyond language by means of vision and action. Polyphony is a better metaphor because it evokes sound and hearing and simultaneity and harmony, not pictures and seeing and sequence and line. Prose accomplishes at most only a kind of sequential polyphony until the reader adds his voice to it.

5. Yes, it is a form of realism; it describes no objects and makes no break between describing and what is being described. It does not describe, for there is nothing it could describe. So much for the idea of ethnography as a "description of reality." Descriptions of reality are only imitations of reality. Their mode is mimetic, but their mimesis creates only illusions of reality, as in the fictional realities of science. That is the price that must be paid for making language do the work of the eyes.

6. Perception has nothing to do with it. An ethnography is not an account of a rationalized movement from percept to concept. It begins and ends in concepts. There is no origin in perception, no priority to vision, and no data of observation.

7. No, it is not surrealism. It is the realism of the commonsense world which is only surreal in the fictions of science and in the science of fiction. Whose common sense? Why, anybody's, which is not to say everybody's as Reid did (1895:692–701).

8. Translation? Not if we think of it as fording a stream that separates one text from another and changing languages in midstream. This is mimesis of language, one language copying another, which never makes a copy anyway, but a more or less contorted original. Though this form of mimesis offends less than that of vision, it is still a silly idea to suppose that one might render the meanings of another folk in terms already known to us just as if the others had never been there at all. It is not for us to know the meaning for them unless it is already known to us both, and thus needs no translation, but only a kind of reminding. So, there is no originating text to play the part of the miss-

ing object. No object of any kind precedes and constrains the ethnography. It creates its own objects in its unfolding and the reader supplies the rest.

9. But what of the experience of the ethnographer? Surely that amounts to something prior since the ethnography is at the very least a record of that experience. No, it is not a record of experience at all; it is the means of experience. That experience became experience only in the writing of the ethnography. Before that it was only a disconnected array of chance happenings. No experience preceded the ethnography. The experience was the ethnography. Experience is no more an object independent of the ethnography than all the others— behavior, meanings, texts, and so on.

10. No origin outside the text—just literature, then, or an odd kind of literary criticism? Yes, literature, but not in the sense of total self-reflexivity, of literature about itself and nothing else. An ethnography does not invite movement from text to text alone. It is not just a collection of clever allusions to other texts, though it can obviously do that as well as any other text. It evokes what can never be put into a text by any writer, and that is the commonsense understanding of the reader. An ethnography is not the author's cognitive utopia since no author can fully control the reader's response. Her text depends on the reader's supplementation. The incompleteness of the text implicates the work of the reader, and his work derives as much, if not more, from the oral world of everyday expression and commonsense understanding as it does from the world of text.

11. Postmodern ethnography denies the illusion of a self-perfecting discourse. No corrective movements from text to object and back again in the manner of empiricism, and no supplemental, self-reflexive movements from flawed sublate to scatheless transcendent mark its course. Each text retains a separate sense within the discourse without being subordinated to a grand evolutionary myth of ultimate perfectibility. Each text is akin to a Leibnitzian monad, perfect in its imperfectability.

Postmodern ethnography foregoes the tale of the past as error and denies the myth of the future as utopia. No one believes anymore in the unconditioned future. The past at least has the advantage of having been. Modernism, like Christianity, taught us to value postponement, to look ahead to a scientific utopia, to devalue the past, and negate the present. In contrast, the postmodern world is in a sense timeless; past, present, and future coexist in all discourse, and so we may say with equal sense that all repetitions are fictive and all differences are illusions. We may say that conservation is not of objects but of time. Objects change, but time does not, which makes it reasonable for us to say that when we see the same object twice it is not the same. No thing is the same, just time, which is no thing and not perceivable. To speak in the language of identities, to say "I saw the same thing," or "it has changed," or "it has moved" requires a changed time and changeless objects and subjects, but a discourse can make all three—time, subject, and object—what it will. It is not enslaved by the hegemony of the noun, by the perception of changeless objects by changeless subjects.

Dispersed authorship mirrors this dispersed self, this inconstant subject, just as the incompleteness of the text mirrors the dissolution of the object, but postmodern ethnography is not thereby anonymous in the manner of bureaucratic discourse or of a television serial. It is neither the DMS III (Diagnostic and Statistical Manual), that terrorist bludgeon of the psychiatrist, that faceless ponderosity of "the manic-depressive personality is characterized by," nor the exploitative pseudonarrative of *Dallas,* with the insidious hiss in the ears of the poor of "see, the rich are rich but miserable."

An ethnography is a fantasy, but it is not, like these, a fiction, for the idea of fiction entails a locus of judgment outside the fiction, whereas an ethnography weaves a locus of judgment within itself, and that locus, that evocation of reality is also a fantasy. It is not a reality fantasy like *Dallas,* nor a fantasy reality like the *DSM III;* it is a reality fantasy of a fantasy reality. That is to say, it is realism, the evocation of a possible world of reality already known to us in fantasy.

12. The critical function of ethnography derives from the fact that it makes its own contextual grounding part of the question and not from hawking pictures of alternative ways of life as instruments of utopian reform.

13. A conflicted form? Yes, full of unresolved conflict, but not agonistic, not violent like science or an instrument of violence like politics. It has none of the rape of the scientist's "looking at," or of the macho braggadocio of "let's see," or of the deployment of armies of argument, or of the subjugation of the weak in the politician's "doing to." Seeking neither the reason that makes power nor the power that makes reason, it founds in the receptivity of "listening to" and in the mutuality of "talking with." It takes its metaphor from another part of the sensorium and replaces the monologue of the bull horn with dialogue.

14. I call ethnography a meditative vehicle because we come to it not as to a map of knowledge nor as a guide to action, nor even for entertainment. We come to it as the start of a different kind of journey.

BIBLIOGRAPHY

INDEX

BIBLIOGRAPHY

Adorno, Theodor
1977   *Aesthetics and Politics.* London: New Left Books.
Aristotle
1924   *Rhetorica.* In W. D. Ross, ed., The Works of Aristotle, vol. XI.
                Oxford: Oxford University Press.
1928   *Categoriae,* and *De Interpretatione,* and *Topica.* In W. D. Ross,
                ed., The Works of Aristotle, vol. I. Oxford: Oxford Univer-
                sity Press.
1931   *De Anima.* In W. D. Ross, ed., The Works of Aristotle, vol.
                III. Oxford: Oxford University Press.
1952   *De Interpretatione.* In R. M. Hutchins and M. J. Adler, eds.,
                The Works of Aristotle. Translated by W. D. Ross. Chicago:
                Encyclopaedia Britannica.
1970   *Aristotle's Metaphysics.* Translated by Hippocrates E. Apostle.
                Bloomington: Indiana University Press.
1973   *De Sensu* and *De Memoria.* Translated by G. R. T. Ross. New
                York: Arno Press.

Arnaud, Antoine
1865   *Logique de Port-Royal.* Paris: Hachette.

Asad, T.
1986   "The Concept of Cultural Translation in British Social An-
                thropology." In James Clifford and George E. Marcus, eds.,
                Writing Culture. Berkeley: University of California Press,
                pp. 141–64.

Atkinson, Robert C., and R. M. Shiffrin
1968   "Human Memory: A Proposed System and Its Control Pro-
                cesses." In K. W. Spence and J. T. Spence, eds., *Psychology of
                Learning and Motivation,* vol. 2. New York: Academic Press,
                pp. 176–212.

Auerbach, Eric
1953   *Mimesis: The Representation of Reality in Western Literature.*
                Translated by Willard R. Trask. Princeton: Princeton Uni-
                versity Press.

Augustine, St.
1950   *Confessions.* New York: Dutton.
1958   *On Christian Doctrine.* Indianapolis: Bobbs-Merrill.

Ayer, Alfred J.
1956   *The Problem of Knowledge.* New York: Penguin Books.

220

Bibliography

Bacon, Sir Francis
1951   *The Advancement of Learning*. London: Oxford University Press.

Bakhtin, Mikhail
1984   *Problems in Dostoyevsky's Poetics*. Minneapolis: University of Minnesota Press.

Barthes, Roland
1972   "Structure of the *fait-divers*." In R. Barthes, *Critical Essays*. Translated by R. Howard. Evanston, Ill.: Northwestern University Press, pp. 185–95.

Bartlett, Frederic Charles
1932   *Remembering: A Study in Experimental and Social Psychology*. London: Cambridge University Press.

Benjamin, Walter
1978   *Reflections*. Translated by Edmund Jephcott. Edited Peter Demetz. New York: Harcourt

Benveniste, Emile
1969   *Indo-European Language and Society*. London: Faber & Faber.

Bergson, Henri
1912   *Matter and Memory*. London: Allen & Unwin.

Black, Max
1959   "Linguistic relativity: The Views of Benjamin Lee Whorf." In R. O. Manners and D. Kaplan, eds., *Theory in Anthropology*. Chicago: Aldine Press, 1968, pp. 432–37.
1968   *The Labyrinth of Language*. New York: Mentor.

Bloom, Harold
1973   *The Anxiety of Influence: A Theory of Poetry*. New York: Oxford University Press.

Bogen, Joseph
1969   "The other side of the brain: II. An appositional mind." *Bulletin of the Los Angeles Neurological Society* 34:136–62.

Bohm, David
1980   *Wholeness and the Implicate Order*. London: Ark Paperbacks.

Brownowski, Jacob
1978   *The Origins of Knowledge and Imagination*. New Haven: Yale University Press.

Carothers, John C.
1959   "Culture, Psychiatry, and the Written Word." *Psychiatry* 22:307–20.

Chafe, Wallace
1980   "The Deployment of Consciousness in the Production of a Narrative." In Wallace Chafe, ed., *The Pear Stories*, Norwood, N.J.: Ablex Publishing, pp. 9–50.

Clifford, James
1983   "On ethnographic authority." *Representations* 2:112–42.
1984   Conrad, Malinowski, and the Lie of Culture. Unpublished
                MS.
1986   "On ethnographic allegory." In J. Clifford and George Mar-
                cus, eds., *Writing Culture*. Berkeley: University of Califor-
                nia, pp. 98–121.

Cole, Michael, and Sylvia Scribner
1973   *Culture and Thought*. New York: Wiley.

Craik, Fergus I. M., and R. J. Lockhart
1972   "Levels of processing: A Framework for Memory Research."
                Journal of Verbal Learning and Verbal Behavior 11:671–84.

Crapanzano, Vincent
1980   *Tuhami, Portrait of a Moroccan*. Chicago: University of Chi-
                cago Press.
1986   "Hermes' Dilemma: The Masking of Subversion in Ethno-
                graphic description." In J. Clifford and G. Marcus, eds.,
                Writing Culture. Berkeley: University of California Press,
                pp. 51–76.

Derrida, Jacques
1967   *L'écriture et la Difference*. Paris: Seuil.
1972   *Marges de la Philosophie*. Paris: Minuit.
1974   *Glas/Jacques Derrida*. Paris: Éditions Galilée.
1974   *Of Grammatology*. Translated by Gayatri Chakravorty Spivak.
                Baltimore: Johns Hopkins University Press. (First published
                in 1967.)
1974   "White Mythology: Metaphor in the Text of Philosophy."
                Translated by F. C. Moore. *New Literary History* 6:26–54.
1978   *Writing and Difference*. Translated by Alan Bass. Chicago:
                University of Chicago Press.
1981   *Dissemination*. Translated by Barbara Johnson. Chicago:
                University of Chicago Press.

Dumézil, Georges
1958   "Metiers et classes functionelles chez divers peoples Indo-
                Européens," *Annales, Economies, Societés, Civilisations*, 13ᵉ
                annee, no. 4 (Oct.–Dec.):716–24.

Dumont, Louis
1970   *Homo Hierarchicus: An Essay on the Caste System*. Chicago:
                The University of Chicago Press.

Dundes, Alan
1972   "A Naturalist at Large." *Natural History* 8,15:83–86.

Eliade, Mircea
1958   *Yoga: Immortality and Freedom*. New York: Bollingen Foun-
                dation.

Fabian, Johannes
1983   Time and the Other. New York: Columbia University Press.

Feuer, Lewis
1953   "Sociological aspects of the relation between language and
                   philosophy." In R. Manners and D. Kaplan, eds., *Theory in*
                   Anthropology. Chicago: Aldine Press, pp. 411–21.

Fischer, Michael M. J.
1986   "Ethnicity and the post-modern arts of memory." In J.
                   Clifford and G. Marcus, eds., *Writing Culture*. Berkeley:
                   University of California press, pp. 194–233.

Foucault, Michel
1965   *Madness and Civilization*. New York: Random House.

Frake, C. O.
1980   *Language and Cultural Description*. Stanford: Stanford Uni-
                   versity Press.

Fürer-Haimendorf, Christoph von
1979   *The Gonds of Andhra Pradesh*. New Delhi: Vikas.

Gadamer, Hans-Georg
1976   *Philosophical Hermeneutics*. Translated by David E. Linge.
                   Berkeley: University of California Press.

Geschwind, Norman, and Walter Levitsky
1968   "Human Brain: Left-Right Assymetries in Temporal Speech
                   Region. *Science*, pp. 186–87.

Goldstein, Kurt
1948   *Language and Language Disorders*. New York: Grune and
                   Stratton.

Goodman, Paul
1971   *In Defense of Poetry*. New York: Vintage Press.

Goody, Jack
1977   *The Domestication of the Savage Mind*. Cambridge: Cambridge
                   University Press.

Goody, Jack, and Ian Watt
1968   "The Consequences of Literacy." In J. Goody, ed., *Literacy*
                   in Traditional Societies. Cambridge: Cambridge University
                   Press, pp. 1–10.

Grace, George
1981   *An Essay on Language*. Columbia, S.C.: Hornbeam Press.

Grice, Paul
1971   "Logic and conversation." In P. Cole and J. Morgan, eds.,
                   Syntax and Semantics 3:43–58.

Gumperz, John, and Dell Hymes, eds.
1972   *Directions in Sociolinguistics*. New York: Holt, Rinehart.

Habermas, Jürgen

1975   *Legitimation Crisis.* Translated by Thomas McCarthy. Boston: Beacon Press.

1979   *Communication and the Evolution of Society.* Translation of *Sprachgrammatic und Philosophie and zur Rekonstruktion des Historischen Materialismus* (1976), by Thomas McCarthy. Boston: Beacon Press.

1984   *The Theory of Communicative Action.* Translated by Thomas McCarthy. Boston: Beacon Press.

Halliday, Michael A. K.

1967   *Intonation and Grammar in British English.* The Hague: Mouton.

Hamilton, Sir William

1895   Note D: Contribution to a History of the Doctrine of Mental Suggestion or Association." In *The Philosophical Works of Thomas Reid,* vol. 2. Edinburgh: James Thin, pp. 888–910.

1895   *On the Philosophy of Commonsense.* In *The Philosophical Works of Thomas Reid,* vol. 2. Edinburgh: James Thin, pp. 741–803.

1895   "On the Theory of Mental Reproduction: Outline of a Theory of Mental Reproduction, Suggestion, or Association." In *The Philosophical Works of Thomas Reid,* vol. 2. Edinburgh: James Thin, pp. 910–17.

Hartog, Curt

1985   "Matrix Mindsets." *Datamation* (July):201–4.

Havelock, Eric

1963   *Preface to Plato.* Cambridge: Harvard University Press.

Heidegger, Martin

1971   *On the Way to Language.* New York: Random House.

Henle, Paul

1958   "Language, Thought, and Culture." In R. Manners and D. Kaplan, eds., *Theory in Anthropology.* Chicago: Aldine Press, pp. 421–31.

Hobbes, Thomas

1908   *Preface to Homer.* In J. E. Spingarn, ed., *Critical Essays of the Seventeenth Century.* 3 vols. Oxford: Clarendon Press.

Humboldt, W. von

1970   *Linguistic Variability and Intellectual Development.* Miami Linguistic Series No. 9. Coral Gables: University of Miami Press.

Hume, David

1888   *Treatise on Human Nature.* Oxford: Clarendon Press.

Hume, Robert E.

1931   *The Thirteen Principal Upanishads.* Oxford: Oxford University Press.

224

Bibliography

Hymes, Dell
1981   *In Vain I Tried to Tell You.* Philadelphia: University of Penn-
               sylvania Press.
Iyer, L. K. Ananthakrishna
1935   *The Mysore Tribes and Castes,* vol. 1. Bangalore: Mysore
               University.
Jaeger, Werner
1944   *Paideia: The Ideals of Greek Culture,* 2d ed., vol. 3. Translated
               by G. Highet. Oxford: Oxford University Press.
1945   *Paideia: The Ideals of Greek Culture,* 2d ed., vol. 1, Translated
               by G. Highet. New York: Oxford University Press.
Jakobson, Roman
1960   "Concluding Statement: Linguistics and Poetics." In T. A.
               Sebeok, ed., *Style in Language.* Cambridge: MIT Press,
               pp. 350–78.
1971   "Shifters, verbal categories, and the Russian verb" (1957).
               In *Word and Language.* The Hague: Mouton.
James, William
1890   *The Principles of Psychology.* New York: Dover Press.
Jerison, Henry J.
1976   "Paleoneurology and the Evolution of Mind. *Scientific Ameri-
               can* (Jan.):90–104.
Kauffmann, Robert Lane
1981   "The Theory of the Essay." Ph.D. diss. University of Califor-
               nia, San Diego.
Keil, Frank C.
1980   *Semantic and Conceptual Development: An Ontological Perspec-
               tive.* Cambridge: Harvard University Press.
Kelber, Werner H.
1983   *The Oral and the Written Gospel.* Philadelphia: Fortress Press.
Lacan, Jacques
1977   *Écrits.* Translated by Alan Sheridan. London: Tavistock.
Ladd, Robert D.
1980   *Intonational Meaning.* Bloomington: Indiana University
               Press.
Lakatos, Imre
1978   *Mathematics, Science and Epistemology: Philosophical Papers,
               vol. 2.* Edited by John Worral and Gregory Currie. Cam-
               bridge: Cambridge University Press.
Lakoff, George
1982   "Experiential Factors in Linguistics." In S. Simon and G.
               Scholes, eds., *Language, Mind, and Brain.* Hillsdale, N.J.:
               Lawrence Erlbaum Associates, pp. 37–63.

Lakoff, George, and M. Johnson
1980   *Metaphors We Live By.* Chicago: University of Chicago Press.

Latour, Bruno
1985   "Visualization and Cognition: Thinking with Eyes and
                Hands." *Knowledge and Society* 6:1–76.

Liberman, M., and A. Prince
1977   "On Stress and Linguistic Rhythm." *Linguistic Inquiry* 8:
                249–336.

Locke, Don
1971   *Memory.* New York: Doubleday.

Lord, Albert B.
1960   *The Singer of Tales.* Harvard Studies in Comparative Litera-
                ture, 24. Cambridge: Harvard University Press.

Luria, Alexander R.
1976   *Cognitive Development: Its Cultural and Social Foundations.*
                Cambridge: Harvard University Press.

Luria, Alexander R., and E. G. Simmernitskaya
1975   "Interhemispheric Relations and the Functions of the
                Minor Hemisphere." *Neuropsychologia* 15:175–78.

Lyotard, Jean François
1954   *La Phénomenologie.* Paris: P. U. F.
1973   *Dérive à Partir de Marx et Freud.* Paris: 10/18.
1974   *Economie Libidinale.* Paris: Minuit.
1977   *Instructions Paiiennes.* Paris: Galilee.
1984   *The Post-modern Condition: A Report on Knowledge.* Translated
                by Geoff Bennington and Brian Massumi. Minneapolis:
                University of Minnesota Press. (First published in 1979.)

Magliola, Robert
1985   "A differentialist manifesto." *Krisis* 3–4:91–111.

Majnep, Ian Saem, and Ralph Bulmer
1977   *Birds of My Kalama Country.* Auckland: Auckland University
                Press.

Marcus, George
1980   "Rhetoric and the Ethnographic Genre in Anthropological
                Research." *Current Anthropology* 21:507–10.
1986   "Contemporary Problems of Ethnography in the Modern
                World System." In J. Clifford and G. Marcus, eds., *Writing
                Culture.* Berkeley: University of California Press, pp. 165–93.

Marcus, George, and Richard Cushman
1982   "Ethnographies as Texts." In *Annual Review of American
                Anthropology,* vol. 12. Palo Alto: Annual Reviews, Inc.,
                pp. 25–69.

Bibliography

Maxwell, Kevin B.
1983   *Bemba Myth and Ritual: The Impact of Literacy on an Oral Cul-ture.* New York: Peter Lang Publishing.

McLean, Paul
1973   "A Triune Concept of the Brain and Behavior." In T. Boag and D. Campbell, eds., *The Hincks Memorial Lecture.* Toronto: Toronto University Press, pp. 6–66.

Nietzsche, Friedrich
1911   ˙*The Twilight of the Idols.* In O. Levy, ed., The Complete Works of F. Neitzsche, vol. 16. Edinburgh: Foulis.
1913   *The Will to Power.* In O. Levy, ed., The Complete Works of F. Nietzsche, vol. 15. Edinburgh: Foulis.
1968   *Twilight of the Gods and the Anti-Christ.* Translation of *Götzen-Dammerung: oder wie man mit dem Hammer philosophirt* (1889), by R. J. Hollingdale. Harmondsworth, Middlesex, England: Penguin Books.

Ong, Walter, J., S. J.
1958   *Ramus: Method and the Decay of Dialogue.* Cambridge: Harvard University Press.
1967   *The Presence of the Word: Some Prolegomena for Cultural and Religious History.* The Terry Lectures. New Haven: Yale University Press.
1977   *Interfaces of the Word: Studies in the Evolution of Consciousness and Culture.* Ithaca: Cornell University Press.
1982   *Orality and Literacy: The Technologizing of the Word.* London: Metheun.

Paivio, Allan
1971   *Imagery and Verbal Processes.* New York: Holt, Rinehart.

Parsons, Talcott
1949   *The Structure of Social Action.* Glencoe: The Free Press.

Partridge, Eric
1958   *Origins: A Short Etymological Dictionary of Modern English.* New York: Macmillan.

Peirce, Charles S.
1932   *Principles of Philosophy.* In Collected Papers of C. S. Peirce, vol. 1. Cambridge: Harvard University Press.
1932   *Elements of logic.* In Collected Papers of C. S. Peirce, vol. 2. Cambridge: Harvard University Press.

Plato
1963   *Theateatus.* In E. Hamilton and H. Cairns, eds., *Plato: The Collected Dialogues.* Princeton: Princeton University Press.

Pratt, Mary
1984   "Scratches on the Face of the Country or What Mr. Barrow Saw in the Land of the Bushmen." Unpublished MS.

| 1986 | "Fieldwork in common places." In J. Clifford and G. Marcus, eds., *Writing Culture*. Berkeley: University of California Press, pp. 27–50. |

Quillian, M. R.
1966   *Semantic Memory*. Cambridge, Mass.: Bolt, Beranek, & Newman.

Rabinow, Paul
1977   *Reflections on Fieldwork in Morocco*. Berkeley: University of California Press.

Reid, Thomas
1895   *Essays on the Active and Moral Powers of Man*, vol. 3. In The Works of Thomas Reid. Edinburgh: James Thin.

Rorty, Richard
1979   *Philosophy and the Mirror of Nature*. Princeton: Princeton University Press.

Rothenberg, Jerome, and Dianne Rothenberg, eds.
1983   *Symposium of the Whole*. Berkeley: University of California Press.

Russell, Bertrand
1921   *Analysis of Mind*. London: Allen & Unwin.

Sacks, Harvey, and E. Schegloff
1974   "A Simplest Systematics for the Organization of Turn-taking for Conversation. *Language* 50, 4:696–735.

Said, Edward
1978   *Orientalism*. New York: Pantheon.

Sapir, Edward
1958   "Why Cultural Anthropology Needs the Psychiatrist." In D. G. Mandelbaum, ed., *Selected Writings of Edward Sapir*. Berkeley: University of California Press, pp. 569–77. (First published in 1938.)

Saussure, Ferdinand de
1966   *Course in General Linguistics*. Edited by C. Bally, A. Sechehoye, and A. Riedlinger. Translated by W. Baskin. New York: McGraw-Hill Book Co. (Also published in 1959 by The Philosophical Library, Inc.)

Schopenhauer, Arthur
1962   *The Will to Live*. Translated by R. Taylor. New York: Doubleday.

Seamon, John G.
1980   *Memory and Cognition*. Oxford: Oxford University Press.

Shokolov, Alexander N.
1972   *Inner Speech and Thought*. Translated by G. T. Onischenko. New York: Plenum Press.

Bibliography

Spanos, William
1985   "Postmodern Literature and Its Occasion." *Krisis* 3–4: 54–76.

Sperry, Roger W.
1968   "Hemisphere Disconnection and Unity in Conscious Awareness." *American Psychologist* 23:723–33.

Stock, Brian
1983   *The Implications of Literacy.* Princeton: Princeton University Press.

Stoller, Paul
1984   "Eye, Mind, and Word in Anthropology." *L'Homme* 24, 3–4: 91–114.

Tannen, Deborah
1984   *Conversational Style.* Norwood, N.J.: Ablex Publishing.

Tedlock, Dennis
1983   *The Spoken Word and the Work of Interpretation.* Philadelphia: University of Pennsylvania Press.

Thompson, H. S.
1980   "Sentence Stress and Salience in English: Theory and Practice." Palo Alto: Palo Alto Research Center. Photocopy.

Thornton, Robert
1984a   "Chapters and Verses: Classification as Rhetorical Trope in Ethnographic Writing. Unpublished MS.
1984b   "Imagine Yourself Set Down . . .: Conrad, Frazer, Malinowski and the Role of Imagination in Ethnography." Unpublished MS.

Todorov, Tzvetan
1984   *Mikhail Bakhtin: The Dialogical Principle.* Theory and History of Literature, vol. 13. Minneapolis: University of Minnesota Press.

Tulving, Endel
1972   "Episodic and semantic memory." In E. Tulving and W. Donaldson, eds., *Organization of Memory.* New York: Academic Press, pp. 382–404.

Turner, Victor
1974   *Dramas, Fields, and Metaphors.* Ithaca: Cornell University Press.

Tyler, Stephen A.
1969   Ed., *Cognitive Anthropology.* New York: Holt, Rinehart.
1978   *The Said and the Unsaid.* New York: Academic Press.

Vygotsky, Lev Semenovich
1962   *Thought and Language.* Cambridge: MIT Press.

Whitehead, Henry

1916   *The Village Gods of South India.* London: Oxford University
              Press.

Whorf, Benjamin Lee

1956a   "An American Indian Model of the Universe." In John B.
              Carroll, ed., *Language, Thought, and Reality.* Cambridge:
              MIT Press. (Originally published in 1936.)
1956b   The relation of habitual thought and behavior to language.
              In J. B. Carroll (ed.), *Language, Thought, and Reality.* Cam-
              bridge: MIT Press. pp. 134–59. (Originally published in
              1939.)

Williams, William Carlos

1946–58   *Paterson: I–V, Fragments VI.* New York: New Directions.

Wittgenstein, Ludwig

1958   *Philosophical Investigations,* 3d ed. Translated by G. E. M.
              Anscombe. Oxford: Basil Blackwell & Mott, Ltd.
1961   *Tractatus Logico-Philosophicus.* New York: Humanities Press.

Yates, Frances

1966   *The Art of Memory.* Chicago: University of Chicago Press.

INDEX

COMPOSED BY G&S TYPESETTERS, INC., AUSTIN, TEXAS
MANUFACTURED BY CUSHING MALLOY, INC., ANN ARBOR, MICHIGAN
TEXT AND DISPLAY LINES ARE SET IN PALATINO

ᜈᜒ

Library of Congress Cataloging-in-Publication Data
Tyler, Stephen A., 1932–
The unspeakable : discourse, dialogue, and
rhetoric in the postmodern world
(Rhetoric of the human sciences)
Bibliography: pp. 219–229.
Includes index.
1. Discourse analysis.   2. Semiotics.
3. Postmodernism.   4. Ethnology—Philosophy.
5. Knowledge, Theory of.   I. Title.   II. Series.
P302.T95   1987   001.2   87-40149
ISBN 0-299-11270-5
ISBN 0-299-11274-8 (pbk.)